One Minute Before Midnight

A Memoir

By Ruth Mueller as told to Mark Bego

PublishAmerica
Baltimore

Second printing

PublishAmerica has allowed this work to remain exactly as the author intended, verbatim, without editorial input.

Hardcover 978-1-4489-7608-9
Softcover 978-1-61546-187-5
PUBLISHED BY PUBLISHAMERICA, LLLP
www.publishamerica.com
Baltimore

Printed in the United States of America

Dedication:

To Raymond

Acknowledgments

Ruth Mueller would like to thank the following people:
Jane Anderson
Micky Denhoff
Hildegard Eismann
Rudolf Eismann, Sr.
Didier Ficks
Francois Ficks
Micheline Ficks
Larry Friedman
Rose Friedman
Dr. Else Fuchschwanz-Heineck
Adolf Halfen
Frank Halfen
Frieda Halfen
Lisa Marie Halfen
Susan Halfen
Victor Hammer
John McCall
Hedwig Mueller
Mary Mueller
Paul Mueller
Maren Otto
Francois L. Schwarz
Lindley M. Smith (a/k/a "Smitty")
Mother Superior, my cousins, and all of the close friends who are mentioned in the text of this book

The authors would also like to thank Debbie Calvanko, Barbara Jonckers, Bonnie Olson, Tony Noto, , Dave Marken and Dan DeFilippo at Pipeline Talent Management, and Michael Wimpfheimer for their help with the production of this book.

Contents

Prologue:

I have known Ruth Mueller since 1980, and since that time I have been fascinated by her. She is energetic, driven, accomplished, fun to be around, and she always has something interesting and thought provoking to say. Now that she is in her 90s, she is still every bit as lively and adventuresome as she was when I first met her.

Having written over 50 books about celebrities and show business personalities, when the idea of helping Ruth to tell her life story came along, I was happy to have the opportunity to work with her. I spent many hours listening to Ruth's fascinating tales of her escape from Nazi Germany, her early life in New York City, her highly successful business life, and her deep appreciation of art and culture.

I transcribed hours and hours of tapes from our detailed discussions, then together we went back and forth about the tone that the book should have, and how her stories should unfold. I feel that this book reads like an honest memoir in Ruth's own words. She is a great storyteller, and every page retains the tone, flavor, and literary voice that mirrors the lively way in which Ruth speaks. To add another dimension, we were able to include several of her diary entries, and even some of the many love letters that were written to her.

After you have read this memoir, I am sure you will agree with me that Ruth Mueller is not only a true survivor, she is also a remarkable woman who continues to live her life to the fullest.

—Mark Bego 2009

Introduction:

My name is Ruth Annemarie Mueller. I am not a movie star or a figure of public note, but I have had a most interesting life. I started out my professional career earning $13.00 a week in America. By the time I retired, I ran a multi-million dollar international corporation. It made it possible for me to afford a very luxurious existence. I have traveled all over the world in First Class style, and I have seen and done things I never dreamed of being able to do. It is from this vantage point that I now look over the accomplishments of my adventurous life.

In the 1920s and the early 1930s when I was a young girl in Germany, I had a normal and typical life of school and fun activities, which included crushes on the local boys. But the world around me was changing dramatically in ways I could never have imagined. Hitler and the Nazis were taking over my country and planning a reign of terror that no modern society had ever witnessed nor dreamed could occur. Because of this, I missed out on many of the usual activities for teenagers that I had been looking forward to, including Sweet Sixteen parties and other events of that nature.

In 1939, less than a week before it became impossible for anyone to escape from Nazi Germany, my mother, my uncle and I fled the country, just as the doors were closing on the life I had known.

Being as I was only half Jewish and possessing my father's Aryan last name, I had narrowly eluded detection of being perceived as a Jew. As it was, I stood up to the Nazis and—by my wits—prevailed over them on the legendary *Krystallnacht*. If I had stayed in Germany, my luck might not have held out as well as it did up to this point. To this day, when I open up the cover of my mother's German passport and see the large red letter "J" stamped there, I am still filled with rage, horror and indignation.

For my mother, my uncle and I, our new life in New York City in the 1940s was one of survival, wonderment, and magical opportunities.

My first job in America was working as a seamstress. But by the time I ended my business career, the corporation I ran had an annual billing of over $180 million.

In business, as in my personal life, over the decades I found that my wits and my own instinct were my strongest tools. I never married. I never wanted to do so. Instead, it was I who chose my lovers and my beaux. I had a four decade affair with a married man named Francois Schwarz who loved me dearly and showed me that a woman could excel in the Manhattan business world just as successfully as a man.

In the 1970s, after Francois died, I found myself the owner and president of a very influential corporation where I had once been an employee. However, it came to my attention that an unscrupulous lawyer and a creative accountant were plotting to defraud me out of my own company. I had stood up to the Nazis and prevailed! I certainly wasn't going to be outsmarted by this duo of male chauvinist idiots.

When I was finished running this corporation, I sold it for a tidy multi-million-dollar profit. I had enough money to support myself through a couple of lifetimes, so I voluntarily retired to do as I pleased. As someone once advised me, "There is no merit to being the richest woman in the cemetery." From that point forward, I began to really enjoy my life.

Why is it that I chose to write my memoirs at this juncture in time? As I have recently celebrated my 90th birthday, I decided to tell my story because like any other person, it is not mine alone. My life has been shaped and touched by so many wonderful, brave, strong, inspirational and loving people whose memory might be lost if I did not put pen to paper at this time.

I am not superior to any other woman, but I have done and seen things that are quite unique and extraordinary. I have watched the world around me change in ways that no other single century in human history ever has. I have done as I pleased with my life, and I am extremely happy with the results. I am the product of the love of my family and friends, and it is to them that I dedicate this book.

I am Ruth Mueller, and this is my story.

Chapter One:
Escape from Nazi Germany

It was August 27, 1939, and it was becoming increasingly clear that something very evil was brewing in Germany. This was in spite of the non-aggression treaty signed between the Germans and the Russians on the 23rd of the month. Apparently, that was all for show. In the streets of Mannheim and every other major German city, the normal everyday sounds of traffic and pedestrians were regularly underscored with the sound of Nazi soldiers marching through the downtown areas. The well-organized Brown Shirt SA [*Sturmabteilung*] soldiers and the Black Shirt SS [*Schultzstaffel*] troops showed their strength by marching in the streets continuously. Whenever we encountered them marching we were expected to stop and raise our arm in a "Heil Hitler" gesture of solidarity, or face possible arrest.

If we turned on the radio, all we could hear were songs glorifying Hitler and his evil party. Every day in the streets—morning, noon and night—we could see displays of Hitler's power. There were well-organized youth groups and goose-stepping soldiers, marching, singing, and carrying on as though they were the owners of the entire world. As they marched through the streets, the Nazi soldiers took up the entire street from side-to-side, causing all traffic to be unquestioningly rerouted. With children in tow, or hoisted up on their shoulders, Nazi supporters would applaud or shout "Heil Hitler!" as his photo was everywhere. The soldiers were also accompanied by motorcades and police, disrupting everything in their wake. I can still hear the frightening sounds of the loud goose-stepping marchers echoing in my head to this day.

There were flags and banners everywhere with ominous black swastikas on them. Even the currency and the postage stamps displayed swastikas on them as well. According to what Hitler himself stated, Germany would be in control of the entire world for a thousand year reign.

Because of Hitler and Goebbel's mesmerizing and inspiring speeches, one would have believed that the Nazis were fast becoming victorious in achieving all of the goals they had set their sights upon, on their road towards world domination. Their self-proclaimed superiority extended not only to military prowess, but also into the fields of manufacturing, science, electronics, and whatever they could think of dominating. Their propaganda was so all-encompassing, it was frightening to see as it poisoned almost everything it touched.

My immediate family—my mother, Uncle Adolf and I—had actively been plotting to leave Nazi Germany as soon as we could. In fact, we had known that we wanted to escape ever since my father had died two years before. The advent of *Krystallnacht* had only underscored our fears of what kind of injustices were coming if we stayed in Germany. We were uncertain whether war would suddenly break out. We knew we had to escape, and we were just waiting for the right moment to leave Germany.

In Germany at this point, you had to pay an "exit tax" to the government for leaving the country. This exit tax was a significant amount of money, meant to dissuade everyone from leaving. The Nazis would do anything they could to separate the citizens from their money. If they couldn't get it from people by these taxes, they eventually began to simply confiscate it—especially if you were Jewish. Since I was half Jewish and half Christian, it was only a matter of time before the Nazis would consider me an enemy of the state as well.

At that time, you also needed a specific packing permission document to move your own possessions and ship them abroad. We were waiting to get our packing permission documents when suddenly it became alarmingly clear that something disastrous was about to happen.

My mother, Uncle Adolf and I each had American immigration quota numbers that would allow us to come to America. There were specific quotas issued by the U.S. for each country. We still wanted to wait for our German packing permits if we were to take any of our belongings with us. Although we had been issued our quota numbers to emigrate to America, we could not go there until March 1940. Thanks to Pralat Bauer, who was a local Jesuit priest, my mother and I each had a job lined up and waiting for us in England. We would go there first where we would work for the German ambassador, then we would set sail for the United States the following spring. The reason that we were so willing to leave at this juncture came suddenly in the form of a warning. This news came to us first from Adi Griasch, the brother of Mother's best friend, Hansy Griasch.

It seemed just like a normal August day in 1939, when Adi called and asked me to meet him in a café in Mannheim for an ice cream. I could sense by the tone in his voice that there was something he did not want to disclose on the phone, so I agreed. Since everybody in Germany was aware that the telephones were tapped, no one dared say anything important on them anymore.

When Adi and I had finished our ice cream, we took a walk together in Luisen Park. When we were sure that no one was around us to hear our conversation, he told me that he had a "draft notice" in his pocket to report for war duty the following Monday morning. I was shocked. No one knew that war was so eminent. What surprised me the most was the knowledge that Hitler obviously had everything already in place for the war to begin. The orders Adi had in his pocket were called "Stellungsbefehl" which were mandatory. There was no way he could say "no."

Adi elaborated about how soon a war would actually begin. He also brought with him greetings from his sister Hansy, who felt trapped in Germany because she had no place to go. Hansy's message to us was: "You are lucky that you get to leave the country. We have to stay here where the bombs will fall on our heads."

Hearing about Adi's draft notice that day, I was in shock. After I returned to our apartment Uncle Adolf, Mother and I sat together and figured out how we were going to properly react to this war situation. As we sat there—much to my surprise—another family friend, John McCall, telephoned. He told me that he wanted to come and see us immediately. Just like Adi before him, there was a sense of urgency and alarm in his voice.

John was a British citizen, who was employed by the Berlitz School. His assignment in the Mannheim area was to teach English to German businessmen in Ludwigshafen at BASF [Badische Anilin & Soda Fabrique]. BASF was one of the premier chemical companies in Germany. Established in the late 1800s, it quickly grew into one of the largest employers in nearby Ludwigshafen just on the other side of the Rhine River. They made everything from dyes to synthetics and pharmaceuticals. Since it was such a large company, many of its executives needed to speak other languages, particularly English, so it was the perfect "cover" for McCall's real purpose for being in Germany. In reality, John was a member of M6—the British Intelligence. No one in Germany suspected what he was really doing, or had any inkling that he was actually a spy for the British government.

At the time, I was a 22-year-old girl who was well-educated, but I was not all that worldly. Throughout my life I have been thankful to have always had friends to look out for my well-being. John was one of those friends who always cared for me.

He knew all about my plans to go to England and then to America. I will always remember that McCall gave me some of the best advice. Since he had a vast knowledge in linguistics, he had once told me, "Whenever you go to a new country and want to learn the local language, go to a Catholic Church and listen to the Sunday sermons, because the priests speak clearly and they use good language. Listen to the local radio, so your ears become trained to the sound of the new language. And go to the movies, even if you don't fully understand the language, you will get used to the sound, and you will benefit from your exposure to the language." I had no idea at the time as to how soon I would be heeding this advice.

He also told me that once I was in England and needed any help, I could call on his sister who lived in Manchester. John was a very good friend to all of us, and a wonderful human being.

After John's visit that August day, a new and urgent course of action was set in motion. When McCall arrived at our apartment, he told me that he and three of his fellow Berlitz teachers were about to make a hasty exit out of Germany through the obviously very narrow window of opportunity that we now had. "We are all leaving the country tonight. Do you want go with us?" he asked. Without hesitation I instantly agreed.

I turned to my mother and said, "That's the only way to do it. I will leave with John tonight, but you must promise me that you and Uncle Adolf will also leave the country within 72 hours." They had no choice but to agree, as time was clearly running out. Thankfully, Mother, Uncle Adolf and I had already obtained our visas for one-time entry to the United Kingdom. I had in my possession Visa number 24962, which had been issued August 8, 1939. We had been granted permission to enter England at the port of Harwick on August 30.

When I now look back at the sequence of events to unfold within less than two months, I can see how narrow our opportunity to escape really was:

—August 8, 1939, Mother and I were granted our visas

—August 23, 1939, Germany and Russia signed a non-aggression treaty

—August 27, 1939, I leave Mannheim with John McCall and the three teachers

—August 30, 1939, Mother, Uncle Adolf and I are granted permission to enter England

—September 1, 1939, Germany marches into Poland, starting the Second World War

Meanwhile, several other members of my family were also planning to leave the country and successfully crossed the German border without incident. My mother's sister Erna also lived in Mannheim. Aunt Erna was married to Uncle Jub, a citizen of Belgium with a valid Belgian passport. He was able to leave Germany and enter Belgium with his wife and son, which they were planning to do the same week.

If everything went the way we planned it I would leave town with John McCall. Then Aunt Erna and Uncle Jub would look after Mother and Uncle Adolf, and make sure they left Germany safely. We would reunite in Brussels and go over to England together. We were a very close-knit family at this point. Since my father had died, it seemed that Uncle Adolf had basically assumed the role of "father figure" in my life.

So that Mother and Uncle Adolf could leave the house without incident, we devised a ploy. They would leave the pantry filled with jam, there would still be bread on the table, and they wouldn't wash the morning dishes. This way, no one who came into the apartment would suspect anything. At this point in time, we were never certain whom amongst our neighbors were actually Nazi spies, though we heavily suspected one of our upstairs neighbors. By leaving things this way, even if the authorities came to the apartment, it would look like there was nothing out of the ordinary.

In the short hours after Adi and John's messages to us, our thoughts had gone from "maybe there will be no war" to sheer "war panic." We had originally planned on waiting for the permit to pack all of our belongings and transport them to America via boat and take suitcases with us. But everything had changed since Adi called. It was further underscored by John McCall's telephone message that he and the three teachers were leaving Germany that very night. Suddenly, we had a whole new game plan: "Get out of Germany as fast as possible before it is too late."

In Germany at that time, everything we bought was paid for in cash, using Deutsche Marks. Checks were reserved for business transactions, and credit cards had not yet been invented. We had saved as much money as we could, knowing the time would come when it would be needed. In the 1939 economy, the fare for each of the three of us to get "tourist class" passage from England to America was the equivalent of what it is today. In other words, it was a substantial amount of money for working class people.

I took the money that we had at home, went to the travel agency in town, and bought three tickets for the Cunard line from Southhampton,

England to New York with an open journey date. I returned to our apartment and hastily packed a little suitcase for myself.

In the suitcase I put two gabardine suits which I had designed and had made at a tailor in Mannheim. One was grey, and the other one was brown. They were so well-made that they would still be in fashion today. I made sure I packed some flannel pajamas, which would come in handy in England. I took along my diary and couple of embroidered silk slips. I packed a couple of pocketbooks and some new blouses and sweaters. Make-up at that time was very minimal. Eau de cologne "No. 4711" was my favorite fragrance, and I made sure that I had a bottle of that—in fact I still use it today! Lipstick was not that common to have, but I did have one tube in my pocket.

After I was finished packing, I raced out of the apartment, and hurried to the Mannheim train station where I was to meet John McCall at the appointed time. I figured that I would wear a new pair of shoes, as they would last the longest. I unfortunately found that to be a big mistake. By wearing that brand new pair of black pumps, it wasn't long after my journey had begun that the new shoes had already given me blisters all over my feet.

I met John and the three female teachers, and we all boarded a train bound for Strasbourg, France. Once past the German border, we all had different destinations in England. John McCall was on his way to Calais, and then to London. The other teachers from the Berlitz School were to take another route where their respective families lived. And, I had to enter England at Harwick.

There was a nervous sense of anticipation amongst the five of us, as we had no idea what kind of perils to expect at the German border. At this point in time, the Nazi soldiers and border officials could detain anyone they chose—for any reason. As we approached the border, the German customs officers asked us where we were going, and whether we traveled with other people. I announced that I was on my way to London to meet my mother and to work. The teachers told them that they were making this journey to visit with family members. We all tried to act calm when we announced our reasons for leaving Germany. In an effort to sound like he was merely a charming world traveler, John

McCall said that he would definitely come back to Germany for a visit. Somehow this placated the customs officers. They allowed us to pass into France.

What a relief! We had survived the first hurdle on our journey. In Strasbourg, the situation changed. We were away from the Nazi's, now my biggest dilemma was a financial one. I had no money at my disposal, other than the permitted 20 Marks I could have in my possession when I left Germany. It had been just enough to get to the station, have a cup of coffee, and leave my luggage in the lockers.

Everyone we encountered in the train station and in public was outwardly friendly. I was greeted on the streets of Strasbourg by strangers who said "salute!" which is French for "hello." However I saw several soldiers in French uniforms around me. Although it is a beautiful city with incredible architecture, I didn't notice much of Strasbourg. I was too preoccupied with our escape, and I was frightened by all of the obvious preparations for war that I witnessed.

Strasbourg was obviously getting ready for war. There is a huge church there, which is very famous, called the Cathedral of Strasbourg. As we walked by workers were frantically removing the huge stained glass windows and packing them up for safekeeping. They took them away and stored them in a secret place. If the war took place and if any bombs dropped in Strasbourg, they wanted to make sure that the priceless stained glass windows of the church were not shattered.

I also remember seeing an executive officer there in the streets of Strasbourg. He was wearing a French military uniform. What was remarkable about seeing him was observing that he had this little assistant, or servant, who did everything for him. He seemed incredibly attentive to this officer, right down to polishing his dusty shoes for him. I had never seen anything quite like that.

The officer stood about six feet tall, and he was immaculately dressed in a French uniform with gold braids and epaulets on the shoulders. On his feet he wore beautiful leather boots which came up to his knees. The hat he wore on his head was a distinctive officer's hat which was black on the sides and red on the top.

His attendant was only four or five feet tall, and as I understood it, he would be with his "master" for the duration of the war, taking care of all of the more powerful man's desires and wishes. This attendant was dressed in a less showy and less dramatic uniform, as though he was wearing what are known as "fatigues."

I felt this was so unjust, as the attendant appeared in my eyes to be a mere "slave." Since I had never seen the preparations for war, I had to accept this bizarre sight as military protocol.

Well, here we were: Five people seemingly dropped in the middle of the French region of Alsace, like orphans in a storm. None of us had any friends or relatives in France to consult or help us formulate our plans. We only had each other, and we were all running for our lives. So, we went to the only place we could think of going: the English Consulate in Strasbourg.

When we got there, we found that they were helpful to us. The consulate gave McCall a small amount of money, so we all felt much better. They also suggested a place where we could stay for the night. Upon their recommendation, that evening we slept in the "Gallia," or student hostel, which was located on the campus of Strasbourg University. It was situated right in the middle of the city, and it was very noisy that night. There was the constant sound of laughter in the streets, and there was a lot of noise from soldiers having had too much to drink. They were the nervous sounds of a city about to be plunged into war.

The next morning we went again to the British Consulate, and then to the Bank of Alsace, for additional money. Onward through the streets we went in the midst of a sea of young lieutenants carrying luggage in preparation for war service. I had a feeling that this was about the same confusing ambiance that existed according to the descriptions which my Grandmother Halfen gave me of her war experiences in 1914.

At this point I was uncertain what I was going to do next. Then I remembered that my Grandma's close friends, Francois and Meta Schwarz, were in Paris. I thought to myself, "They might be able to help me get money and food and a place to stay for the night." I phoned them from Strasbourg. However, they weren't there. They had left already for Vichy, where the government of France had been moved. So I decided that I would take the train to Brussels to meet my Aunt Erna and Uncle Jub, to hear about my mother and Uncle Adolf's whereabouts and to plan what was next for me.

Suddenly, our party of five was breaking up. The first of us to leave were the three female Berlitz teachers. As we kissed and said goodbye, I only had one desire: "I hope these lovely people will still be here after the war." I sadly watched as the train carrying this trio of women left the station. I was to be the next one to leave.

I purchased a ticket bound for Brussels via Luxembourg. John McCall bought sandwiches for both of us, gave me money, and walked me to my train. I kissed him goodbye and boarded the train. As I looked back at him standing there on the platform, I feared that I would never see him again either. Little did I know, my premonition was correct. This was the last time I would ever see him. As the train pulled out of the Strasbourg station, I felt so very alone.

Meanwhile, I was hoping that with the help or Erna and Jub, Mother and Adolf had gotten themselves safely to Brussels, and waited for me there. In the train, as we passed the city of Saverine, I could see that only soldiers were on the train platform. Already troops were mobilizing. As we approached each of the train stations, city name signs were obliterated by grey cloth draped over them, so we didn't really know where we were. The only way I knew where we were stopping was when the conductor traveling with the train announced, "The next stop is Metz." As we entered the Metz station, everything was so quiet, like the calm before the storm. Everyone could tell the war was coming in a matter of days. It was a fearful silence. No one spoke a word.

There was an eerie atmosphere of doom that seemed to hang over us all. The anticipation that war was going to break out at any moment made me worry that when we pulled into the station I would see the first wounded soldiers there. I was relieved to see the sight of four nurses and four stretchers on the platform, but no signs of wounded troops or bloodshed.

It was a very hot day, and the trains were extremely crowded. People were perspiring and the nearness of each other created a very unpleasant odor. We were packed in the railroad car like sardines in a can. The aisles and exit areas of the cars were standing room only. There were so many people and suitcases everywhere that it made it impossible for anyone to move.

At the border between France and Luxembourg, I encountered no problems at the Customs office. In my mind this was bizarre, but I was very relieved.

I was amazed at how smoothly it went. I was also surprised at how easily I was able to go from Germany into France at Strasbourg. Throughout history, Germany and France had always considered each other enemies. This hatred that these two countries had for each other went right down to the school level. In Germany we even sang songs of hatred about the French:

"Siegreich Wollen Wir—Wir Dürfen Es Nicht Mehr Sagen!...Deutschland Lebe Hoch." which means "Victorious we will fight, but we are not permitted to say whom we are fighting anymore. Germany will prevail above all!"

Fortunately, everything about my escape from Nazi Germany and the war was unfolding according to plan. The path I took to get out of Germany was complicated, with several border crossings. From Mannheim, Germany I went to Strasbourg, France. From Strasbourg I went to Metz. From France, I crossed the border into Luxemburg. From Luxemburg I would travel to Brussels, Belgium. Then I was to go to Rotterdam in the Netherlands. I hoped that Uncle Adolf and Mother were waiting for me in Rotterdam. Uncle Jub's brothers, Hans and Karl, lived there with their families, so we would have a safe place to rendezvous.

So far things were going smoothly. Then I reached the border between Luxembourg and Belgium. Even in my 90's as I write this now, I can still distinctly remember the lonely and terrified feeling that I felt that day. I had a deep fear of what the soldiers and authorities were going to do with me, or to me. I felt so alone in the world, as though I had been deserted by everyone I knew. Without John McCall accompanying me, suddenly it seemed that the people I now encountered were all against me. Yet, I tried to remain calm.

At this point in time, the German government had instituted an unprecedented policy with regard to passports. First of all, the traditional German passports now carried distinctive black swastikas on them. Then, if you were Jewish, a large red letter "J" was stamped onto the first page in indelible red ink, which meant that you were Jewish and considered to be a second class citizen. Since my last name, Mueller, was considered to be a very non-Jewish and very Aryan name, my passport had escaped the dreaded red "J" stamp.

I was instructed to come into the station house. The border guards said, "Well, you have no 'J' stamped on your passport. Why do you want to leave Germany? What is your reason for leaving the country? Are you a spy? Who are you, and where are you going?"

So, I told them that I was going to meet my mother—hopefully in London—where both of us had jobs waiting there for us with the German Ambassador. But they still were dubious about my sincerity, and my intentions.

I felt trapped. What was I going to do if I could not enter Belgium? What would become of me if I was stuck here and the war suddenly broke out? Desperate to talk my way out of this horrifying situation, I said, "Call my Uncle Jub. He is a friend of Minister Franz van Zealand. Franz von Zealand is the man who proposed a single currency for unified Europe. He had been with my uncle as a prisoner of war in the first World War."

The guards telephoned him and left a message. The next few minutes seemed like hours as I sat there and waited for the phone to ring. After several connections with my uncle, von Zealand called the station back and he vouched for me. Upon his word, the guards let me pass into Belgium. I took a deep sigh of relief.

One of the cleverest of our plans involved how we were going to get a few of our belongings out of Germany. Uncle Jub had taken several suitcases from Mannheim about six months before, and deposited them with a friend, Mr. Fivez, in Brussels. I was to pick them up on my way through Belgium. However, when I got there, I couldn't seem to reach Mr. Fivez. I decided that I had to find a place to sleep for the night, in the hope that I could reach him the next morning. I found a hotel near the train station, went without dinner, and went straight into bed.

The next morning, I walked to the train station to find out how I was to get to London. I decided to go to the local travel agency where I would plot my course based on what transportation was available. When I got there, it seemed that everyone had the same idea, and I had to stand in a long line for assistance.

There were maybe 50 people in one single line, and the person at the desk before us was handling everyone's inquiries, one at a time. It seemed like this would take forever. As chaotic as it was, the travel agency was surprisingly well organized, and everyone was behaving in a very orderly fashion. No one standing in line said a thing, and the silence was eerie.

The man who was standing directly in front of me was wearing a navy blue blazer and beige pants. He was leaning over in an odd stance, as though he was tying his shoe laces or something. When he suddenly stood straight up, and turned around, I had the surprise of my life. It was Uncle Jub! Now there was no need to continue to stand in line, because anything that I needed to know, he would be able to tell me.

Jub informed me that Aunt Erna and my six-year-old cousin, Franzel, were waiting in the café across the street. We left the travel agency and went to the café to surprise Erna.

Amidst a week of trying events, it was indeed a pleasant surprise for Aunt Erna. We sat in the café and talked, and we were able to tell each other of our individual escapes from Germany. Erna told me that they also had left Germany in a helter-skelter fashion. They had left nearly all of their belongings and just walked away from their lease, like they were on their way out to dinner at a restaurant.

Between all of us, we had very little cash. However, Uncle Jub insisted on giving me some extra money to help me out on my journey. We talked for a while, and decided that it was best if I left alone for England and they stayed in Brussels. Since my Uncle Jub was a Belgian citizen and he was there with his wife and son, it was the only place that they could safely stay.

Both Uncle Jub and Aunt Erna had small suitcases with them, which they had left Germany with. For Belgian citizens, that was allowed. However, as German citizens without packing permits, Mother and Uncle Adolf were not allowed suitcases at all.

So, anticipating this problem, we had devised our clever plan. Inside the suitcases we had previously deposited with Mr. Fivez were clothes and personal belongings. In the four additional packages were the family's fur coats. There was a gorgeous ocelot coat, a mink coat, a beautiful foal coat, and an additional jacket. That afternoon after seeing Uncle Jub and Aunt Erna, I successfully contacted Mr. Fivez and met him. I picked up the five suitcases and the four packages. I then boarded a train at the station and left Brussels from *Gare du midi,* which means Midtown Train Station.

I was on the train bound for Rotterdam, Holland, and miraculously everything was still unfolding according to plan. However, a few things started to go wrong. In Rosendaal, the Border Control Police came to me and didn't want to let me into Holland.

The officer said to me, "You have to leave this country in the fastest possible way. Your visa is only good for transit through the country, and you are not allowed to stay here at all."

I said, "I need to get there, to see my mother." So they telephoned family friends who lived there. After they spoke my friends and to the authorities, I was granted a permit allowing me to stay for 24 hours in Holland before leaving for England.

I also anticipated getting to Rotterdam and seeing my mother and uncle, where they were supposed to be staying with these same friends. However, according to them, Mother and Adolf's plans had suddenly changed and they had left Rotterdam on the last boat leaving from Hoek Von Holland bound for England. The last ship had already sailed from Hoek Von Holland, and they had no idea when they would resume service. That is why my mother and uncle could not wait for me.

After everybody investigated, we found one last possibility for me to sail for Harwich, England from Rotterdam, Holland. With the money which Uncle Jub had given to me I purchased a one-way ticket for passage across the English Channel and headed for the port.

On the boat, we were not permitted to have any light, including matches for cigarettes. We had special lookout patrols for sighting German U-boats, because they knew the Germans already had U-boats patrolling the area. Fortunately, my boat trip went without incident. When I reached Harwich, England and went to the Customs Office, they wanted to know if I had anything to declare. It was August 30, 1939. I told them, "I came from Germany, I have no belongings of value." When I asked, "Do you want me to open the suitcases?" they said, "It's no problem, just go." Again, I breathed a deep sigh of relief. If they had confiscated my suitcases, we would have no clothes or winter coats to wear in England. Another problem existed too, as I only had the key to open one of the suitcases. In all of the confusion, Uncle Jub had forgotten to give the rest of them to me.

The British immigration officer stamped my passport with: "This day on condition that the holder registers at once with the police and does not enter any employment other than as resident in service in a private household." Household servants were needed in England, and having those prearranged positions was the only way we could enter the country.

I went to the local train station and purchased a ticket for London. When I arrived in London at Victoria Station, I found that some 4,000 other people had arrived there at the same time as well. On one hand it was a crowded scene of sheer bedlam at the station, yet there was still a proper sense of order to it. Fortunately, tables were set up on the railroad platforms as Information areas with volunteers to help me. I tried to find the whereabouts of Mother and Uncle Adolf, and went to one of the volunteer tables. The volunteers were very efficient at uniting us. What a sense of relief all three of us felt that evening in London. Somehow we all made it out of mainland Europe unharmed, and managed to find each other as well.

In London we saw even more signs of impending doom. One of the sights I saw there was that of people in the streets spending the night filling sandbags. These were going to be used to stop fires from spreading from one building to the next. All of the frantic behavior I saw before me in London made me realize that every minute counted, and every decision we made could be a matter of life or death. A horrible feeling of dread came over me. The city seemed to be a sea of frantic activity and fear. We were informed that Hitler had already bombarded Poland. Had England declared war on Germany? We were not sure, but we could see that they were evacuating children, and there were British troops everywhere.

We were scared, but we were determined to do everything we could to survive this. We had an appointment at the Bloomsburry House, which was an organization of volunteers to help all of the refugees. Since Mother and I had been issued working permits to be in England, we were able to find accommodations for the two of us thanks to the people at the Bloomsburry House. It was nearly impossible to find somewhere the three of us could stay together. Uncle Adolf had a different kind of permit, so he had to find other accommodations. Adolf was fortunate though, in that Uncle Jub had put an amount of money in an English bank in his name, or he wouldn't have been able to leave Germany as easily. At the time, to enter the country, the government had to have a way of proving that Adolf had a traceable source of money. If he could not supply proof that he had money to live on, he would be put into a camp with all the other male refugees who came from Germany.

With the money Uncle Jub had deposited for him, he rented himself a room in a place apart from Mother and I. That night, all Uncle Adolf had with him were the clothes he was wearing and a pair of pajamas, which were wrapped up in newspapers.

The volunteers who helped us out had given Mother and I billets for our accommodations for that night. But they also delivered some bad news to us: the jobs we supposedly had working for the Ambassador from Germany to England no longer existed—because the Ambassador had left London that very morning. With his hasty exit, our cook and chambermaid jobs were suddenly non-existent. Now what were we going to do? At this point we were absolutely exhausted. We decided that we would have to resolve our job dilemma in the morning.

Mother and I finally got to the room that was arranged for us to stay in that night. Instead of being relieved, we were horrified at what we found there. There were dirty linens, and not a clean towel to be found. I went to bed that night with my pants on because it was so filthy in the bed.

After Mother and I tried to settle down in this filthy boarding house for a couple of hours, I was still unable to sleep. As I lie there, I devised a plan to get us out of there—immediately. I got up and did some investigating, and I found that there was an 11:45 p.m. train, bound for Manchester. I realized that we had to get out of London, since our only contact in England was John McCall's sister in Manchester. We had to get there and see if she could help us.

I had the address and telephone number where Uncle Adolf was staying, and I phoned him at 11:00 p.m. to tell him that the train to Manchester would leave at 11:45, and we were going to be on it. I wanted to get out of London immediately, for fear of our safety.

Tired, and at the end of his patience, Adolf argued with me on the telephone. "You are chasing me around the globe," he exclaimed, "and I won't have any part of it!"

I said to him, "The train to Manchester leaves at 11:45 tonight, and you had better be there."

"I just got settled for the night. Every time I settle in, you chase me out."

"Fine," I said, "then you stay in London on your own, we are going Manchester—tonight!" I was furious with him, and I was not going to take "no" for an answer.

Finally he agreed, once he realized there was no changing my mind.

Mother and I went back to Victoria Station, found Uncle Adolf there, and the three of us boarded the train. The night train to Manchester passed many villages along the way. Most of them had no lights anywhere, and it was a very scary sight to behold. It was a continuation of the frighteningly unnatural atmosphere that all of England seemed to have been plunged into.

As dawn was breaking, we arrived at our destination. In Manchester, a taxi took us to a boarding house. It was 5:00 in the morning. The woman who opened the entrance door to the boarding house was dressed in an old brown checkered man's housecoat, slippers, and curlers in her hair. Several of her teeth were missing. She informed us, "We have only one double bed." We took it. We all laid down upon it, just long enough to catch our breath.

At breakfast, we found one large table and six miners seated at it, before their shift in the coal mines. They were having breakfast— "family style" with eggs, bacon, and potatoes. All of it was as greasy as can be. There was no butter, but there was something there to spread on toast. We didn't know what it was—lard perhaps. We ate as much as we could, then we went back to our room.

I didn't want to touch anything, because everything was as incredibly filthy as the boarding house in London had been. Much to my horror, we found that the sheets were dirty, and filled with bedbugs. The bedbugs bit us and didn't let us sleep. I tried to sleep with my pajamas on, but the bedbugs were determined not to let me get any rest. I finally attempted to sleep in the bathtub. In spite of the shockingly dirty accommodations, the people there were so wonderful to us, all of them. They welcomed us with no questions asked. We stayed one night at this boarding house. When we checked out, we paid, and shook our belongings in the bathtub very well in hope that the bedbugs were not traveling with us.

In London we had been informed that once we got to Manchester we should go to an organization of volunteers who were helping out the refugees find lodging and jobs, known as the Kershowhouse. After our second breakfast at the dirty boarding house, we took our belongings and went to the Kershowhouse.

Mrs. Barash-Kershow, who ran the Kershowhouse, was very friendly and helped us to find a room for my uncle. She also promised to find some work for my mother and myself. Since the jobs promised to Mother and I in London were now non-existent, we had to immediately find a way to support ourselves. And, since our boat passage to America was not to take place for several months, we had to come up with new living accommodations.

At that time England permitted female household help to come into the country, and to be paid, because there was a great demand for that type of work. Men were not so lucky. There were no jobs for immigrant men. Thank God that Adolf had his money in the bank, or he would have been trapped in a dreaded refugee camp.

Mother, my uncle and I then went to St. Gabriel's Hall, which was an address given to us by John McCall. It was 91 degrees that day and everything was unbearably hot, except for the convent at St. Gabriel's. There we were greeted and taken into the parlor. We were served tea and crackers. Mother Superior came down to the parlor and met us. She was a very charming and strong person, and she was in charge of all of the nuns. Mother Superior's official title was the head of The Convent of The Cross and Passion, St. Gabriel's Hall, Victoria Park, Manchester, England. After we told her where we came from, and what we had been through, she had tears in her eyes. She took me by the hand, and led me into the chapel to "pray with me."

After we returned from the chapel, Mother Superior said she was going to help us out. As a student-aged girl, I was given a room like all of the other students who stayed in St. Gabriel's Hall while attending university. This worked out perfectly. I helped out in the dining room, the most desirable part of the house. Because there were no students in attendance at the moment, due to between-semester vacations, I had very little work to do. I was so thankful for our accommodations that I wanted to be helpful as I could while I was there. I even offered to help polish the floors.

"No, no, no," said Mother Superior when she found me doing that.

"But I can do that job," I said.

"You can't do that, because we have other people waiting for that job," she explained. There were several poor people, and the sisters would feed them and it was their job to polish the floors in exchange for food.

Sister Gabriel Thérèse was my superior, a very calm and collected nun. She often gave me little treats. One day she presented me with an apple. Another day, it was toffee. One of the ladies from the faculty told me, "What you lost in earthly belongings was really nothing. You will get it back very soon. It won't be long before everything will be great again." I was happy to hear her words of comfort, but I also sensed that things would get much worse before they got better.

I saw the war coming, with bombs, gas masks and air raid shelters, just as my grandmother had described the earlier World War. Even my dreams of America moved far away from my horizon of view. I felt again that I was alone in the world. Not long afterward came the sounds of sirens, and orders that all windows be shut and taped over with black paper, to make certain that the city was difficult for the Nazis to bomb at night.

At night all of the cinemas were closed. Theaters were closed as well. It was like a whole different world. Not only did the war make it all so surreal, but the way things were done in England were so different than what I was used to experiencing. I really felt so alone in this strange country full of people who seemed to eat everything half raw. I found that English food was prepared very differently than what I was used to eating in Mannheim. In Germany we cooked meat until it was very well done, so I never got used to the still-bleeding beef and flavorless mutton that they served in England.

While at St. Gabriel's Hall, I had plenty of time to ponder what war was all about. Why did it have to be this way? Had people already forgotten the wounds inflicted after the First World War? No. Nobody wanted war except one: and that was Hitler. Those who followed him were either the fanatics under the thumb of Hitler, or destitute bankrupt people who had been left with no hope. The other people who supported the war were very wealthy industrialists who stood to benefit financially from supporting him.

I wrote in my diary: "Poor people, I can not do anything else for you but pray. Poor people who have nothing else to lose but their lives."

In England it was an unusually hot September, reaching 90 degrees many of the days. The room I was given at St. Gabriel's Hall was small, but it was a decent room. Cool and quiet. In return for staying in the room, I helped out in the kitchen, otherwise I was treated like any of the other girls in the student body. Since I spoke both English and German, I was able to teach some of the nuns how to speak German. I never did question why they were fascinated with learning German from me. Perhaps it was that they wanted me to feel that I too had a sense of self-worth, and that I had knowledge to impart on them. Or, maybe they were anticipating and fearing an invasion by German soldiers. Surely, a grasp of the German language would work to their benefit if that happened. In teaching the nuns my own language, it gave me a sense of security and belonging, amidst the bizarre and frightening state of the world.

Meanwhile, Mother's situation was different than mine. The people at The Kershowhouse had found her a job so that she could earn money as well. That way she could afford to have a roof over her head, and all three of us could live for our several months in England until our quota numbers came up.

Mother's job was with a family by the name of Goldsmith, who were the owners of a department store in Manchester. She took a job as their cook, but soon became the "chief cook and bottle washer" for the family. Every morning a helper known as a "charwoman," came in to work for the Goldsmith's as well. She was a lovely jolly woman and one of her first tasks during the day was to chop wood, because the heating was via the fireplace. One morning my mother didn't want to wait for the Charwoman to come, as she wanted to make the coffee. So, Mother took on the Charwoman's job of chopping wood in the morning. When they found out my mother could bake, they praised her and encouraged her to do more baking. After that they found out that her ironing was so superb, she got more and more to iron. Mother held this job from the time we arrived in Manchester, until we left the country.

So our days in Manchester were filled with my mother and I working. I was at the convent, my mother was in the employment of the Goldsmiths and she lived there too. Since I was just working to maintain a roof over my head, I actually made no money.

After the terrifying ordeal of narrowly escaping from Nazi Germany with our lives, my life in the convent in Manchester was like a blessed sanctuary. It was cool, quiet, and stable. Several times during my stay at the convent I felt like I had awakened from a nightmare. Who knows what fate would have awaited us had we stayed in Mannheim.

But, of course, the nightmare was far from over. My mother, uncle and I were lucky to have not only escaped from Nazi Germany, we also avoided becoming bombing casualties in London. The Second World War had officially begun. We avidly read the newspaper reports and listened to the radio. The first foreign soil the Germans marched onto was Poland on September 1. By September 27, they had demolished the complete Polish Republic. Hitler and his circle of Nazi advisors had developed a new method of surprise attack. Since the First World War was mainly fought in trenches with machine guns and Germany had lost, a new tactic had to be devised. This rain of fire upon Poland is what is known in war terms as the *Blitzkrieg*. In the German language, the word *Blitzkrieg* literally translates to mean "lightning war." This term was coined because this war strategy utilized lightning fast advances into enemy territory. These advances would combine attacks both from the air, and from the ground. It was a combination of machine gun fire, armored tank advances, and bombs dropped from airplanes. The Nazis would push further and further into enemy territory, expanding their control day by day until they occupied whole cities and countries. Now the war was in full swing, and no one knew if they were safe anywhere in Europe.

There were several peace treaties in place after the First World War, which Germany had agreed to as part of their surrender. However, once Hitler came into power in 1933, it was his plan all along to go to war. He had already bulldozed his way into controlling all of Germany, and in September of 1939 he implemented his plan of taking over one European country after another, which were to fall like a successive line of dominoes.

By 1938 Hitler had already escalated the manufacture of a legion of Panzer armored tanks. The head of this new division of tanks was Heinz Guderian, who had studied the British books on the principles of tank warfare.

Another key to Germany's successful Panzer tank division was the use of radio transmission, which was utilized to communicate with the individual tank operators. They were able to plow their way into foreign land as a single unit, advancing in a single line of destruction. One of the keys to this strategy was for the German army to secure key bridges before the enemy could destroy them. This gave the Nazi's a way to rapidly advance without significant delays. Because these Panzer tanks were so well armored, they could successfully stand up to machine gunfire or the bullets from conventional guns.

Hitler and his army had taken years to plan their strategies. The army was fortified in numbers and with capabilities that the countries they were invading did not possess. For instance, in 1940, French tanks still did not have the advantage of unified radio command. This worked in the Nazi's favor, especially combined with the sheer element of surprise. One by one, in the coming months, Germany would use the *Blitzkrieg* strategy to invade Poland, France, Yugoslavia, and Greece. Hitler had his eye on controlling all of Europe, and during the beginning of the war, he successfully invaded one unsuspecting country after another.

When we left our home, we knew we had to get out of Germany to ensure our own safety. Luckily I left August 27, 1939. The September 1 invasion of Poland was the beginning of implementing this *Blitzkrieg* tactic. Suddenly all of Europe was plunged into a war.

I distinctly remember November 5, 1939 in England, as I wrote about it in my diary.

That was the day I did something very cavalier and uncharacteristic for me. Although the cinemas were closed at night, there were matinees. That afternoon I went to the movies with a very nice Englishman, whom I had just casually met.

He was very polite and well-spoken. He was tall, lanky, and he very much empathized with my situation of being in a strange country and not knowing anyone. Speaking to him, he very much fulfilled my vision of what a perfectly mannered and well-spoken Englishman was all about. He had a very dry sense of humor, and he put no demands upon me. He felt that he would make my dreary stay in England a little happier. He was correct in that fact, because for a couple of hours that day, I felt good, and was able to temporarily forget the war. This young man was invited to a dinner party that evening, and he invited me to come along with him. I told him that I could not accompany him, but I was flattered by his offer.

It was so unlike me to have gone to the matinee with him that day, since he was a perfect stranger. Why would I suddenly do such a thing? The reason was simple. None of us had any idea what was going to happen next. Would the German army drop bombs on England any minute? Was the evening about to be pierced by the sound of an air raid or machine gun fire at a moment's notice? All of our lives seemed so uncertain at this point. Ultimately, it was a nice several hours with this young man, however I never did see him again after that evening.

Father Kennedy very often came to St. Gabriel's Hall for tea in the afternoon, and for different talks with the young ladies who were students as well as the faculty members. I was always wondering what it was like to have taken a vow of celibacy. So, I was inspired to write in my diary:

How hard it must be for such a young and beautiful priest, to find himself in the company of 24 young and beautiful girls, where he could never have any relationship. In my eyes, this is a terrible way to be. I wonder if these young priests often feel regret for having committed themselves to a life of celibacy. I have long thought about this with regard to Father Kennedy. I personally would like to vote for abolishing this senseless "vow of celibacy." Life is sometimes so strange. Who knows what is right? Who knows what is wrong? Do you live a life not to feel anything? Or do you just choose not to make your life a beautiful thing? Is this just my opinion? Try as I might, I just don't understand what the Catholic Church is all about.

Although I had escaped from Germany and was in one way relieved, during my time in England I still found myself depressed. When I think back on all of this, I really would have thought that I could find someone who could console me. Somehow I thought that I would have found some help. At least I could cry there at the convent, and nobody noticed. Or, so I thought. One day Mother Superior saw me with tears in my eyes, and she realized that there was something not quite right with me.

She asked me what was wrong.

I didn't want to tell her what I felt and thought, but I really felt like a piece of nothing: something inconsequential, like dust. Why was I living? What for? Nature is beautiful, and gorgeous. I saw all of this beauty around me, but what is here for me? I just couldn't comprehend it. I felt so very lost as the entire world I had known seemed to fall apart.

I'd looked upward like a child, early the previous morning, and saw the moon and the trees. In the clear blue sky of dawn, it was still nearly dark. But the night gave way to the day. And, like a child I felt the whole thing was a dream. It is like a deep nothing, not to know, not to *be*. From the beauty of nature overhead, I realized what a little nothing I was in the grand scheme of things.

But I also realized that I had no time to dwell on such thoughts. I had to go on and on, and hope that very soon we would be in America. In my mind, America was the promised land of freedom and opportunity. I had to concentrate on my future.

Because of our visas, we had to leave England in March of 1940 or miss our chance to escape altogether. To make matters worse, much to our horror, we found out that we had to purchase new tickets to America. Since the war had broken out, we found the tickets we had purchased in Germany with Deutsche Marks were deemed to be void. Cunard Line was unable to obtain the money from their Mannheim ticket office—or any German office for that matter. In the eyes of Cunard, although I had the actual tickets in my possession, they were no longer valid.

Without enough money for the three of us to purchase new passage to the United States, what were we going to do? It was Mother Superior who came to our rescue. She ended up giving us the money for the tickets, out of the little money she herself had. I never questioned where this money came from. It was a lot of money at the time, probably the equivalent of several thousands of dollars. I do not remember what the price tag on the tickets was, but I felt it was a magnanimous gesture. I vowed to repay her any way I could as soon as I was in America.

When the day finally arrived that we were to board the ship for America, we went down to Southhampton, England; happy that we were finally making the last leg of our voyage to New York. But when we arrived at the harbor, we were really very, very sad at the sight that greeted us. As far as we could see, there were ships standing half way up in the water and half in the mud. They had hit mines and were destroyed. Was that to be the fate of our ship as well? We had no idea what was to come, and this sight horrifically illustrated what was possible.

Once we boarded our ship we were told that we were going to be traveling in a convoy which should have been a very comforting thought, but I felt that a convoy would attract more attention than a single ship, and it made me even more uncomfortable. As our ship left the port there was no gala goodbye, no hoopla. This was nothing like the exciting ship launches I had seen in newsreels and movies. There were no streamers or confetti. Quite the opposite. Everyone was very somber when we boarded. We were leaving certain danger for a land of uncertainty.

Uncle Adolf was very happy that this was the last leg of his flight from Germany. He said to me, "Every time I settle down somewhere, you come and tell me 'Move, move.' So, I have constantly been on the move. First in Mannheim. Then in London. Then in Manchester. I hope this move to New York City is my last trip, and that I can finally have some peace and quiet in my life." He sincerely hoped that this would be the end of our travels for a while.

Our journey across the Atlantic was an adventure in itself. I was amused to find that the soldiers on the ship wanted to talk to me. They wanted to know about Germany and I wanted to know about where we were going, and what to expect on our voyage. However, I didn't get any answers from them because they were in uniform, and this was "classified" information. All I knew was that I was finally on the way "home," or at least to what was going to become my new home.

We had left Liverpool on March 9, 1940. I wrote in my diary that night:

We are barely away from the pier, and already we are having a drill for the lifeboats. Tonight I explored the boat, and again found how beautiful the world can be with a little more money. Some of these people are really traveling in luxury. But one has to be happy we are even on board. Never mind the accommodations. On board the S.S. Lancaster we have many soldiers. And, who knows what else—in terms of war supplies and firearms—are also aboard. We—as the passengers—are not permitted to have any sort of light at night. There is a strict rule that no cigarettes can be lit anywhere on the ship at night, as the illumination from a match or a burning cigarette might possibly give away our position on the sea, putting us in danger of being sunk by German boats patrolling the area.

Mother, Uncle Adolf and I had a tourist cabin together. We sailed very slowly so that we didn't make too much noise and alert the U-boats in the area. We sailed in darkness and hoped for our safe arrival in New York.

The ocean was rough. Few meals were served to the handful of people in the dining room—the ones that were not seasick. One of the people in our group was on deck during turbulent conditions. The wind was so strong that when he leaned over to vomit, his passport blew out to sea. The man was hysterical and rightly so. What can one do with no identification card, no passport? He was so upset that he beside himself with horror.

Most of the passengers were refugees from various countries. They were from Germany, Austria, and England mainly. On board we met a couple from Vienna. We kept a friendly relationship with them for quite a long time: Mr. and Mrs. Treuer, and their daughter Lizzie who was my age. Lizzie and I became quite good friends on the ship, and we vowed to stay in touch with each other in America.

Everyone was very much concerned with where we were going. Would we arrive? What did we leave behind? Whom of our friends would still be alive when the war was over? The uncertainty cast a dark cloud over the journey. It seemed that no one we were traveling with on the ship knew what we would find in America. We all hoped New York would fulfill our dreams of the wonderful city with freedom and equality for all. Our first stop in North America was the city of Halifax, Nova Scotia. The soldiers got off at that point. We only stayed in the port of Halifax for a short time, and we did not leave the boat. Then we set sail for New York City.

As we entered the New York harbor, our sailing by Ellis Island was a breath-taking sight. For so much of our voyage, we had no idea if we were going to live long enough to see this vision at all. Seeing the Statue of Liberty brought to life all of the pictures I had seen in cinema newsreels. I felt awestruck. So many emotions came washing over me.

Mother, Uncle Adolf and I were all on deck for this inspiring sight. It was a cold March morning, and we all wore wool gloves on our hands, and wool caps which we had pulled over our ears. I got goose bumps all over me at the sight of Lady Liberty welcoming us into the harbor. We had been waiting for such a long time to actually see this moment arrive, it was amazing to witness as it became a reality before our very eyes. I had done everything I could to make certain that Mother and Uncle Adolf and I made it safely out of Nazi Germany. Now what awaited us?

As the unmistakable cityscape of Manhattan and all of its skyscrapers came into closer focus, I was in awe to see that we had arrived in the city with the streets were supposedly paved with gold. What exactly would we actually find there? Would we be able to make a living for ourselves? Would it be wonderful or horrible? Would all of our hopes be fulfilled? Whatever the answers would be, the war was currently raging on the continent we had just left, and we were thankful that we had narrowly escaped from the hands of the Nazis. I had witnessed signs of their brutality already. On this cold March day, the one thing that I did know for certain, was that this was going to be the beginning of a whole new chapter of my life.

Thanks to all of the wonderful people who helped me, I had narrowly escaped with my own life. I was so grateful that Mother, Uncle Adolf and I had actually made it out of Nazi Germany, and we were now safely in America. It was as if I had made it out at the very last minute. If my window of opportunity to leave Europe unharmed was to close exactly at the clock's stroke of midnight, then surely I had narrowly escaped at *One Minute Before Midnight*…

Chapter Two:
My Childhood

My name is Ruth Annemarie Hedwig Mueller. I was born January 21, 1917, an Aquarius. It was in Mannheim, Germany, the County of Baden, where I first saw the light of the Sun. As I found out later on, I came out three months ahead of time because my parents were only married the previous August. I was born too early, but there I was. That was how I started my life. It obviously set up a lifelong pattern, because even today I arrive ahead of time for any appointment.

The economic and political situation at that time was not too wonderful in Germany due to the effects of the First World War. It wasn't long before the economic inflation left a big imprint on me as well. One of my first memories is of my father coming home one day with a purchase he was proud of having bought—a beautiful wooden carved owl.

My mother instantly flew into a rage and said, "We do not need such a thing! What did you go and do that for?"

My father logically explained, "When I get up tomorrow, the money will not buy even a wooden owl, so I figured that we may as well have that as opposed to nothing." He called it "running away inflation."

I was often told the story of the owl. These were very hard times for my parents. My father was an engineer for Mercedes Benz at that time, and we lived in Frankfurt. When my grandmother, my mother's mother, came to visit she always brought me presents. During one such visit, after she gave me my present, we sat down for coffee and she asked for milk. But, there was no milk.

And in my three-year-old way of speaking I said, "I can drink black coffee."

She was horrified to find that a little girl was so nonplused at the lack of milk.

That was another family story that was often repeated and laughed about around our house.

My grandmother was such a wonderful influence on my life, from the day I can first remember her, up until she died.

I will never forget when she later came to America, towards the end of her life, she said to me, "If I had only come to this beautiful country early in my life, I would have done a lot of things that could have made a difference." And she could have, because she was so bright. She was a wonderful person, and a lot of people loved her dearly.

Another incident in my childhood I distinctly remember was one day when I was in my baby carriage in front of the house. At the time baby carriages were very high off of the ground—by at least three feet. My nanny was supposed to be taking care of me. While she was rocking the carriage back and forth she had her back to me and was flirting with her boyfriend, and not paying attention to me. I was very lively, as I always was—and still am today. Nobody thought at that time of tying down a baby in her carriage.

Suddenly, my father came running down the street and saw that I was trying to get out of the carriage at that very second. He ran up and grabbed me, and told the girl, "You are relieved of your job. I never want to see you again."

He took me upstairs and told my mother, "This girl almost let Ruth get killed if I hadn't come by at that moment." That was the last I saw of that particular nanny.

My mother was a very warm and wonderful person. She was very good to everybody, and she loved dogs very much. My father had brought a dog, a boxer, into the marriage before I was born. It was a lovely dog, but very protective of my father. And when I came into this world the boxer did not like it a bit. At one time, she was standing up against the baby carriage, lifting her paw, trying to hit me in the face. Maybe she wanted to play with me. Again, my father saw this from far away, and he ran up and grabbed the dog. Soon afterward, that dog was given away to some good friends. My father saw that she had a good life, but not with us. Again, I escaped from mishap.

As I said, I was very active as a child, and very mechanically interested as well. We had a car which was parked in front of our house. At the time, parking spaces were very easy to get, and the car was always parked right there. For whatever reason, I liked being in the car. It was a sure way to keep me quiet. Another of my happiest things at the time was to have a hammer in my hand. People would walk by and look into the window to see what a little girl with a hammer was doing in the car. There was something about the power of the hammer that I liked. Keeping me quiet at that time was very easy—all you had to do was to put a hammer in my hands and put me in the car.

Another vivid early memory of mine took place on a beautiful sunny day. We were going somewhere and my father was going through his morning toilette routine. All of the windows were open and he was singing in a beautiful voice. People were passing by and listening to him sing the aria's of various operas. "*O solo Mio*" was my favorite. I was fascinated to watch as passers-by on the street would stop to listen to him. I so much enjoyed my father's singing voice, and obviously people outside the window enjoyed his voice too.

That evening, my mother came to my room and started singing to me "O Solo Mio." I said to her, "Mama, no singing! Not singing 'O Solo Mio!' Only Papa singing 'O Solo Mio.' Mama singing 'Wuz im Garten!'" Apparently I was already a music critic. In my mind "O Solo Mio" was my father's song, but from Mother I only wanted to her "Wuz im Garten," which is a lullaby about a pig in a garden: "Can you see the pig in the garden, how they toil the soil…"

As a child I very quickly developed a great sense of what I wanted to do, and what I didn't want to do. That is commonly known as having a stubborn streak. At one point, my father wanted to leave on a trip, and everybody said goodbye to him, but I wouldn't. I didn't want to say goodbye. My father hit me on my behind, and I still wouldn't say goodbye. So, he hit me on the behind again, and still I would not say goodbye. I would give no reaction—except to start to cry.

This went on until my mother came in and yelled, "Stop this nonsense!" He would not let loose of me, and I would not give in. Finally, the two of us ended up on the couch. He sobbed, and I sobbed. He was so upset that he didn't go on his trip, and my mother had to console both of us with cold compresses on our eyes.

I loved my father very much. One day when we had people at the house, the question was raised: "Who would you prefer to live with if your parents divorced? Your mother or your father?" I was baffled by such a question. "How could that be?" I thought to myself. "That wasn't possible!" But the adults posing the question laughed and joked about my confused reaction.

I knew that my mother could not drive and would not have the car. Instead of saying either of their names, I simply said, "I will go with the one who keeps the car." Everyone thought that this was a completely diplomatic move on my part and had a good laugh over my reply.

Both of my parents had strong personalities and they were both very giving and generous people. We always had a lot of friends at our house for dinners and get-togethers. I enjoyed having company. I particularly remember one time when my father gave a brand new suit to a friend who was in need. I thought it was a wonderful idea, but my mother felt he should have given an older suit away, not the best suit which he had just bought. I resented my mother for reprimanding him. As far as I was concerned, my father could do no wrong.

As a young girl, when he walked with me and put his arm around me, I felt not like his daughter, but rather like his girlfriend. Only years later did I see that an *Oedipus Complex* definitely existed. *Psychoanal,* the dictionary of psychology, defines *Oedipus Complex* as: "the unresolved desire of a child for sexual gratification through the parent of the opposite sex. This involves, first, identification with, and later, hatred for the parent of the same sex, who is considered by the child as a rival." This, however, is part of the inner dynamics of all families. All children experience some anxiety about the confusing relationship of their parents.

One lovely Sunday morning, while my father was singing—as usual—before we went to church, I heard him swearing and tearing something apart. What happened was that: the collar of his shirt was too tight. He never liked to have starch on the collars of any of his shirts. In this instance, he could not even button it. As his wife, it was understood that it was Mother's job to instruct the laundry that his collars were not to be starched. So, he blamed my mother for failing in this task. He became so enraged that he tore the shirt into shreds. Although I too blamed my mother for the incident, I also promised myself at that very moment that I would never permit myself to display such anger.

When I was four years old, my parents were amidst negotiating to open a store in Braunschweig. I was left in the care of my grandmother and grandfather. I was very small at that time. They lived in an apartment building which had a wide, sweeping marble staircase which went up to the first floor. A couple of my unmarried uncles lived there as well. They all lived together on the first floor in a large apartment.

One day, I came running up the stairs yelling, "It's the first time! It's the first time! It's the first time!" I cried, and I jumped up into my uncle's open arms, and said, "It's the first time!" That was all that I could say, over and over.

Finally he was able to calm me down and asked, "What was the first time? What are you talking about?"

It turned out to be the first time I had seen a rat! There on that beautiful white marble staircase of the apartment building was a big brown rat and I was beside myself with horror.

Very often the phrase, "it was the first time" would be used in the family. And for me, the first sighting of a live rat on the staircase of "C.2.1" was a big deal for me. Well, the second time that I saw a rat, it wasn't such a big and traumatic event as the first time. But that first time had a very dramatic and innocent feeling.

The housing in Mannheim was laid out in squares. The city was divided in a fashion which is very similar to the island of Manhattan in New York City. From the castle to the river, all of the apartment buildings and houses had both numbers and letters to denote their position amidst the concentric square organization of the streets.

The division in the middle of town was exactly one kilometer from the castle to the Neckar River Bridge, and the squares were set up in between. One square block would be A.1, the next A.2, the next A.3, and so on. Then heading south one would find B.1, B.2, B.3, etc. This way no one could get lost trying to find an address. At the time, Grandma lived in building "C.2.1."

At the age of five my Aunt Erna took me to the bank with her. While she did her banking, she instructed me to wait for her in the lobby. When she returned she was startled to see me standing on a banquette, speaking to a gathering of people who were listening, laughing and applauding at what I was saying to them.

I am not quite sure how I fell upon the subject matter that I was addressing them with, but I was telling them all of the off-color words and terms that I had been taught never to say in public.

"'Asshole' is a bad word," I proclaimed from the banquette. "And the word 'fucking' you should never say." And, my entire repertoire of blue language came out. Each forbidden word would be followed by the phrase, "You must never say that."

My poor aunt was horrified to hear what I was pontificating to the crowd at the bank that day. In my mind I was not doing anything wrong because I told them, "You must never say these words."

I was severely reprimanded that day for my public display, regardless of my good intentions. And my shocked aunt vowed that she was never going to take me to the bank with her ever again!

At one point my parents were living in Braunschweig where they were running the bicycle, baby carriage and sewing machine store. I went to live with my grandmother, and although I loved living there, one day I decided to run away.

As I recall, I had been reprimanded by my Uncle Adolf for something. I don't remember exactly what it was about. But, being a hard-headed Aquarian little girl, I ran out of the apartment and into the street. I didn't know where I was going, I just knew that I was running away from home.

They were so horrified I would do such a thing that they were absolutely crazy with worry. It was about 5:00 p.m. and I just ran as fast as I could. I did not know where I was headed. Being alone in the street as the sun was going down I became frightened of my own courage and felt a great relief when I heard the footsteps of my two uncles trying to catch me, which they did.

"What happened to you?" "Where did you go?" "What has gotten into you?" I was met with all of these frantic questions when I suddenly returned to the house.

I defensively said, "Well, I didn't like this, and I didn't like that. And I just decided that I had enough and I was leaving."

My Uncle Adolf said to me, "You are too hard to handle. If you don't straighten up young lady, you are going to go back to Braunschweig to live with your mother and father."

Oh, no, I didn't want that!

After I thought about it, I was much better off with Grandma. She was wonderful to me. We had such great times together. When I realized what my options were, I opted for staying with her.

Living with Grandma was much more fun than staying with my parents. It was very funny that later on in life I learned that my father had done something very similar in his youth. He was about 14 years old, and he had received bad school marks. His parents gave him a big lecture, which he did not like, so he went to the toilet, jumped out of the window, and away he went. His poor parents were worried sick, and finally the police found him in Switzerland where he was working in a bakery store making bread. The movements of people at that time were very much known by the police because you had to register with the Post Office. And in Switzerland, records were very well kept of every person who came or went across the border. Once the Swiss police located him, his parents boarded a train and retrieved him. Back in Germany with his parents, he got better marks in school and behaved properly from then onward.

At the time I realized that I didn't need to run away because I was having a much better time with Grandma and Grandpa than I did with my own parents. Grandma would send me to the store to buy freshly pressed cider. She had a big pitcher of that and Calle, the big fat white braided bread with butter. I also remember that I would peel fresh walnuts. When walnuts are fresh, you peel off the skins, and they are sweet as can be.

Grandma loved her crossword puzzles. She would have me help her with the puzzles that would appear in the newspaper every day. I would help her with the words. I remember there was one clue that said: "River in Italy." Two letters only.

I said, "Po." And she would cheer the fact that I knew the right answer.

She really admired me for getting words like that. I will never forget it. And she also loved the serial stories that would run in the magazines. She would be waiting for the postman to bring the latest issue so that she could continue reading the story she was following.

Another thing that she let me do was to stay up late into the evening. If it was just the two of us at home, she let me stay up as late as she did. We had such a great time together.

Grandma had a masseuse named Mrs. Kurz who came to visit her every morning. The masseuse had eight children and very little money. Grandma liked the massage that she got, but she also wanted to help Mrs. Kurz.

I said to her, "Grandma, I want a massage too." And Mrs. Kurz very willingly would give me a massage as well.

I remember saying, "Oh, how wonderful! Oh, how wonderful!" I loved it so much. I still love massages today.

I have all of these wonderful memories of life with my grandmother. When she was growing up, her father had a great library. Whenever she couldn't be found and they were looking for her, they would find her somewhere in the library, up on the ladder reading a book.

In school the teacher said to her, "Now we are going to study Shakespeare."

And she replied to the teacher, "Shakespeare? I read Shakespeare already, when I was just a little girl."

And the teacher exclaimed to her, "A little girl? And what do you think are you now?"

She said, "I don't know. But I read Shakespeare already."

On one occasion the teacher requested that Grandma's father come to school and talk to the principal. The principal told him, "This girl is so bright, let her study and become a teacher. She is so ahead of everyone in her class, and her grades are far above average." Today we might say, "She had a high I.Q."

Her father said to the teacher, "Under no circumstances will I permit such talk. My daughter is going to get married, have children, and live happily ever after. And don't put any more of these bees in her brain. I don't want this."

Unfortunately, when she married, she married her first cousin. Everyone was horrified: "Oh my God, the children are all going to be idiots!"

Well, nothing happened, and they all turned out to be very bright and they were all perfectly healthy.

Whenever anyone in the local town spoke about my Grandma and Grandpa, they always referred to them as "the beautiful couple." They also said, "They have so much money that they will never live long enough to spend the interest on the family fortune that they have between them."

That was how it looked in the decades before Germany changed so drastically. However, things turned out quite differently. The economy shifted dramatically after the First World War.

My grandfather was a very good natured and a good looking man, but he had absolutely no business sense whatsoever. They owned a lot of property between them. However, one day Grandpa decided that he was going to sell the land. It was taking a long time to get the money from the new owners.

At one point, their fortunes were in seriously bad shape. My grandmother asked him, "What is taking them so long to pay us?"

He replied, "Oh don't worry about it. They will pay us eventually. Don't be so hard on them."

He went so far as to say to the new purchasers, "It's okay, pay me when you can." In reality, they never intended on paying him. Lawsuits were not common in those days, and Grandfather was totally ineffectual.

So my grandmother decided that she was going to take the reins of this situation. She took over the whole business deal. At the time Mannheim had around 300,000 inhabitants, and she decided that they needed to move there. She started her own real estate business, selling property, and finding properties for people who were looking to purchase a home.

She became so well known in Germany that on one occasion she received a letter from America, which was addressed to "Frau Frida Halfen, Germany." Miraculously it made it to her, addressed with that alone! Everyone really admired her. She was bright and had a lot of initiative.

Grandma knew how to make and cultivate contacts, and she was perfect at it. She made sure that she ruled the roost at home, and sent all of her children through school. She also kept a big book of all of her business dealings, and she was really quite remarkable as a business woman.

She told Grandpa, "Please don't do anything. I will earn the money in this family. You have done enough damage. All of your attempts at business deals are costing me too much money. Whatever you do, please do not do anything." She was happy running the family business, and he was equally happy doing nothing.

Grandpa only lived to the age of 65, and he didn't work for 30 years. The last straw had come when he had decided to sell off all their income-producing land, and sold it short, eliminating a large source of their income. They also had stocks and bonds, however when inflation came, they became absolutely worthless.

As my father once said to me, "Those shares of stock are only good as wallpaper for the toilet."

Unlike Grandpa, Grandma knew exactly what she was doing, and because of her the family survived. She was always living in an apartment in the best area of town. Their children were always dressed properly, and there was always food on the table. She was the mastermind behind the family's survival.

Grandma was also very clever as a writer. She once wrote a poem for Kaiser Wilhelm, and it was published in the local newspaper. The Kaiser even sent her a wonderful "thank you" letter. That was before the First World War, because that was the event that originally deposed the monarchy in Germany.

She was also the kind of person who was very social and she knew a lot of people. From time to time parents would come to her and say, "Don't you know of a nice man for our daughter to marry?" She would get in the middle of those kinds of transactions as well.

Grandma eventually became famous for playing matchmaker in town. At one time she said to a man who was her client, "Ok, I have arranged an afternoon tea. You come there and meet us for tea. And if you don't like her, you take your car keys and put them on the table. That will be our sign that you are not interested."

My grandmother would always tell the story of this particular incident in which she said, "We came to this very lovely coffeehouse, and the three of us sat down. We hadn't even fully gotten settled in our chairs, and out came the car keys. That was it! Tea was over."

She would always tell the story of this poor maiden who sat there in all of her finery, waiting to meet her Prince Charming. He came and took one look at her, and the keys were on the table already.

I remember that my grandparents had an apartment that had a tile stove in the entrance way. You would put hot coals in there, and that was how the room was heated. It would be in a corner so that it would heat two different rooms at once. There was also an opening on the side of it where you could put apples, and when the roasted apples came out of this stove, they were absolutely delicious.

I remember on one occasion when I was six years old. I was home alone—no adults, and Emma the housekeeper was there with me. Grandma was in town shopping, and she said to herself, "Oh my God! I forgot to tell Emma how to make the potato pancakes!"

When she came home the potato pancakes and apple sauce were ready to be served. Emma informed Grandma, "Your granddaughter took a little step stool, and told me exactly what to do and how to do it."

As per my instructions, she had washed the potatoes, peeled them, and shredded them. I remembered every detail, including drying the shredded potatoes before mixing them with flour, salt, and eggs. Grandma was shocked that I had remembered how to make the potato pancakes all by myself.

To this day, potato pancakes and apple sauce is still my favorite dish! I have to give thanks to Grandma for that recipe, and so much more. I think that my business sense came from her as well.

Chapter Three:
My Teenage Years

As a child, I wasn't really in love with going to school in general. I can't say that I liked it at all, in fact. Rather, I accepted it as a necessary evil. I was not good at academic studies. I was more the type who excelled at the physical activities. I played field hockey, I swam, I ran, I jumped, and I did gymnastics. I was really a good swimmer. I just learned it by watching other people. I picked up lots of things by imitating others. In fact, I learned to play tennis that way as well.

When I was taught to swim, I also wanted to learn how to dive properly. I mastered the Jackknife going forward, but I had trouble with that dive backwards. The instructor said to me, "I am going to hold onto you, and you and I are going to dive off the diving board together, backwards. I am going to grab you around the waist, and just do with your body what I do with mine. Pull your knees up when I tell you to do so."

That was all it took, I just imitated what he did with his body, and I suddenly understood the sensation of diving backward into the water. Then I did it on my own, and before long I had mastered "the jackknife" dive backwards by myself as well.

On one occasion I was doing a dramatic dive, and I didn't realize how close to the diving board I was. I had to jump up above the board, and as I headed down towards the water, my face had to pass the board. Right afterward I was terrified to find out that my head had passed by the board by only a fraction of an inch. As I was going through the dive, I could actually hear onlookers gasping with horror over what I had done. I could have been instantly killed. After that incident I made certain that I dove farther away from the board to avoid such a tragedy.

In fact, a friend of mine was killed exactly that same way. I was about twelve or thirteen years old by then, and it left a lasting impression on me.

I also played field hockey in school. I loved to play field hockey. I remember one day we were playing the game, and I was playing the "right outside" position. It was my intention to hit the hockey puck towards the middle of the field so that one of my team members could take the puck and ultimately make the goal. I hit the puck dead on, but instead of making it to where I intended, I inadvertently hit one of the defense team's players squarely in the trachea area of the throat and instantly cut off the air to her lungs.

She fell over backwards, unable to catch her breath. She even started to turn blue. From where I stood, I thought that I had killed her and I started to cry. I threw my hockey stick down on the ground and to run towards her to help revive her.

Fortunately she was not dead, and everybody on the field ran immediately to her side to help her to breathe again. I am happy to say that there were no bad after effects, and she was okay. But that incident scared me half to death.

During the years when I was playing field hockey, Emma, our housekeeper, wouldn't let me come in the front door when I was all full of dirt and grass stains from the hockey field. She would make me enter the house through the kitchen, where I would get cleaned up. I remember that she always seemed to have a fresh pot of coffee there, and I loved that.

I remember on one occasion, I single-handedly drank the whole pot of coffee, and ate the whole loaf of white bread, butter, and jam by myself. I have such vivid memories about that kitchen to this day. I can still see the kitchen tiles, the room, and everything in it.

Emma, who was about 28 years old at the time, had an illegitimate son. Emma stayed in the upstairs area of Grandma's apartment, known as the "Mansard," where she had a private room. It was not to be confused with being a penthouse. Grandma graciously allowed Emma to have her son come and stay with her on the weekends.

In those days, having an illegitimate child was treated like a huge scandal and kept a deep dark secret. No one even talked about such a thing. It was considered "shameful" to have a child out of wedlock. However, Grandma was such a progressive thinker that she thought nothing about extending a kindness to Emma, regardless of what society might have thought.

Aside from swimming in school classes or competitions, I also enjoyed swimming with my friends for fun. Where we lived in Germany was on the beautiful Rhine River where the tributary river, the Neckar, meets it. The Rhine runs all through Germany, and it has a powerful and steady current. Ships delivered all kinds of merchandise on the Rhine, since it was cheaper than shipping goods by railroad. In Mannheim they had aluminum air-filled pontoons with a swimming area and changing rooms. It was called Herweck. The pontoons held up swimming decks and they would have wooden floors under them with gaps in between the planks of wood so the fresh water could flow through them. That way, you could swim in the fresh river water, without being washed away in the current. You would go in, pay, and change your clothes in the small cabins that were there. There were also several diving boards: a shorter one for the young ones, and a higher one for the adults.

Herweck, with its pontoons, was the classier of the bathing areas on the Rhine. There were also other swimming areas along the river, including one where the more blue-collar workers and their families would go to swim and socialize.

We were all good swimmers, my friends and I. And at one point we became daring enough to go down into the river, under the pontoons at one end and out the other. It was extremely dangerous but there we would go, into the river, and under the huge pontoons. Later on, when I was an adult, I saw these and thought to myself, "We could have been killed! We must have been really stupid." But at the time we all thought we were invincible.

We also used to sun ourselves at the swimming areas, almost to the point of being like a piece of crisp bacon. We would pour on ourselves a concoction of baby oil with iodine in it to really become dark. I am sure this started what has been—in later life—precancerous cells, which I have had removed on my body seven times to date. However, at the time we considered it wonderful to be tanned nearly pitch black. It was called at the time *arbeitslosen farbe* [unemployed color]. We would get so dark, roasting ourselves in the sun like turtles on a rock. We thought we were really something.

Another thing we would do is ride our bicycles out to the *strandbad* where we basked in the sun. Then we would get into the water and swim up to the barges passing by which were heavily loaded with cargo, so they were low to the water. Since the river had a strong current and the barges were heading upstream, we would get on them and ride up-river. Then we would dive off and let the current take us back to where we started.

Sometimes we would be helped up by one of the guys who were swimming with us. We would get our legs over the side, and the guys' outstretched hands and arms would help us up. But one time I didn't see that the "train" of several barges had these metal ropes which would link them together to a single tug boat. All of a sudden one of the guys yelled out from the barge, "Watch the wire! Didn't you see, the metal rope? If you got caught in it you could be crushed onto the side of the barge!" I didn't see the metal rope this particular time. I was really surprised and frightened when I realized that I could have been killed.

When I got on the barge, one of the guys said, "Had you gotten caught in that, you would have gone up and down and under the whole barge and drowned!"

If I had caught my foot in the metal rope, that would have been it. One wrong move and I wouldn't have been alive to tell this story. What kids will do, never thinking of the consequences, always amazes me. It was a rather stupid thing to be doing, but at the time we had a lot of fun doing it.

Meanwhile, in my family life, there was always something going on. My parents were something of central characters in the lives of their parents and siblings. My mother had a nickname in the family. She was known as "the lawyer." Whenever there was a conflict or a problem, it was she who prevailed on everyone to get along. She was the healer in the family, and she was able to find solutions to every problem.

Mother and Uncle Adolf were always of the same opinion while their younger sister, Erna, and Adolf never had a great understanding. Also the other brothers, Robert and Walter, never had as close a relationship as my mother and Adolf did.

First of all, Mother had a complete understanding and was very nonjudgmental about Adolf's personal life. Uncle Adolf was gay, which was something of a guarded secret. At the time, in Germany it was not legally permitted to be gay. In fact it was a criminal offense according to Paragraph 175, and the death penalty was one option that was open for the judge. All of her life my mother felt very close to Uncle Adolf, and she was very protective of him.

As it is nowadays, Holland was a big vacation destination for gay men, because of their relaxed attitude about people's sexual preferences. Adolf and a couple of his friends would often go there. I have photographs of Adolf and his buddies at a swimming area on the Atlantic Ocean by the name of Scheveningen.

Among the photos that Uncle Adolf brought back from one of these particular vacations were snapshots of him and his friends with a small private wooden bathhouse on wheels. These would be rented for the day. They would have them pulled out into the shallow water for private use. There they could disrobe and put on their bathing trunks, which they would wear with a proper sleeveless swimming top. This way they could swim all day and then swim back to their little bathhouse on wheels and change their clothes, and then the horses would pull them back to shore. These days, when people wear practically nothing to swim in, this seems absolutely ridiculous. My how things have changed in the last 80 years!

It is interesting to note how the world's opinion of gay behavior has changed so much over the years. A joke told to me in the 21st Century is a perfect illustration: "A man has his suitcase packed, and he wants to leave Germany. When asked, 'Why do you want to leave?' he answers: 'First being gay was a criminal offense punishable by death, then it was tolerated, and now it may become mandatory!'"

Meanwhile, my Uncle Robert was very good looking and a real ladies man. One day he sent a telegram to Adolf asking him for money because he had to pay a doctor bill. Adolf sent him the money and went to the town where his younger brother was working at the time. Adolf expected to see Robert in ill health and not feeling at all well. On the road to his poor brother's apartment, he had to stop for a parade that was blocking the roadway. Well, Adolf was more than surprised to find his brother Robert leading the parade down the street on a white horse, dressed in gala attire.

"This is the reason for the needed funds of DM 500?" Adolf thought to himself. Come to find out, Robert did have a doctor bill, but it had nothing to do with his own health. He was paying for a girlfriend's abortion.

Robert was a real Lothario, and the girls fell for him very easily. This finally got out of control. My grandmother was visited one day by a very lovely young lady who informed Grandma that she wanted to marry her son Robert.

"Why, may I ask you?" Grandma said.

"Because I am pregnant with his baby," the girl replied.

Speaking the honest truth, Grandma informed her, "That's impossible, because Robert is already married and has two children."

The girl told her she had no idea.

Grandma took a deep breath and asked the girl, "How can we settle this situation? There are only two possibilities. One is abortion." At this suggestion the girl emphatically said it was "out of the question."

So, the second choice was, "How are we going to settle for the education of the child?"

The poor girl had no clue. Finally, a sum of money was agreed upon between Grandma and the girl, and this problem was solved.

No sooner than Grandma believed she had correctly and strongly reprimanded her son for his irresponsible and careless actions, when a second girl came to Grandma and wanted to see her about her son Robert—for the exactly same reason.

Again, for the second time, Grandma made a payment to an unwed pregnant girlfriend of Robert's. However, she had reached the end of her patience. At the time she told Robert, "No longer am I going to be the paymaster for your follies. That was the last time I bail you out of one of these situations!"

This was before the First World War, and the immigration laws in the United States were not as stringent as they later became. Immigration to America was easier then. So, Grandma had a new solution for this recurring problem with Robert. She purchased boat tickets for Robert, his wife Berta, and their two children Rosie and Lee. In addition, she gave Robert a small sum of money he could live on until he could find a job and get settled in America. Sending him across the Atlantic seemed like a logical solution to this problem.

In America, Robert found a job working at a butcher shop, Schaller & Weber. Berta died several years later, and Uncle Robert married a woman who was a nurse. He later retired and lived in Florida with his second wife who took very good care of him.

When the Second World War was looming and Mother, Adolf and I needed to leave Germany, the affidavits that were needed for us were given by Robert's daughter's Rosie and her husband Larry. In the affidavits someone had to vouch for us that in no way would the three of us become wards of the state. They needed to make sure that we had family living in the U.S. to rely upon if anything went wrong.

In other words: if Grandma hadn't sent Robert to America when she did, we might never have escaped Nazi Germany ourselves. It is funny how things ended up working out for us like synchronicity.

At the time my grandmother and grandfather lived in Dahn in Pfalz [Palatina]. They had lots of acres of land, and they had a butcher shop, so they were very well-to-do in town.

Dahn was a very small town, a real village. But it was known to have very good air there, so it was a favorite destination for people who had trouble with their lungs. For this reason, it was a very small resort area. I remember Grandpa sleeping in the foyer with his head right next to the oven to keep warm. He was a man who was not very ambitious in life. But, for he and Grandma, it worked out fine. During their long and happy life together, he and my grandmother had five children together.

Grandpa died in Mannheim later. I don't know specifically what he died of, but I do recall that he had arthritis. I think that he was resigned to the fact that he was no longer of use to anyone else at that point, and physically he disintegrated. Some people do that. They simply lose their will to live, and their health just wastes away.

After Grandpa died, I would sleep in the bed next to her. As we would turn out the lights she would recite a passage from an opera. According to the opera's lyrics: *"Gute Nacht, Gute Nacht, ich habe mir die Ehe ganz anders gedacht."* And, then she turned out the light. It interpreted into, "Good night. Good night. I had thought that the wedding night was different."

Naturally, as a child, much of my time was occupied with going to school. When I was 12 or 13, geography was one of my favorite subjects. I loved drawing maps. In fact I liked it so much that when one of my friends complained about having to do some homework in that subject, I volunteered to do it for them. I liked the subject so much.

It was hard for my teacher to find new challenges for me in geography. The teacher said to me, "What am I going to do with you? I know. You now have to do a map that outlines air travel schedules."

At this time, the idea of traveling by air had just started. It was a new thing, and seemed there was no plan or goal. There was a piece of paper, and it had departure and arrival times on it. I made this map which encompassed a departure time here, an arrival time there, and so on. The popularity and demand for leisure and business air travel was not that widespread at that time since commercial air travel was in its very beginning phase. I remember when Mannheim had its first airport. I thought that was just wonderful and exciting.

As part of my geography assignment, I had to figure out, if you took your plane from here to a certain destination, "How many hours would it take to get from Mannheim to 'where ever?'" The geography teacher devised this just to keep me busy, because she didn't know what to do with me, since my grasp of geography was so much greater than anyone else's in the class.

I was very happy to do that. It seemed like a fun subject to me, because geography I really loved. I didn't know then that I would be able to travel to so many different faraway places in my life.

At that time I had only heard about the giant air balloons that Germany was also developing for air travel: the giant Graf Zeppelins they were constructing. They were known at that time, and I had read about them, but I never saw them. Later of course, came the tragic May 6, 1937 crash of The Hindenberg.

I also liked gymnastics in school. There were the suspended rings which you grabbed and swung on. There was also the sawhorse that you did gymnastics on to land in a pile of sawdust. There was also the parallel bars which you would swing on. There were various routines we would perform. With our hands on the bar supporting our bodies in mid-air, we would swing our legs over the left bar, then to the middle, then to the right bar, and then over the other side of it to exit. I loved all of these activities, especially the parallel bars upon which you could perform all sorts of acrobatic stunts.

The rings were a particular favorite of mine, and there were also tumbling exercises that I enjoyed. I also was very good at doing handstands. I would have loved to have become a Physical Education teacher.

At the time, my best girlfriend was Lory Meyer. She had a twin sister named Ann. Lory was tall and slender. We were at an age where we were developing from girls to young woman, and Lory was decidedly flat chested. This is amusing to think of from today's perspective when everyone seems to be over-endowed. As a matter of fact, she wore a man's tie around her neck. We used to kid her, "You just wear that so we can tell which is the front of you, and which is the back."

Around the age of 14, my focus shifted from gymnastics to boys. If I really wanted to, I could write a whole chapter on the boys I had crushes on during my school years. One of my favorite boys was Fritz, who was the brother of my best friend Lory. He looked like a young Tyrone Power. One day he asked me if I would go to the movies with him. I was sitting on his bicycle on the front where the handle bar was. I remember sitting right there as we drove through the city, and feeling that it was just wonderful. We went to the movies, and this was so exciting. First of all he was three years older than I was. At the time I was 14. That was definitely the highlight of the day. There were a couple of more guys I was quite fond of, and I recall a tall one who was six-foot-two.

I was quite a daredevil in those days. I would ride my bicycle backwards, sitting on the handlebars while I pedaled the bike and steered, unable to see where I was going. It was really quite dangerous. When I think of it today, I can't believe the crazy chances we took. But at that time I had a beautiful bike. It was white. We would bicycle together and we had picnics. There would be a lot of people there.

There was also one guy who moved away from Mannheim to Berlin, and that was just terrible for me at that time. I was crushed. However, it wasn't long, and he was forgotten.

I was still a young teenage girl when one of the most important people in my life entered the picture. And the way that it unfolded was quite unexpected and unplanned.

Francois Schwarz was a friend of the family, and his wife, Meta, was actually going to visit my grandmother. I was five years old at that time. That's how I met him first, but I did not know him really. Francois was about 19-20 years older than I was. He was born in 1898. My grandmother and his wife knew each other very well.

When I was 14, I met Francois again. That was on December 6, 1932. I will always remember that day. I was living in Mannheim at the time. At school there was an upcoming Christmas event. It was a Saint Nicholas—or Santa Claus—party. We were going to put on a school play, and I needed a pair of black velvet pants for it. My Aunt Erna made arrangements for me to go to the Schwarz's apartment to borrow the pants.

I went there to have lunch with Meta and her husband Francois. It was a weekday, and Francois came home for lunch. That was the normal European thing to do at the time, to take a midday break and come home for lunch for an hour or two.

He came home, and I was absolutely intrigued by him, because he was a very, very attractive man. He was charming and really knew how to dress and carry himself in a sophisticated way. He always wore a hat and coat and tie. He had manicured hands. This was very much out of the ordinary, as men were not supposed to do that. He was not a young man in my eyes, but he was extremely elegant.

When I got there, I remember being served a big piece of chocolate cake by Francois. Ironically, as he served me the chocolate cake, he made a comment to me about my weight, and how I should lose some of it.

He instructed me how to do some exercises which would reduce the size of my stomach. I followed his instructions, and laid down on the living room floor. He then put a heavy sandbag on my tummy, and showed me the exercise.

The three of us—Meta, Francois, and I—all had lunch there that day. Afterward, he needed to go back to work, and I had to go home. As I prepared to leave their apartment, he asked me to wait for him, and he would accompany me part of the way.

So, Francois and I rode down the elevator together. While in the elevator, he leaned down and kissed me on the cheek. Well, I was 14 years old, and he was such a dashing looking man. He was known as this handsome man in town, whom everyone admired and looked up to, and here he bent down, rested his nose on my cheek, and kissed me. I remember in the books it says you don't accept anything like this from a man, but I ignored that and put my two arms around him and squeezed him. And, that was the beginning of it.

For those brief seconds alone together with Francois in the elevator, it was like a fairy tale, and I was the princess. Then the elevator arrived at the ground floor. The elevator door opened, and the fairy tale ended.

He walked with me for a few blocks. I felt like I was walking on air. Then we parted ways. He proceeded to his destination, and I went my way. Well, it was a very small town—not a tiny town—but in a town of around 300,000 people, everyone knew of certain people there, and everyone seemed to be very aware of Francois.

It was like a dream. I was only a teenager, but I was suddenly madly in love with this man. How unfortunate for me that he was a married man, with a very charming wife. I was a naughty little girl for having the thoughts that now danced through my mind, but I loved him. I just couldn't think of anything but him for a long, long time. After this brief encounter, how could I think of any of the awkward boys my own age!?!

I was absolutely smitten by Francois. I was deep in the midst of a young girl's "crush" on a handsome older man. This went on for several months.

Of course I couldn't ask Francois for a photograph of him, but I saw that my Aunt Erna had a sepia colored professionally taken portrait photograph of Francois in a frame in their apartment. In the photo Francois had a broad and warm smile, and wore a dashing hat. As soon as I saw this photograph, I wanted it for myself. However, I didn't dare tell anyone that I had a crush on this older married man who was such a good friend of the family.

Suddenly I had an idea. I was living with my grandmother on the first elevated floor of the apartment building, and Erna and husband Jub lived on the ground floor of the same building. I cleverly took the photograph—frame and all—from their apartment and put it in my bag. I then took it to a local photographic shop, had them shoot an "inter-negative," and make a print of Francois' smiling face.

After I went to the photo shop and picked up the finished print, I took the original and kept it for myself. I then took the duplicate photograph, inserted it in the frame, and took it back to Aunt Erna and Uncle Jub's apartment, and returned the new black & white photograph, and put it where I had found the original. I was surprised to find that no one noticed that the sepia colored photo of Francois had suddenly changed colors to become a black & white print. Somehow, no one was any the wiser, and I got to keep the photo that I so wanted. This was in August 1934.

Very shortly thereafter, I had a school reunion and I found myself over at Francois and Meta's house again. This event was to be a bazaar, and Francois gave me some money to spend at that outing.

My Uncle Jub and Aunt Erna were best friends with Francois and Meta. As a quartet, they seemed like a four-leaf clover they were so inseparable. They went everywhere together, they were never apart. They went out to dinner, they went to the theater, they went all over the place as a foursome.

It was about two years later Francois suggested to the other three, "Why don't we take the little one along with us?" Of course I was very excited about this prospect, as I still had quite a crush on Francois. I didn't know what was going to happen that evening.

It was my first real adult evening out. My aunt took care of dressing me for this special outing. She gave me silk stockings and said, "Put on your blue dress, and you'll be ready to go to the cabaret with us."

I was a very young 16-year-old at this point. I remember the dress I wore, the shoes and everything. The dress was a light blue sleeveless knit skirt and jumper. At that time the fashionable hem line was knee-length. There was a white flower appliqué on the dress just below the left shoulder.

When my aunt saw me she said, "Oh my, you look much older in this thing. You did a good job of putting yourself together."

Then my aunt put a bit of make-up on me, and when she took a look at me, she was pleased with the young lady she saw in front of her. When she was finished she announced to me, "Let's go."

This whole glamorizing routine was something that I had never done before. This was not the kind of a thing that my mother would ever have shown me how to do, since I was still very much a shy young girl at the time. The idea of putting on make-up and wearing beautiful evening clothes was all so exciting and new to me.

So, off we went to this cabaret. I was getting into something I had heard of but never had seen with my own eyes. It was a classic German cabaret, with a bar and drinks and performances and so on. And, to top it all off, I sat on a bar stool. Before that day, in my mind, bar stools were for whores—not proper young ladies. Never in my imagination did I ever think that I would find myself sitting on a bar stool of all things.

I sat on the bar stool there and watched all of the people with great fascination. There were very beautiful girls there, and several of them came around and kissed Francois. They were bartending girls and waitresses. Now that was too much for me not to notice.

I thought to myself, "God, what are they doing? They shouldn't do that!"

Obviously Francois was very well known there. He spent money here and there and everywhere. I was so in awe of the whole experience that I was frozen to my bar stool. It was such a unique adventure. I will never forget it.

It was all so new to me. The environment was so different, and Francois was so sweet to me too. He came over to me and he embraced me.

"Are you enjoying yourself?" he asked me.

I was so happy that in my mind it felt like I was dancing. Not only was I intrigued by this whole scenario that I found myself in, but I was intrigued by him as well. I found the whole ambiance of the cabaret so fascinating. How the girls went to him, and how he danced with them and flirted with them. And the most bizarre thing was that his wife was right there and looked at this behavior and permitted all of this. I had never seen anything like this before. It made me wonder what his relationship with his wife was all about.

My aunt and uncle didn't act like anything was out of the ordinary for this behavior—all of these strange girls kissing Francois. I didn't know what to make of it.

Then there was the show at the cabaret which mesmerized me as well. The performer was Crog, who was a very famous clown. He did this sort of silent mime act. He was very well made up, and he was the Number One European clown act. He was known as *Nit Moeglich* ["not possible"] which was the only thing he said. He could be compared to a Marcel Marceau kind of a silent performer. He was a mimic and he did all of these wonderful things.

Then there was a girl who played the guitar. She was skimpily clad in a hula-style grass skirt. Around her neck she had many chains and a Hawaiian flowered lei. And she had very dark skin. According to my impression at that time she was probably *café au lait* in color, but I had rarely seen a person that dark. She was singing a song about, "In Africa are brown the girls, with teeth as white as snow."

When I went home that night I mimicked that song, "In Africa…" This was the era when Josephine Baker was the rage in Paris, and everyone was intrigued by black performers in Europe. They were considered to be exotic to European society.

That was a wonderful experience I had with Francois, and I remembered it for a long time. Then came a hiatus when I only admired him from far away. This cabaret outing was one social interlude. It was an afternoon event on a Saturday, a matinee. But it made a big impression on me.

I didn't see him for a long time. My aunt and uncle continued to socialize with Francois and Meta, but I didn't have any personal contact. I went back to my life as normal. I went back to school, and that was all.

I knew that Francois was a very, very good looking man and that everyone was in awe of what he had accomplished, because he was working for Prince Max. He was involved in reparations for Hungary. Francois and Prince Max were also involved in a business deal that had to do with buying wood for telephone poles.

I heard through my grandmother and my aunt all about Francois' business dealings. I indirectly knew about what he was doing. That was my only information about him. I would see him every once in a while around and about town, but I was still secretly deeply in love with him. But, what did I really know of love at the time? This was basically a teenage girl's crush.

Other than hearing about him through my family, I had no other encounters with Francois. They had no children, and to my knowledge, it was his fault—as I was told. Or, so I gathered.

When the war was coming, Francois and Meta escaped from France via Portugal to America. They had left Germany much earlier than I did. In 1934 he asked Prince Max to move the firm he was working for to Paris when he realized what was coming.

He had observed what was going on with Hitler and Germany, and he told Prince Max, "You have to move me to Paris." Prince Max very politely obliged. Sylvania was the firm that he worked for at the time. From that point forward, Francois was the chief of Sylvania Paris. He had a beautiful, beautiful apartment. It was a wonderful place which I visited after the war. It was located at Rue Raynouard in the Passy district. After the Americans liberated France, the apartment was occupied by Col. Carter, who later became our employee at the Francois L. Schwarz Company at 630 Fifth Avenue. But that was all a long way away.

While I was a teenager, I was very intrigued by this slightly older boy by the name of Hans. He was part of my circle of friends in Braunschweig. He had earned his diploma as an engineer. And he had asked me to be his *Couleurdame*, which was the equivalent of "going steady" in academic circles. It was a way that the young men could show off a desirable young lady socially as his *Couleurdame*.

I knew that if this relationship were to progress into a serious one with Hans, I would eventually have to produce perfect proof of being 100% Aryan. At this point in time we realized that Hitler's demands for a Germany populated with only an Aryan race, combined my family tree—being half Jewish—would never work in this situation. At that time in Germany, a law had even been passed that a Jewish household could not employ an Aryan.

I went through my diary from this era and found what I had written about Hans:

Hans has trouble today because of my descent, and he has to take an Aryan girl as his *Couleurdame*. As a Diploma Engineer at the Technical High School, it is impossible for him to date me. On 12 February, 1937, Hans invited me to the Architects Ball. He is the son of the brewery owners in Oggenheim, and he is a very good looking young man. But Hitler's Aryan Paragraph in the German Constitution killed every possibility for such a union. I don't know why we are all so stupid and do not see the writing on the wall everywhere.

I had made plans after I would graduate from the school in Braunschweig, I would start an atelier [an exclusive boutique] for women's clothing for high end fashions. But Hitler's laws are making it more and more strangulating. No Jewish household can have an Aryan servant, cook or any other employee.

Another of my classmates was Bubi Hirschberger. I wrote about him in my diary:

I visited Bubi in Arbeitsdienst [similar to the National Guard] in Marienburg. We all have some friends who encouraged us to take the whole Hitler Doctrine not too seriously. We permitted "ostrich-like" behavior, by putting our head in the sand. We think that we will somehow be spared. At about the same time, I went to Heidelberg and visited the Castle where I met Gunther Leiner's father who said to me, "Do you know Oppenheimer? He writes very positive things from America, I thought you would have been gone a long time ago?"

To which I answered, "No, just the opposite."

How stupid of me at the time, not to accept reality of how Germany was changing into a segregated society were Jews were no longer considered legal citizens. Here, even the father of one of my friends realized how dangerous it was for me as a partially Jewish girl to stay in Germany. However, I was so arrogant and cocky in my determination to stay in the country that I thought was my home.

At the time, since my father was still alive, and was still an Aryan man, he felt that he would be able to protect his family from any potential peril. Since he had this opinion, and since he was the head of our household, I adopted this same stubborn attitude. I blindly thought that since I was half Aryan, nothing bad would ever happen to me by remaining in Germany.

Guenther Leiner was a friend of mine from my Hockey Club cronies. He was a real lovely, educated young man and he invited me for a trip along the Rhine in his light blue Mercedes convertible, which was delightful.

Guenther was such a caring and mature person for his age, that I found myself really liking him. After a game of hockey, we had the habit of going *en masse* to one of our families' homes. One afternoon after our hockey game, we went to Guenther's parents' house.

I remember a long table set up with desserts and tea and coffee for us. There were some little cakes which consisted of a chocolate cake in a small roll, about the diameter of a pencil, and they were filled with whipped cream.

Being teenagers, someone got the bright idea to put the end of one of them in his mouth, and he blew the whipped cream across the table at someone. This started a war of whipped cream being blown all over the place. Much of the whipped cream ended up on the tablecloth or on the wallpaper.

Guenther was so level headed, instead of panicking, he just said, "Don't worry, I will take care of cleaning up this mess."

That's how Guenther was. At one point, his younger sister, Urs, went to a department store and charged a bunch of items that she could not afford to pay for. Guenther simply said to her, "Don't worry, I will take care of it." He somehow cleverly arranged it so that their parents never received the bill, and neither of them got into trouble.

Guenther and I drove to Braunschweig, where it was my intention to have him meet my parents, as I thought I would eventually marry him. Guenther was so formal and delightful at the same time, I couldn't help but be in love with him.

After he met my parents, my mother later told me, "I like him very much, but he will never get permission from the Nazis to marry you, so it can never be."

I was so disappointed to hear her say this. I so badly wanted to end up marrying Guenther, but my mother was right. It was an impossible situation.

As a young girl, I often wrote my thoughts and my frustrations in my diary. Amongst the entries I wrote were the following thoughts:

Life blows away like leaves in the wind—but love stays forever. I hope that my idea can be accomplished, namely I want to be successful in my chosen work and my highest expectations are for me to see them through. Why doesn't life behave the same as nature? We should start, and have a spring, and a wonderful life, and then go to rest like nature does in the winter, and everything again would come up fresh and renewed in the spring. Why can't life be like that?

The field flowers on the roadside along the way, and the day is fading away making room for the night. All I want at the moment is a little bit of money, so I can stay here until the end of the world. Life should be more like nature. Namely, the human body should go into hibernation, and we could wake up like the blossoms in the spring, and all of this Nazi nonsense would be gone. And the renewal of the cycle would be beautiful, and the bad would be gone.

At the time I was just a teenage girl living in an ever changing Germany. While the face of the world was changing—and not for the better—I was still preoccupied with my own young life. However, it was becoming increasingly hard to ignore the ways in which the Nazis were slowly ruining Germany, and leading us into a war against ourselves and against the rest of the world.

Chapter Four:
Nazi Germany

Around 1932, my parents were in Hildesheim to discuss with a friend by the name of Emil Levy, the possibility of starting up a branch of their store in Braunschweig, which my parents would run.

Emil Levy was married to Mathilde, who was the sister of Gustav Jenner's wife, Clementina. Gustav was an older man—a D.O.M. (Dirty Old Man)—but he was always very properly dressed. He always had on a tie. He was tall, stately, and very good looking. Wherever he went, he had with him a little black velvet bag which was about three-inches-by-five-inches. It was about the size of a hand. Everybody was always curious to find out what was in this bag. Finally, one day I said to him, "Okay Uncle, enough of this mystery. Show me what is in that bag of yours!"

He smiled and said, "Okay, come over here, and I will show you."

He had collected in there all kinds of diamonds, in various shapes and grades. There were also several other precious stones in there: emeralds, sapphires, and a glittering assortment of gems.

He said, "The day may come when I might not be able to take anything with me, but this little black bag. As long as I have it, it will make life easier for me while I'm here."

Gustav Jenner had the biggest shoe store in Hildesheim. It was situated in a beautiful house in the middle of town, and on the first two floors was his shoe shop. On the third and fourth floors were the living quarters where Jenner and his wife lived. Everyone knew her as "Clem," which was short for Clementina. They lived there with

Gustav's son from his first marriage, Armin, and Clementina's son Heinz from her first marriage.

Clem had been married for the first time to a man named Novak. Novak died in the First World War, and after that she married Gustav Jenner. When Clem married Gustav, she had the savings of her first husband, which Gustav took, controlled and used. It was typical of a European wife at that time to subjugate herself and let her husband use the money as he saw fit. In later years this enraged Heinz, as he felt this money was from his father for his education. He never forgave his mother for not fighting for his rights. Later, my parents stepped in and helped him to get a job at Buesing, which was the manufacturer of trucks in Braunschweig.

When the Nazis came into power in Germany, shocking things started happening to people. It must have been a terrifying feeling when Mrs. Jenner saw her sister Mathilde, her sister's husband Emil who was Jewish, and their two grown up daughters, being walked down the main street on the way the railroad station. Clem could not do a thing, or dare say a thing as she watched this horrible sight. The impulse would be to scream and yell and run out into the street to protest this. However, that would have made the concentration camp her own destiny as well.

The brown-shirted Nazi soldiers led them down the streets, and took them to the freight cars that would transport them to the concentration camp. To further humiliate them, they were required to take brooms and literally sweep the streets as they took their last walk to the railroad station.

Fortunately, Jenner was not Jewish, and he was very well known in the town as a great philanthropist. Clem was a typical Christian / European housewife with blue eyes and natural blonde hair. She had a very quiet and reserved attitude, in contrast to Gustav's forceful and dominant disposition.

After the Second World War and the *Währungsreform* was over, Jenner used the contents of the little black velvet bag to buy shoes and gasoline in Pirmasens. At that time no one wanted to sell anything for the very devalued and undesirable German currency. He however had his little black bag of gems. Jenner drove to Pirmasens, and the shoe manufacturers were very happy to sell him all the shoes he wanted in exchange for his precious gem stones and diamonds. Jenner loaded his car with shoes. In fact he jammed the car with every pair of shoes he could get his hands on and returned to Hildesheim to sell them in his store.

When he returned, the people of Hildesheim were ecstatic to see new shoes for the first time in ages. Ultimately, Jenner's theory about keeping his wealth in diamonds and gemstones served him well.

As part of the field hockey team in school I met several other people through playing local teams in other towns. On one occasion we drove to Hamburg to play against Uhlenhorst, Hamburg. I stayed overnight with the parents of my counterpart on the Hamburg team. I played the position of "Right Outside" on our team, and the girl whom I stayed with was the "Right Outside" player from that club. That was in 1936, and it was a very nice experience to be with the girl and her gracious family.

That year I was a young and optimistic nineteen-year-old girl having new adventures. I had every reason to believe that my young adulthood in Germany was to continue to be one of filled with wonderment and new experiences. It was easy for me to ignore the shift in the government's politics, and to concentrate on my teenage social life, boyfriends, and parties.

One of the things that I was looking forward to was attending the 1936 Olympics which were held in Berlin. It was fun to see athletes from all over the world, competing in what I thought was a friendly fashion. I was fascinated by all of the events, and I loved seeing the Indian team win the field hockey game.

However, behind the scenes, it was a very controversial year for the Olympics. It was the beginning of Nazi Germany, and this was Hitler's chance to show the superiority of his Third Reich teams. Because of Hitler's preoccupation with his Aryan Race ideas, he didn't want the black athlete, Jesse Owens, to participate in the games at all. However, the Olympic Committee won out and insisted he was to compete. Jesse competed in the 100 meter hurdles, and he ended up winning the Gold

Medal that year. There was a big stink about it. Anything that was not Aryan was looked down upon. In Hitler's eyes he was making a race that would top everyone else.

In 1936 I not only went to the Olympics, but I went with my youngest uncle, Walter, to Obersdorf-Hirscheg/Riezlern. It was part of Austria, but butting up against an enclave which belonged to Italy. The mountains prevented people from getting in and out easily. It belonged to Italy by all rights. However, because of the mountains, access from the Italian side was not possible. We had to enter it through Austria. I was with a group of people, and one of the guys saw a small shrine in one corner. There was a crucifix and some flowers there. This German man said in an irritated manner, "What is that over there?"

The landlady defiantly announced, "That is Jesus."

To which the man replied, "Why isn't our Führer up there?"

The landlady turned around, looked him straight in the eyes and said, "Listen, Jesus is there. He was there before Hitler was born, and he stays there as long as I live."

She was not in Germany, but in Italy, so she could get away with making a statement like that without getting killed. At that time, Italy had not yet succumbed to the Nazi / Mussolini way of thinking.

It was a good little vacation for me. We would go dancing in the evening, and skiing during the day. That evening one guy who was a German doctor asked me to dance with him. He was so tall, and I was literally in the air—my feet could not touch the ground! It was like he was carrying me around on the dance floor.

He asked me what my name was. And I said, "Ruth Mueller."

He said, "Oh, that's as good as old aristocracy. You don't need an Aryan passport, you have your aristocrat status with that name alone."

That irritated me, his arrogant Nazi attitude. But what do you do but grin and bear it? I thought inside, "You son-of-a-bitch." He was a doctor, but he was also a Nazi from the word "go." What could I say to him but, "Oh, yes, thanks."

After that I got away from him as fast as I could.

My Uncle Walter looked everything but Jewish. He was a boxer, he had a slightly broken nose. He had blue eyes, white skin, and the blondest hair that you can imagine. So, nobody would ever dream of him being anything but Aryan.

My blood still boils at the mere thought of the arrogance of those Nazis. The very idea that Hitler should be superior to Jesus, and Jesus should disappear. It was outrageous.

It was impossible not to notice what was going on in Germany and the rest of Europe. The Nazis had by now become an unignorable force. In 1936, the highly desirable Port of Danzig, Poland became a target for the Nazis. Poland owned it, and Germany wanted it. It wasn't going to be long before Germany got its way. That same year Poland and France signed a non-aggression treaty between the two of them. It was getting to a point where each of the individual countries within Europe were choosing sides between them.

As an only child I had lot of advantages, but I also had bad times to digest. When my mother had the store selling sewing machines, bicycles and baby carriages, people often bought them on installment payments. One salesman, Herr Payem, who was Jewish, did not deliver the money he collected, but cashed it in for himself. When my father met him accidentally in the street, he confronted him about this and "boxed his ears." My father meant only to smack him to make his point; however, poor Herr Payem lost his balance, fell, and hit the edge of the pavement. When his head struck one of the stones, he was killed instantly.

This was a very terrible situation. My father did not want to kill him, but he did. I remember long conversations with the lawyer who represented my father. There were many hours of discussions at home which I witnessed. Since I was the only child, there were no siblings for me to share the weight of this situation in the household.

My father and the lawyer had to construct the defense statements very carefully so my father would not be charged with murder. The court's conclusion was that this was an "unfortunate accident," and not a case of "premeditated murder."

To illustrate what the times were like in Germany, the court was very much in favor of my father's case because Herr Payem was Jewish, and my father was an Aryan. Instead of a strong judgment against my father, he was simply required to make a financial payment and that was the end of the case.

This whole affair was very stressful in our household. However, my parents loved each other very much, which was very evident to me during these trying times. Somehow we made it through this unfortunate event.

While the political situation was changing for the worse in Germany, something tragic happened within my family. It was a lovely Sunday afternoon in 1936, and my father took the car out. He had his mother in the car next to him. In the backseat of the car was my mother and a friend, Theo Griasch. The four of them took off, and I drove with some friends of mine in an open convertible automobile. Our final destination was a wonderful place where we were going to have a Sunday luncheon and sit in the lovely warm September air on the promenade at a lake.

From Braunschweig this was a lovely little tour, and my father had the scenic route all planned out. It was going to be a wonderful day the way he had scheduled it. We were all having a great time in the cars, driving along as we had planned. My father's car was several vehicles ahead of the automobile that I rode in. All of a sudden there was a long line, and we had to stop. All traffic had to come to a halt, as there was apparently an accident somewhere up ahead.

All of a sudden, like lightning a vision came to me. I instinctively knew that the accident involved my father. I jumped out of the car, and ran all the way until I reached my father's vehicle. I finally reached the car, and there was my father holding his left arm.

Come to find out, he was in the driver's seat with his left arm resting on the sill of the car window. Another car had struck my father's vehicle and it had flipped over towards the left side, and cut off his left arm at the elbow. It was a horrible sight. I saw a friend of mine named Axel there with a car, and I grabbed him and said, "Axel, help me! Help me!"

We helped my father into Axel's car, and drove him immediately to the hospital. At the hospital the attendants came down with a stretcher, and my father was still so much in shock that he grabbed for his arm, and I saw the exposed bone as his severed forearm bone fell on the ground in front of me! I just lost my mind for a moment. It was so terrible to see, I was completely wiped out with horror.

But I caught myself, and I watched as the orderlies took my father to the doctor into the hospital. I waited for Mother to come in the other car. There was such a commotion when she arrived. What started out so nicely, turned out to be a horrible, horrible summer day.

All of the other passengers in my father's car were spared any major injuries. My grandmother had a few bruises, but that was all. The people in the backseat—my mother and her friend—also had a few black and blue marks here and there, but nothing of any consequence.

The only one who had any major injuries was my father. There was a big article in the next day's local newspaper, telling of the events. According to it, "A very serious accident occurred on the main street in Wolfenbüttel. A car was hit by a man who came out of a side street. The other driver had been issued his driver's license two weeks prior, and he had been drinking a bit of alcohol. He was not paying attention to the accelerator and the brakes at the time. He thought he was pressing down on the brakes, but in fact had his foot on the gas pedal."

There was a big crash as the other man's car hit the vehicle that my father was driving. He hit my father's car so hard that it flipped it over. In addition to losing his arm, he also suffered a concussion. The newspaper account said that his injuries were very, very serious, and they hoped that he would survive.

Somehow, he made it through the accident, but this was a long, and drawn-out affair. Ultimately, the doctors had to amputate his left arm above the elbow. After he came home from the hospital, my mother very courageously bandaged it every day.

I couldn't look at it at all. I had to leave the room while she did this. But, Mother was so brave and wonderful, and took such good care of my dad. Her devotion was really lovely and inspiring to see.

Meanwhile, Grandma Halfen, my mother's mother, was set to emigrate to America early in the year 1937. She was going to live with my Uncle Robert whom she had sent to the United States several years earlier. Grandma had a passport, but the passport had to have a certain "exit" stamp on it from the German government, and it had to go to the authorities.

It was decided that I would go alone to the authorities and obtain this stamp so that she could safely leave the country. I took her passport and I went down and came to this dimly-lit place. There was a man sitting there who was in a high position in the Nazi organization.

There were lots of people sitting in chairs all over this office. They were mostly older people who all seemed to be seeking the same kind of exit permits in their passports.

I came into the room, and the official asked to see me immediately. I felt very uneasy about it because there were all of these other older people who were all ahead of me.

I went up to speak to him. I told him the situation, and explained what I wanted. We talked, and somehow he was able to make an immediate appointment with me. In other words, he wanted to have a date with me. I agreed to it. I made a date with him because I sensed that this was the only way I could get the stamp in Grandma's passport. I got the stamp, but it came with the stipulation that I would see him again. For the sake of Grandma's passport, I had to agree to meet him at an appointed place and time.

I got all of my papers together and left the office. After I got out on the street, I said to myself, "What am I going to do? I don't want to go out on a date with this Nazi officer."

I was sweating bullets, I was so scared that I didn't tell anyone about it. When the appointed time and day came for my date with the Nazi officer, I went to the pre-arranged spot. I didn't know what I was going to do when he showed up.

Fortunately, for me the Nazi officer never arrived for our date. I never heard from him, and was I ever relieved!

What I suspect happened was that he figured I was so young that he never really took it seriously. Whatever the reason, I so happy that I never heard from him at all. Needless to say, it was a huge relief.

I was sincerely afraid, because that was a time of extreme paranoia. Whenever the telephone rang, you were never sure who it would be. We had gotten to the point that we were almost afraid to answer it.

This was an odd time in Germany. We really never knew what was possible. If the doorbell rang, our first instinct was to shudder with fear, because we had no idea who would be standing on the other side of it. The Nazis could come to our door without a warrant, and demand that we open it up. They had the right to just show up and insist on whatever they wanted.

It wasn't until several days after my arranged "date" with the Nazi officer that I finally relaxed. I was really sweating it out. Had he shown up that day, God only knows where he would have taken me, or insisted on doing.

Anyway, having obtained the stamp in Grandma's passport, she was allowed to leave the country in 1937. A couple of days after her papers were in order, Grandma had to go to Stuttgart. I went with her. We had to go the passport office, and then we had to go to the American consulate. I took Grandma to get all of her documents in order, and we stayed at a hotel.

After Grandma got her visa, her passport, and all of her paperwork all together, we were all breathing a sigh of relief. We were so afraid that she wouldn't be allowed to make this trip. Finally, I had my peace of mind.

Grandma and I took the train to Mannheim again. Weeks later, Grandma and her youngest son, my Uncle Walter made the voyage to New York together on the boat.

My mother and I would have loved to have left Germany at the same time that Grandma did. But, we couldn't. We didn't have our entry papers to America yet, so we had to wait. There were quotas in place. America had specific quotas from every country, and no more were allowed. So, you had to wait until your number was called to fill that year's quota. You would have to go to the American Consulate and get a number, and wait until your number came up. We didn't want to wait, but we had no choice. It would take another six months to a year. As things developed, it would be foolish to wait for a Packing Permit to take your belongings. It was getting to the point where we would just have to run to save our own skins. A lot of people in the same situation hesitated and didn't do it, and it was a decision that literally cost them their lives.

Meanwhile, my other grandmother, my father's mother, was very non-opinionated about what was going on in Germany. She neither took the Nazi party seriously, nor did she harbor any hatred for them. She was so non-political in her way of thinking, she too thought that all of this Nazi nonsense was just a passing phase, which in time would all be gone and forgotten.

Her only concerns were for her children and grandchildren, and she couldn't have cared less about the political climate of the country. This just further illustrates how we all were able to feel that eventually this Nazi nonsense would all go away like a passing fad, and Germany would return to normalcy.

On my 21st birthday, January 21, 1938, the mother of my friend Bubi Hirschberger arrived at our door to present me with six red long-stemmed roses and a book, *Zarathustra* by Nietzsche. Her son, Bubi, was still at the Arbeitsdienst, which was like the German National Guard at the time.

Little by little, the times were changing. It was getting harder and harder to ignore the Nazis and what they were doing to Germany. They were ruining it, and fear was creeping into every aspect of normal life.

During this era, I wrote in my diary:

One thinks that life has to stand still, it cannot go on like this, but then one realizes you can not do the things you would like to do, and resign to the fact that, "Life is renunciation, and renunciation is life."

Today everyone in school started saying "Heil Hitler," in the morning. There is no more saying "Good morning." That really hit home. Some of my friends visit us no longer...others arrive when nobody can see them, as they are wearing their Nazi uniform with an arm that has a "swasticaband." The deceitful quietness about this situation more and more interrupts our lives, and finally you have to see the truth about what is going on. Friends say to me, "Nobody will do anything bad to you. We will take care of it." We are starting to realize that this is wishful thinking.

In school, my art teacher was talking about the new Nazi flag that now replaced the old one. He said, "I prefer the old color combination of red, gold and black, to the new red, black and white one." After he said that, he realized what he had said, and how this could be misconstrued as a denial of the Nazi regime, and quickly covered his statement by remarking, "I say that, only because of the artistic color composition. I don't want anyone saying, 'Mr. Moor does not like the new Nazi flag, but prefers the old one.'"

Meanwhile, while my father mended from the car accident and his amputation, he seemed to be in good spirits and in good health. Then, almost a year later, my father suddenly became very sick. He was in the house of my grandmother, and he said to me, "Oh, darling, go away, I am so sick. I have a stomach ache." What he thought was a stomach ache was actually a heart attack. It was his own self misdiagnosis.

He went to the toilet, and he came back and laid down on the couch. I called a good friend, Dr. Elizabeth Thresher, who was not a member of the Nazi Regime, and asked her to come to our house immediately. She was a fine human being, and the cousin of my mother's best friend.

When she was getting out of her car and coming into the house, this brainwashed Nazi fanatic who lived above us came down and accusingly yelled, "You are not going to treat anybody in this Jewish household, are you?!?"

She looked at him, but didn't answer. She just came in, and tried to help my father. Unfortunately, all she could give him was an injection of camphor directly into the heart. It didn't help him either, and he died right then and there.

Regarding that man upstairs: how can you say that to anybody, and to a doctor of all people? To command them not to go and help a dying person. That was horrifying. It was over 50 years ago, and it still makes my blood pressure rise to think of how brainwashed and how cruel this stupid man was. But, that was the way it was in Nazi Germany. The Nazis had traded compassion for hatred and bigotry.

My father died in September of 1937. It was very hard for me to accept that he was gone. But, in retrospect I don't know what would have happened if he had been alive when it later became time to plot our escape from Nazi Germany. With father still alive, we wouldn't be able to leave him alone in Germany as an invalid.

I realized that his passport was only good until September 13, 1939. And, we had to leave shortly before that expired. It is sometimes hard to understand how certain things work out. In retrospect things look as if they are planned. But, who plans them? Who pulls the strings? Who is the guiding factor in our lives? A lot of questions arise. Regardless, when my father died, that was a very tough, tough time for me.

In 1937, Hitler set about getting rid of people in power who made him uncomfortable. He fired a lot of people who were not his disciples. I knew then, it was time for us to leave. It was really getting bad.

It was in 1938 that Germany really started to become much more aggressive within Europe. Hitler took control of the *Wehrmacht* [German army] from now on he was in charge and he fired top generals like Van Ribbentrop, Minister of Exterior.

On March 12, German troops marched into Austria, where they were greeted with open arms. Since Hitler's plan was to reunite all of the Germanic people, this did not seem like such a radical move for Austria.

On March 14, Austria officially agreed to the *Anschluss* [the connection] of Austria to Germany. To make it official, on April 4 the population of Austria voted for this *Anschluss,* and they were now part of Hitler's new German Empire. Things seemed to escalate very quickly after that.

The date of November 10, 1938 was to be known as Kristallnacht. It marked the beginning of the legal abuse of Jewish people. In the eyes of the German Nazi government, the Jews were no longer considered to be legal citizens. Personal money and property was confiscated from the Jews, the Nazi's destroyed Synagogues, and they would write the word *Juden* on the glass of Jewish shop windows to denote that they were Jewish-operated businesses.

I remember the *Krystallnacht* quite clearly. For me it was a terrifying experience. That was when the German Aryans—mainly students—took it upon themselves to destroy the Jewish people's residences. They took families' glasses and porcelain and threw them into the streets, causing the sound of breaking glass and cracking crystal hitting the pavement to be heard all over the city.

At the time I said to my mother and my Uncle Adolf, "All of you leave the house, and go over the hill to the other side of town to Uncle Jub and Aunt Erna's. I will stay here when they come."

So I had my apron on, and I waited for them to arrive. And surely they came by, from one house to another. They rang our doorbell, I opened the door, and they came storming in like they owned the place. As they did so, they left the door wide open. They went into the big room of my grandmother, and opened the doors on the bird cage for the little parakeet to fly out. They opened drawers from the desk and proceeded to throw all the papers they found there, out the window and into the street.

At that point, I tried to negotiate with one of the students who was in charge, who seemed to be a little bit more civil than the others. I told him that I was at the home of my grandmother, and that I was a member of the student body, and I studied this and that. As a distraction, my ploy worked for a few minutes.

The fanatical man who lived above us with his family, came out of his apartment when he heard the commotion. He shouted as he stood in the landing of the staircase between their apartment and ours, "You must go to the cellar! They have a machine there where they are printing propaganda against our regime, against our Führer, our beloved Adolf Hitler. And you really have to look there."

So the young Nazi looked at me, and I looked back at him and said, "Okay, let's go downstairs and have a look. No problem."

Since I had charmed him a bit by talking to him as one student to another, I could tell by the look on his face that he was dreading going downstairs and finding anything that would turn the rest of the mob against me. In those brief moments we had struck upon something of an understanding together. He was now afraid on my behalf that the others might find something and do something to me.

I simply said, "No, no, no. We will go downstairs together, please." We got down there, and we lit matches to illuminate the cellar. There was a small, single piece printing press. I ran my finger across it, exposing the fact that there was about a half an inch of dust on this old machine. I didn't think that anybody in their right mind would think that this was used in any way recently. It certainly could be used to print the propaganda that the man above our apartment insisted to be examined, but it was quite obvious that it had not been touched in years. In fact the whole cellar was filled with dust, because no one ever went there to clean up. It was just used to store things.

So, we talked a little bit, and then he told the other guys, "On to the next house."

What an amazing sense of relief I felt to hear him say that. I was very happy that I had temporarily saved all of our belongings from destruction. I waited until my uncle and grandmother had come back. When they returned everyone was happy and relieved that nothing had happened to me or to our belongings.

That night was a terrifying experience, one that could very easily have turned ugly if I had said or done the wrong thing. I knew that inside me I had the ability to maintain a calm sense of confidence in the face of danger. I was quick at thinking on my feet, and this really put me to the test.

It would be foolish of me not to say that I was very much afraid of what would happen if anything went wrong. This was one situation where anything could happen. If the wrong guy would have come to us, they would have taken me away for all that I know. And one never knew who was around to incite the Nazis to commit an act of violence.

I don't know if it was quick-witted instinct or unbridled fear that motivated my actions that evening. But I had a firm belief that I could handle it, and handle it I did. That was *Krystallnacht*, which I braved against the Nazis alone.

The Nazis made it quite clear that they were against organized religion in general. Obviously the Nazis wanted to defile synagogues, but they seemed to leave the churches alone. Although they allowed the churches to exist, they wanted to make sure that Christianity had no real power in Germany. Some of the priests were really very much against the Nazis, and some of them were imprisoned for expressing their views. It all depended on where the individuals stood with the Nazis. No one who valued their lives would publicly say anything against the Third Reich or against Hitler.

You could secretly have thoughts against the Nazi regime, but you had to keep your thoughts to yourself. You wouldn't dare oppose what was going on by 1938. It was too far gone. It was like being strapped to a roller coaster—you had absolutely no control of what was around the next turn.

It seemed that the majority of Germans clung to the idea that things would get better, because the times were so bad. There were visible signs that the economy had improved under the Nazi rule. However, things were about to take a turn for the worse when Hitler began to show his true colors against the Jews.

Whenever you have a really bad economic situation, people say, "Well, let's change. Something's got to change. Maybe it will be better. It can't get any worse. Let's go with this new idea and see if it works."

If an economy is really bad, a dictator can make changes which show outward signs of improvement. However, there is "absolute power" related with dictators. When their whims suddenly take a turn for the worse, there is no opposing a dictator. Yes, the economy had improved in Germany. What people didn't realize is that it was all for the war machine.

The Nazi regime was masqueraded at the beginning as a way to improve the awful post-World War One economy. Hitler's cranking up the war machine took its toll on German society. While he was stockpiling ammunition for the war he was about to start, some of the luxuries in day to day life began to disappear. We didn't have butter anymore, but we had bullets.

In the First World War, the German people—Jews and all—would turn in all of their gold in return for a useless iron medal to pin on your coat to show their solidarity towards the country. Now, here we were again in a position where war of some sort was obviously brewing in Germany.

It was in 1938 that America started the escalation of their military forces, sensing a possible conflict. On September 28, 1938, President Franklin D. Roosevelt sent a telegram to Adolf Hitler to help to protect the peace.

That was also that year in America that the C.I.O. (Consolidation of Industrial Organizations) was founded. It was in contrast to the A.F.L. (American Federation of Laborers) which was much more radical. They were both determined to improve the lives of workers.

On April 15, 1939, Roosevelt sent another message to Hitler and Mussolini in an effort to avoid war. But it seems that everything was already set in motion. Hitler was determined to have a thousand years of German supremacy, and he would stop for nothing in his path. There was a song which was continuously played, and it referred to Hitler's "Thousand Year Germany." The translated lyrics mean, "Today Germany belongs to us, and tomorrow the whole world will belong to us too."

There was another German song at the time, which I found to be very revolting. The song's lyrics included the line: "When the Jewish blood flows from our knives, our work will go much better."

Within Germany we all followed the news of what was going on around us. On March 23, 1939, the Germans made a military treaty with Italy. This caused a military unification, thus canceling the previous concept of a German/British shipping armada. There was also the cancellation of the Polish non-aggression treaty. It was only a matter of time before Germany marched into that country. Everyone seemed to be taking sides, so 1939 was the year that the United Nations accepted the declared neutrality of Switzerland.

By 1939 the Nazi's had infiltrated everything, starting with the school children. Nobody suspected that I had a Jewish grandmother and grandfather. I had a document with a swastika stamped on it. It had to be on there whether you liked it or not. The complete infiltration of all of German society was so complete that it was ingrained in everything, from the schools on upward.

There were marches and meetings and rallies. Everyday on the radio they would broadcast pro-Nazi propaganda. It was unbelievable how early on they took over everything—newspapers, radio stations, schools.

Finally, by August of 1939 we felt like we were living on a powder keg which could erupt any minute. That was when Mother, Uncle Adolf and I started to prepare for immigration to America.

There was such a very uneasy feeling within Germany in 1939 and 1940. Then Russia was expelled from *Voelkerbund* [The League of Nations]. England blocked Jewish immigration to Palestine. On September 1, 1939 Hitler was to start his *Blitzkrieg* by marching into Poland, thus creating the collapse of the Polish Republic. This officially marked the beginning of the Second World War.

After September 1, 1939 a lot of things happened in very fast order. Hitler was clever enough to realize that to hatch his plan to conquer the world, he was going to have to rely on some innovative thinkers, whether or not those people agreed with him politically or not. For instance, Max Planck, who was born in 1857, was a German physicist who tried to stand up to Hitler. Subsequently he was thrown out of Germany. But Planck came back and stayed in Germany, where he returned to lecture at the University in Goettingen.

Planck had developed his quantum theory known as "Planck's Constant." A lot of atomic research was later based on that. That is why Hitler wanted Planck to come back to Germany alive, so that he could exploit Planck's vast knowledge. Planck was somehow lured back to Germany. Although Planck's return to Germany caused him to be viewed as a traitor by those on the outside, he was later exonerated by his peers.

As the war progressed, so did Planck's hatred of the Nazis. In 1944 he was involved in the assassination plan for Hitler which failed. For revenge, they took Planck's only son and hung him up on a butcher hook.

Three other people studying the idea of harnessing the power of the atom were Otto Hahn, Fritz Strassman and Dr. Lisa Meitzner. Dr. Meitzner, who received her PhD in Vienna—was the first woman to do so. She went to Stockholm to flee the Nazis. The trio of Hahn, Strassman and Meitzner were working on discovering how to split an atom. They found light weight atoms by bombarding uranium with neutrons.

While in Stockholm, Dr. Meitzner received a telegram from Hahn and Strassman, which read: "Happy Birthday." That was their code message meaning, "We split the atom!" What an important step for all our lives as this led to the creation of the atomic bomb, which ultimately brought about the end of World War II.

Enrico Fermi, an Italian with a Jewish wife, received the 1938 Nobel Prize in Sweden for the first nuclear chain reaction. He was allowed to go to Sweden to accept the Nobel Prize, and was expected to return to Italy. Instead, he never went back to Italy but went from Sweden to America and worked in Los Alamos.

In 1946, Hahn received the Nobel Peace Prize for his work on Nuclear Fission. By rights he should have shared this honor with Lisa Meitzner, but he never stepped forward to give her the credit that she deserved. Although she received some lesser awards, that Nobel Peace Prize, by rights was half hers.

According to Popular Science.net, in reviewing the book *Lisa Meitzner: A Life in Physics*, by Ruth Lewin Sime, "Meitzner's career was shattered when she fled Germany, and her scientific reputation was damaged when Hahn took full credit and the 1944 Nobel Prize for the work they had done together on nuclear fission…Deprived of the Nobel Prize she so clearly deserved for her contribution to the discovery of nuclear fission, Lisa Meitzner has never been given the attention she deserves in the history of twentieth-century physics."

One might speculate what would have happened if Planck did not return to work in Germany. After the war, Planck was exonerated by his friends. He then died in 1947.

The Nazis were so entrenched in German society at that time, it was impossible to escape their influence. In every apartment house throughout Germany, on the first floor there was a designated Nazi party member who was an informant for the building. On every floor of every building there was designated a party member to spy on everyone on that floor, and to report everything that went on amongst the residents of that floor. In other words, everybody was spying on everybody. In every building there were seven or eight Nazi party members who were spying on everyone who lived within that building.

They reported on who was Jewish, and who wasn't. They spied on who was coming and going in and out of the building, and at what hours of the day or night.

Every building had one official to whom every floor's spy reported to, and he in turn had to report to the head official of that block. And every block head had to report to an even higher up official who was responsible for a ten block area, and so forth. It was impossible to do anything without someone spying on you.

When you think about the kind of organization it took to mastermind this, it was astonishingly effective. It was sensationally diabolical and meticulously organized. One has to give the Nazis credit for their organizational skills. It would have been wonderful if they had used it for humanity and put it towards a good cause.

The person who did all that was Joseph Goebbels—the guy with the club foot—and his propaganda machine. He was the murderous brains behind the Nazi regime.

It was Goebbels who influenced Hitler greatly. No one had the right to raise their head up and say "no" to him, or to question the authority of the Nazi party. If you did question the Nazis, or if you said or did anything to oppose them, you were simply taken away. You disappeared, never to be heard from again. Anyone who opposed them was killed. There was no standing up to them.

It was so insidious that children in school were absolutely brainwashed. They would come home from school and say to their parents, "I am so glad that you haven't said anything against our beloved Füehrer, or I would have to report you to my teacher."

They brainwashed everybody. My girlfriend Else was married to a man who was totally controlled by the Nazi regime. Their last name was Fuchsschwanz—which means "foxtail" in German. Else was a great friend of mine. She was always an extremely wonderful girl, and I liked her a lot. I was very close to her during our school years. She was a good friend of mine all my life, pretty much. Else and I were about twelve or thirteen years old when we met.

At that time, we wanted to know all about life, and how it starts. There was another girl from school, whom Else and I knew, who came from the wrong side of the tracks. But, she knew everything—and then some. We would not go right home after school. We would go into the park and Else and I would say, "Tell us, tell us, the facts of life."

She told us all sorts of stories, which might have been true, or might not have been true. But, we were absolutely in awe of her, and we made her tell us all about sex. This is how we learned. Erna Teufel was her name. The word *teufel*, translated into English means "devil." I will never forget her: Erna Teufel—our sex instructor. We were very much interested in what she had to say, and she gave us all the answers to the questions we had.

Else studied in Heidelberg to become a doctor. She said "yes" to a very good looking chemist's proposal of marriage. His name was Heineck. While she was studying she got pregnant and had two children. She had missed attending a lot of classes, because she had to take care of these two children. But, she had studied her text books and knew the material even though she hadn't attended the classes. When it came time for the final exam, her professor would not let her come to take it. She insisted that she knew all of the material, and that she had the right to take the exam and prove it. She told them, "I know what I need to know to pass the exams." She was insistent, and she really fought for it. Finally, the consensus was that she was allowed to take the exams.

She wanted to finish with the rest of the class, and she finished on time. In the end, she passed the exams with flying colors, and graduated on time. This only happened after a long struggle with her professors. She was very determined, and in the end she got what she wanted—she was now a doctor.

Her father was also a very interesting man, an executive of the Manesman Company. I remember one Sunday morning before she was married, I was in Wiesbaden and I stayed with Else and her parents. Else told me, "Be very punctual. My father is very punctual. We are going to take a trip in the car." It was an open car, and a beautiful one at that. The top was down, and it was a lovely summer day. We were all in the car, and we were on the streets of Wiesbaden. All of a sudden, her father turned the car into a driveway, he then turned the car around in a sharp turn, and zoomed off in the opposite direction. I nearly fell out of the car he drove so fast.

I couldn't believe what he had just done, until he explained, "Do you think I'm crazy enough to raise my hand to 'Heil Hitler' for those idiots marching down the streets?' Naturally, he meant the Nazi soldiers who were marching in the direction we had originally been heading. "It is a sunny day and these guys really get my goat," Else's father complained.

Had we gone on our original path, we would have had to stop for the marching Nazi soldiers, and all raise our right arms in allegiance, or there would have been very bad consequences. This is why he made his erratic turn, over and down and in reverse, and then full speed ahead in the opposite direction.

If you did encounter the Nazis, and you did not raise your arm in solidarity, you would be interrogated, or arrested, or any number of things. It would have been very bad for us.

When the Nazis marched down the streets, they did so with such formality, with flags and all of the banners. When the car made it erratic turn I didn't know what hit us. I didn't even see the marching Nazis. But, Else's father certainly saw them, and wanted to avoid them at all costs.

Else's father was a really wonderful person, and I liked him a lot. He hated the Nazis with a passion.

However, her husband Heineck was of a different mind. But Else loved her husband, and she had her practice in this town. Together they had a very nice home, and it was where they raised their children, so that leaving her husband was out of the question.

Then her husband came to her one day and said to her, "If I knew that you listened to the BBC broadcasts out of England, I would have to report you to the authorities."

"What?" she said to him in disbelief. "You would not permit me to listen to the BBC?"

"Under no circumstances," he replied.

"Really? You would report me? The mother of your children!"

"I'm sorry, but I owe this to my Führer."

At that point she realized that Heineck had become a real fanatic.

She decided not to discuss it any further with him. And she would go up in the attic when he was not home, and put a Persian rug over her head and over the radio, and she would continue to listen to the broadcasts of the BBC. That was my friend Else! No one could tell her what to do.

Her husband was not only mesmerized by the Nazis, he was brainwashed by them. He fell for their devious lies and propaganda. He was so brainwashed that he would turn in his own wife over to the Nazis—knowing they would kill her for treason.

Else is a perfect example of someone who did not approve of what the Nazi's were doing, but she could not do anything to oppose them— let alone stop them.

She stuck it out with her husband until the war was over. Then she got a divorce as fast as she could and got him out of her life. She was glad to get rid of him. He ended up moving down to Bavaria where no one knew him or about his political beliefs. In Bavaria he became a car salesman, while Else had her practice in Wiesbaden.

Throughout our lives Else and I had several very happy times visiting each other. She came to America to visit me. She brought over her daughter, and her daughter-in-law, who had married her son Lutz. Both of her children became surgeons. And, needless to say—none of them were Nazis—even though their father had tried to brainwash them into it. They wouldn't have any part of it.

During one of her visits to America we went out to East Hampton. When I asked her why she did not remarry, she said to me, "At this point I am too young and too old."

I said to her, "Else, explain that to me."

She said, "I am too old to go into another situation where we would have to grind the rough edges. And in a marriage, that's what you have to do. I am too old for that, but I am too young to settle for an 'old age' situation. I am not that kind of a person either."

Years later she married a very nice man named Fritz, who was a real darling. He was the manufacturer of small furniture. Although she had said she would never remarry, Fritz was much closer to her own age, and it was a wonderful match. He was not possessive in any way, and he let her keep her practice in Wiesbaden. It was her way of demonstrating her own independence.

We met once at The Schloss Hotel Buelerhoehe, above Baden-Baden, Schwarzwald-Hoch Strasse, and we had a wonderful luncheon, during which we reminisced about the good old times. And, we turned the time back to what used to be—and how we got to the present point.

Fritz died in the meantime, but it was a wonderful relationship they had and they traveled a lot together. At the end, unfortunately, Else had trouble with her eyes. She had "macular degeneration." And that was very, very bad, because she could no longer drive. Afterward, she had someone who drove her, and I still met her. She took everything very much like a trouper, I must say. She rearranged her life so that she could accommodate a driver, who was a very nice woman who was an aristocrat but had no financial means. As we used to say: "a *tittle* but no middle."

On another occasion, while I was in Europe I contacted Else and we met at Europaeischer Hof, a famous hotel in Heidelberg. We had a wonderful lunch, and turned the clock back many, many years. After our lunch Else and her driver went back Wiesbaden and I went back to Spechbach.

She came over here to America and we had great times. We went out to East Hampton and had a lot of fun. After Fritz died, she had a very lovely friend, a young man, who did spend a lot of time with her going to the theater, concerts, and other events. He treasured her friendship until she died in January of 2004.

Else's daughter would come over here as well and she would go skiing on the glaciers in Canada until 2002. She had a group of men she went with, and she was the only girl. They used a helicopter to get to their starting point up in the mountains on the glaciers.

I wrote her daughter a long letter after her mother died. I told her how Else and I played together, and all about the fun things that we did. She wrote back and said, "You really gave me a view of another side of my mother that I didn't know."

The Nazis were very clever about bribing and brainwashing the people. At that time, there was widespread inflation, and the common people could not afford any of the luxuries of life. To win them over to the side of the Nazi party, they would give them special government sponsored things to make the Nazis look like glorious saviors of the German working class. There was an organization called *Kraft durch Freude*. It was unheard of for a working class family to afford a vacation in those days. But through *Kraft durch Freude*, there were ridiculously inexpensive trips to the sea for the common people. In this way, it looked like the Nazis were revolutionizing Germany, and baiting those German citizens of the Aryan race with luxuries that had previously been unaffordable to them.

This was one of the clever ways that the Nazis worked their way into the hearts and minds of society. What they didn't say however, was that if anyone opposed them in any way, they would be hauled away and would either be beaten or killed. Or, a person would simply disappear one day, never to be heard from again, or be shipped off to one of the concentration camps.

Many Communists, writers, poets, free spirits, and free thinkers, would simply be sent to the concentration camps. The camps were not for just the Jewish people, they were for anyone who opposed the Nazi regime.

In the beginning many Jewish people would say, "If it was not for the question of me being Jewish, I would buy his concept." That was how insane it all was at the time. The Nazis made it so palatable, so wonderful to join their ranks, that many of people thought it was the right thing.

There was no unemployment anymore. So, now it looked like Hitler was doing a wonderful job of running the country. However all of the work was being done for the war machine.

By the time many German citizens got wise to what was really going on, it was too late to protest or even voice your opinion. The Nazis had worked their way into all levels of society, and we didn't know who was or was not against us.

In 1933 when Hindenburg gave the position of Chancellor to Hitler, my grandmother said to us, "My darlings, sit down." She cried bitterly as she told us, "We have no idea what is going to happen to us now.

This is the most terrible thing in history." She could tell how ruthless and power hungry Hitler was, and she could tell how he was going to lead Germany to ruin. The day he became Chancellor, she could tell that this was going to be disastrous.

The Nazi armed forces were very well organized. Amongst the Nazi troops there were the SS, or Black Shirts. These were the most ruthless ones. And they had sometimes selected young men for their ranks, who were branded with a hot branding iron with the initials "SS" under their arm. Then we had the party members of the National Socialist Party, wearing brown shirts. And then there was the regular army personnel, who would wear a grey/green uniform.

Fortunately, there were some Germans who weren't sucked into the Nazi propaganda. The old aristocracy, and the Junker families, produced the few anti-Nazis like Von Stauffenberg, who unfortunately, was not successful at killing Hitler. Because the bomb in the brief case he had did not detonate at the right time, his plan failed. When his plot was exposed, he was killed for it. There were a few people who tried to assassinate Hitler, but they were all unfortunately unsuccessful.

Of professional soldiers, very many were young noblemen from good families. They were soldiers by profession, but they were true to the Emperor [Kaiser Treu] and the country. In other words, they would blindly follow the orders of their superior.

They were not into the politics. They were very well trained, and very polite. When I was in Cannes with my aunt in 1956, we had a bartender who heard us speaking German. He said to us, "When the Germans were here, it was very good. They were orderly. They didn't take our women, they didn't do anything. They had their pleasure, and they kept to themselves. When the Americans came, they took my silver can, they took my sugar, and they bribed our women with nylons and chocolate. The next thing we knew, the American soldiers were drunk in the gutter. On the other hand, the German soldiers always had starched collars, and they were prim and proper. You never saw them doing anything like that."

I said, "Yes, but the Germans were occupying France."

And he said, "Yes, but they were a good occupying force. They never behaved badly like the Americans did."

That just goes to show you how the German soldiers in the war didn't dare do anything wrong or step out of line, or they would be punished.

A lot of very powerful people gave money to the Nazi's. It was said that Krupp & Oetker and many other factory owners gave the Nazi party a lot of money. There was one particular man who was a real Nazi, and he gave them everything. Then, after the war was lost, the workers really took revenge and tortured him in the yard of the factory and left him there to die. One of his kidneys was seen on the floor. They nearly killed him, but a doctor came and fixed him up again.

Before the war started, there was one guy who was a friend of my parents, his name was Berthold. He came one day, in his brown uniform, to the store. And my father said to him, "What the heck are you doing?"

He said, "I am a 'hamburger.' I am dressed in brown on the outside, but on the inside I am red. I belong to the Communist Party, but I don't dare say it, or they would kill me. I have to play along with them."

The Nazis would routinely send people around to interrogate citizens. There would be a knock on your door. People were shivering with fear. If they took somebody in for interrogation, they would really torture these people.

Our friend who made the comment about being a "hamburger," came by one day and he was visibly upset. I said to him, "What happened?"

He said, "They called so-and-so in for interrogation. They tortured him right in front of me, and I couldn't say anything or I would be the next one tortured. It was so terrible to see. I am just sick to my stomach." He was very, very hurt by the sight of this and the realization that he was absolutely unable to prevent it.

He had a girlfriend who was in the theater, and she was Jewish. He said, "I cannot even see her. I cannot call her. They will be on my trail. I don't know what to do, or how to do it."

Finally, the Nazis came and got her and took her to the concentration camp at Auschwitz. They started doing these things on April 27, 1940. That was the date which Heinrich Himmler began the systematic genocide of the Jewish people. The Auschwitz concentration camp was located in Poland near Oswiecim.

The common citizens knew nothing about this. People would just suddenly be gone without any explanation, and everyone thought, "No, no, no, this cannot be going on!" It was unthinkable that such things would be happening. Finally, when people did find out that it was indeed true, it was too late to protest or you would end up on the next train to the concentration camp.

I remember thinking, "This cannot be!"

Recently, I saw a woman interviewed on the television. She was a twin. She and her twin brother were in the concentration camp, and Josef Mengele was the notorious doctor who was there. He was doing all sorts of sick medical experiments on humans, supposedly in the name of "science." Mengele was doing all sorts of things with twins, while claiming to be studying them. He somehow took a liking to this child and her twin brother.

He did something horrible with her brother in the process. Mengele often killed the subjects of his experiments. Then he would do a detailed report of the autopsy. The experiments often went wrong, but he wrote down the effect of things, which were gruesome.

Somehow the brother managed to escape from the camp by jumping over a wall. The sister also managed to get out of their clutches. In the process they were separated, although she and her brother somehow managed to find each other again after the war. Even so, it was a true horror story.

When I saw and heard her speak, it is as though she is not all here. She speaks like she is in a trance as she recounts what she went through. The television documentary is called *Rene and I*. It was absolutely hair-raising to hear how people could do such horrible things to other human beings. But, these are the things that the Nazi's did in the concentration camps before and during the war.

Pre-war Germany was a very liberal country. It was also very international. They had all of the scientists from Italy and other places coming over to Germany to exchange ideas and technologies.

Goebbels' propaganda machine was heralded in the newspaper called *The Stürmer*. Its editorial cartoons showed horrible Jewish faces as caricatures, helping to turn many people against the Jews. The Jews routinely and systematically got blamed for everything. They would also be blamed for giving their money to anti-German causes.

The public was so brain-washed they began to believe that the Jews were the bad guys. It was like they became the scapegoats for everything that was wrong. First of all, the Jews were the money lenders. However, what most people don't realize is the fact that this was due to the teachings of Christianity. It was the Christians who started this tradition, not the Jews. According to ancient Christianity, Christians were not permitted to lend money to others. So, the Jews came in, and were able to lend money, and to collect interest for doing so. The Jews didn't come up with this system, the Christians did— according to their teachings. It was the Christians who made the Jews the moneylenders. Anyone can go back into history and see that this was the way it was set up.

Obviously, my friends and relatives were all caught up in what was going on within Germany. My Uncle Adolf fought in the First World War and was wounded in the battle of Hartmansweiler Kopf near Belgium. He was an 18-year-old boy when they took him into the army. He was carrying ammunition to the front when a hand grenade detonated and cut his lower jaw wide open. An American doctor saved his life and put him together again.

My mother visited him later in the hospital. But, when she arrived at the hospital and was told what floor he was on, she went there and could not find him. Finally, another patient told her Adolf was the one who was "over there." As she looked, she could see that his whole head was wrapped up in bandages—even his eyes were covered, because splinters of metal went into his eyes. Later the splinters were removed by the use of magnets.

Upon the sight of Uncle Adolf with his head fully bandaged, Mother fainted right there. This was her most beloved brother, so she stayed on for weeks while he recuperated in the hospital. While she was there she helped many of the other wounded soldiers in addition to Adolf. Later, when Hitler was crucifying the Jews, Uncle Adolf thought that he was going to be immune to such treatment. According to him, "I am a German war veteran, nobody will do anything to me." That was early amidst the Nazi regime. Later he was convinced differently.

Uncle Adolf was a quiet man. He lived with his mother, whom he loved very much, and he went off on his vacations to Holland with his friends, where he had a really good time.

He had been employed by a department store, but by 1939 he had retired. While Adolf was waiting for our papers to immigrate, he took a job as a salesman selling wooden decorative pieces for coffins. He had made an excellent sales quota, so the owners could not understand what went wrong when he all of a sudden quit. As part of his job as a salesman, he had to visit the carpenters in the small towns. He had a good rapport with all of them. One day the owner of a carpenter store said to him, "You are a great guy. I like you very much and I tell you, if one of these Jews would come in my store, I would take this board," he said as he lifted up a wooden board, "and I would hit his head with it until he was pulp." Needless to say, my uncle never went on the road again—in order to avoid any conflicts. It was not required to wear the *Juda Star* on your sleeve at that time yet. Uncle Adolf, like so many of the German Jews, were greatly assimilated into society.

In 1934 I had began attending the Braunschweiger Handwerker und Kunstgewerbe Schule and I learned clothing design, and designing. As a final project in my last year at the school in 1938, I had to design a garment on paper, then create and cut out a life-sized pattern, and make it in white muslin. Then we had to cut the pieces according to our patterns, sew them together, and wear the finished garment like a model, for our graduation.

Our mistress of the sewing room was a previous head of the famous *haute couture* house of Lanvin in Paris. She was a very lovely, always smiling, short person. She later on married the man in charge of the school's architectural department.

Graduation from the class found us all clad in our white muslin creations. It was wonderful. We had photos taken at the graduation in the garden of the school in the outfits we designed and created. However, the idea of eventually landing a job as a dress designer or dressmaker in America seemed like an impossible dream.

The first year, in 1934, I had received a general education. The years from 1935 to 1938 were completely devoted to the end result: a degree in designing and dressmaking.

After my graduation ceremony, the Nazis began enacting a new practice of acid etching the word "JEWS" on the windows of any shop or establishment which was owned by Jewish people—so that no one would set foot inside. This included my mother's bicycle shop. This significantly impacted our income as a family.

After years of being "ostriches," we finally woke up and took our heads out of the sand. Now we realized that much more than our income was at stake, our lives were suddenly in jeopardy. In Germany, Jews were now treated like lepers.

As Germany was preparing for war, some parts of my life continued on a normal course, even though there was a prevailing sense of doom that something catastrophic was coming in the very near future. On the 20th of February, 1939, I went to a Mardi Gras ball in Mannheim, I still have pictures of it. I wore a nice Dirndl dress. We danced, and my date that evening was a lovely man whose uncle was a Baron. Everyone knew him in town. So, I felt awfully elated that he asked me to the ball and we danced and had a good time.

However, in the middle of the dance, all of a sudden he got a nosebleed. There were marble floors there, and we put him on the floor, and I was sitting there trying to help him, and they stopped his nose from bleeding. But, in spite of the nose-bleeding incident, I will always remember it as a wonderful evening.

A second cousin, or some sort of other distant relative of mine, was also there that night at The Park Hotel, which was held in similar prestigiousness to The Plaza Hotel in New York City. My date and I ended up sitting there and talking until 2:00 in the morning, and it was wonderful. He called me afterwards, but he lived out of town, which complicated things. It seems that after he got the nosebleed, he was so embarrassed that was the end of that affair.

With everything else that was going on in Germany at the time, I hastily left the school without officially picking up my graduation papers. Suddenly I realized that I might need my certificates of graduation, and I requested that the school give them to me. When I finally received them, they were dated April 21, 1939.

Within the next few months it was clear that parties and dances and dates with handsome young boys were all trivial concerns compared to what was going on in Germany and the rest of the world. Was war about to break out? Were the Nazi's ruining Germany? Were any of us safe from what was going on around us? It wasn't long before this era of mystery was to end, and grim reality was destined to take its place.

Chapter Five:
New York City

When we arrived in New York, I had this set vision of what the city would look like. We got off of the boat, and my cousin Rosie came to the port to meet us. Cousin Rosie and her husband Larry, who lived in Laurelton on Long Island, had given us the affidavits to come to America.

Rosie had come to this country with her parents when she was two years old. She then married Larry who was the sweetest and most wonderful man. He was so generous that he gave money to all the beggars in the street who were asking for money. His theory was: "They need it more than I do." That was just the kind of guy he was.

At the time that we came to America, everyone had to have someone legally vouch for them before they could immigrate here. Immigrants had to prove that they had sufficient funds available to them, so that the government would never be responsible for them through the welfare system, the health department, or any other governmental organization.

If we had this same method of strict immigration quota systems today, it would surely save a lot of the problems that we are currently experiencing. However, it would be a challenge to implement that nowadays. Back then, you had to have a lot of money in the bank or a way to support yourself to come here.

I will never forget, upon arrival at the pier, my cousin Rosie took me in her arms, and I tried to tell her of our experiences in Germany. She only told me, "You will forget it soon, and maybe it wasn't all so bad."

She really had no idea how horrible things were in Germany at the time, and to hear her say this really took me by surprise. Did she not hear of Auschwitz—Guers—Therensienstadt, etc., etc.?

Rosie had good advice for me. She said, "There is a song that we have here, and you should really learn it. 'Laugh and the world laughs with you, cry and you cry alone.'" I didn't know what to say, so I just smiled. It was as though she was blind to the horrors that were underway in the Germany we had just left.

As we drove past Fifth Avenue in Manhattan, I said, "Wonderful! This is exactly the New York City that I had imagined in my dreams!" I was so thrilled by the sight of this legendary avenue, with its expensive shops and all of the people there who were fashionably dressed. It was just like I had envisioned that it would look. I was so excited to be here! It was as though my wildest dreams had just come true. However, my elation was very short-lived.

We drove north from the upper east side of Manhattan Island, and somewhere along our route, we made a turn into the Bronx, and all of a sudden my grand dreams of what my new life was going to be like in New York City were shattered. Once we crossed the East River into the Bronx, the vision was something quite different. I saw the look of poverty, the dilapidated buildings, and the lower rent dwellings of the urban American lower class. This was not the New York City with the streets "paved with gold" that I had envisioned living on—Fifth Avenue was more of what I had in mind! As I looked at the unhappy faces we passed on the street, I was so disappointed that I began to cry.

This was nothing like I had expected to find. When we arrived at our destination in the Bronx, we came to a fourth floor walk-up apartment building. While everyone supposedly had their own room, they were tiny rooms, with just enough space for a bed and a table, a lamp, and a chair. The rooms themselves were so small in fact that they were more like little cubby holes.

It was a seven room apartment for my Uncle Adolf, my Uncle Robert, my Uncle Walter, my mother, my grandmother, and I. Everybody had a tiny room of their own, except for me. My bed to sleep upon was to be the couch in the living room.

These arrangements were all made by my Uncle Walter. My grandmother's second-oldest son, Robert, had been here in America before the First World War, when he was shipped off to America by my grandmother. And, his two daughters—my first cousins Rosie Friedman (married to Larry) and Lee—had grown up in America. It was they who brought us to this place.

It was in this fourth floor walk-up apartment where my Uncle Adolf, my mother, my grandmother and I, were to live when we arrived in America. It was located at 666 East 164th Street in the Bronx. It was from there that we were to start to make our living in this new country.

The apartment was on the top floor of the building. This was not to be confused with the penthouse in any sense of the word, it was just the top floor.

I was terribly disappointed with what I saw. The Bronx was ugly, and disheveled. There was such poverty around me in the streets. But what was I to do? I was in America now, and I knew that I just had to make the best of it. I had to consider myself lucky that I had made it to America at all, as opposed to staying in Germany where there was nothing but a horrifying sense of doom.

The next day, my Uncle Walter took me into Manhattan. We went to Times Square in the Broadway theater district. Now, the lights of Broadway absolutely mesmerized me. It was marvelous, and I was happy as a lark.

We went to see a movie. Then we went to a cafeteria, which was a unique experience in itself. It was one of the famed Horn & Hardart's automats that were so popular back then. I was fascinated to see the revolving glass doors full of food. You would put a nickel in the slot, the turntable would open the door, and you could take your food out, and walk over to the table and eat it. I had never seen anything like this before.

I was full of vim and vigor after all those fun experiences. Now, that was the New York City that I had expected to see, and had anticipated coming to America to become a part of all this excitement. Then we went home to the grey and ugly Bronx again.

At night my uncle went to some sort of committee meeting, and I went with him. I was asked to sit in the back during their meeting. I was told that they might have some sort of a job for me if I couldn't find anything else, and that I should come back in a month.

From there we went to the Catholic Society, and they took down all of my information and talked to me. They told me that I should not think that I was qualified to land a job in the area of my education. They told me that the only thing I was qualified to do was in the area of being a maid or some sort of other household help.

They told me, "If you work in a house you won't have to have any real dialogue with anyone, you can just work. In our opinion, that is the best way for you to get a job and earn a living."

I went back to the Broadway area, and finally I thought, "What a beautiful city New York truly is!" I was just in love with Manhattan at that point. I felt, "I just have to get a job, and then everything will fall in place for me."

Diary Entry:
It is the third day we are in the United States. Today my Uncle Robert said to me, "Well, what are you doing? Get up and go look for a job." So much for the last of my "streets paved with gold" dreams.

I looked in the newspaper and I found a job listed for a fitter at Best & Company. I went there, but my English wasn't good enough. I answered several ads, and didn't land any of the jobs. I thought to myself, "This is ridiculous."

Diary Entry:
Now I am four weeks in New York City, I have been looking for work. I either get, "We don't have any work," or "Don't call us, we'll call you." It is hard to get used to accepting rejection.

After much trial and tribulations, some of the other immigrants in the building helped Mother and I find jobs. First, there was Mrs. Goldsmith, who lived downstairs helped Mother to get a job at the

Chinese laundry, which was around the corner from where we lived in the Bronx. She was busy ironing drapes and curtains all day.

Mrs. Goldsmith at the time worked at a manufacturer called Wollner & Klist. It was a factory that was located down on Bleecker Street in Manhattan, and she was able to get me a seamstress job there. The first job I had was sewing together chenille cotton strips onto canvases. Ultimately these became toilet covers and bathroom mats.

It wasn't long before the supervisors could tell that I was very good at sewing. There were a lot of older women there who did nothing but operate the sewing machines. As a young girl with quick and nimble fingers, I was very good at my job. I was so good that they decided not to waste my talents on the chenille toilet covers.

On the fourth or fifth day on the job, I was moved to the area where nine-foot by twelve-foot carpets were being sewn. These big carpets were for Hollywood customers which were now all sewn by me.

This was my first job, and I earned $11.83 for one week's work. My mother also got a job at the same place, sewing chenille onto canvas which produced carpets and smaller rugs, toilet seat covers, and things like that. It wasn't a fantastic job, but we both had work and an income, and we were in America—safely away from the Nazis and the war that was raging in Germany. For that, I was very happy. It felt wonderful.

One of the first things that we had to do when we became established in America was to pay back Mother Superior's incredible generosity. I borrowed the money from Cousin Rose and sent it to Mother Superior. Every month I sent care packages to Mother Superior with all of the things that it was impossible for her to obtain in wartime England, with all of the rationing. She would send me the loveliest thank you notes, which I cherished.

I wasted no time getting into the swing of things in New York City. I was doing several of the things I wanted to do, and I was also having some great adventures.

In addition to my job, I also attended English language classes at Morris High School in the Bronx. One of the other students was a young man from Bogota, Columbia, by the name of Hernando Otera Haigan. He took a real fancy to me, but I was not interested in dating him. I told him that between my work and my classes, that only left my Sundays free, and on Sundays I was busy with my family.

Frustrated by this news, he said to me, "Where I come from, and two people are in love, nothing comes between them. Couples marry at an early age in Bogota."

Much to his disappointment, this revelation did nothing to change my mind about dating him. On one occasion there was a school outing to Bear Mountain, and I was with Hernando. This particular boat ride was very nice and presented a very attractive view of the scenery, as one could see the beautiful estates from the Hudson River. In the bright sunshine, it presented itself as a very desirable home life. It looked especially attractive from the boat on the river, because you could just see the big houses. Who knows if the people were actually happy in the houses, but from where I saw it, these houses appeared to present a very glamorous and happy existence. Perhaps it was all in my imagination, but it made quite an impression on me that day.

In May of 1940 I graduated from night school at Morris High, and a very good looking councilman gave the Commencement speech, advising all of us to study and become good Americans. His name was Howard Hilton Spellmann. As he gave his speech, it seemed to me that he spoke as if I was the only person in the room. But, I rationalized that it was just my imagination.

After the speech was over, people began circulating and socializing. A couple of my school chums came up to me and told me that they realized that the speaker couldn't keep his eyes on anyone else but me, and they became very jealous.

One of the girls said to me, "Howard is so rich and so good looking."

In my head, all I could think was, "No, no, no."

Both statements seemed to be true. But I was just a young girl, and it was such fun to be flirted with.

Howard found a way to speak to me alone, and proposed that we have a date. We made plans for me to come and visit him in his office on Saturday which was my day off.

But it was so much fun to be pursued by him. I was young and I figured, "Why not?"

On Saturday I arrived at Howard's office downtown, which was located somewhere on Broadway. It was a beautiful office. The walls were lined with beautiful and rich looking mahogany book shelves covered with volumes of books. Much to my surprise, there was nobody there but he and I. Needless to say, he tried to get me to in a compromising position. He only partially succeeded.

He told me right away that he had to see me again. He announced that he was in love with me. However, he was married, and had two children—twins no less.

He proposed that I should move to the West Side of town, and tell my mother that I am going to be his mistress, and that I would go with him on a holiday to Florida. He was going to make sure that I would get a different and better paying job.

The second time we met he took me out to a restaurant, and we had a wonderful dinner there. Then he walked me to the subway, and we made plans that we were going to see each other again.

He kept telling me that I should tell my mother that I would be his mistress.

I finally told him, "Forget it. This is too much for me." I really didn't want to get involved in any way. I said to him, "This is a very nice interlude, but: no, no, no, no, no."

I thought that I had broken it off, and that the affair was over. However, he called me and I met him again. And of course he looked handsomely young and wonderful. And right away he gave me a kiss, and started again with his whole line of wanting me to be his mistress.

"Whatever you want, you can have," he promised me.

In the meantime he was trying to get the Cunard Line to refund the money I paid for the unused tickets which I had purchased in Deutsche Marks before the war. This was obviously another way for him attempting to keep me on the hook.

He told me, "I am absolutely smitten by you. Thinking about you makes me crazy. I must have you. I don't know what to do! How can I prove my love for you?"

He then told me that he wanted to speak to my mother personally so that he could work out the arrangements for him to be my lover, and I his mistress.

I told him, "Absolutely not, under no circumstances are you going to meet my mother."

Then he asked me, "Would you marry me if I were free?"

I told him, "Yes." However, I didn't really believe that he was serious about divorcing his wife for me.

In my mind, this love affair just couldn't go anywhere from here. He told me that he was going to quit his law firm, and we would move up to Canada together to live.

I think that he was actually relieved that I didn't loose my head over all of this and accept his plan to divorce his wife and run away with me. I knew in the end this was all just a line he was handing me to try and get me into bed. I may have been a young girl at the time, but I was wise enough to figure this out.

It finally came to the point where I had to essentially tell him, "Get lost. I am not going to do it. Finished. That's it." And, finally that was the end of that.

During my first summer in New York City, I had another suitor who was infatuated with me. Siggy Laemle was a friend of my Uncle Walter's and he was a very handsome and nice gentleman. I remember one particular sunny Sunday in July of 1940, when I went with Siggy to the 1939-1940 World's Fair in Queens.

It felt very good to be with Siggy because he was very typically European in his mannerisms, and he was very attentive to me. He was charming and he paid me compliments about my new hairdo. We went on several of the rides, and viewed many of the exhibits that afternoon, all of which were very entertaining. While we were at one of the restaurants at the World's Fair someone at the next table remarked to us that we made such a nice couple. Then they asked if we were married. Siggy replied, "I wish it was so."

I thought to myself, "Oh no, this is much too soon for this." I remembered the words of my grandmother who said to me, "To be unhappily married, it is always too early. And to be happily married, it is never too late."

I was actually very flattered that Siggy was so passionately in love with me. However, for my part, I didn't feel any spark of love. I didn't want to settle for a very secure existence merely for the want of the very *Bourgeois* lifestyle that he was offering me. I just wasn't cut out for this kind of life. There were far too many things that I wanted to experience.

So, I decided we were going to have to go our own separate ways. He was still very lovely and nice to me. But I made sure that he understood my viewpoint.

Not long after that his job transferred him to Boston. His last words to me were, "Be careful, watch out, but if you have too much fun, name it after me."

He later got married to a girl in Boston and they had two children. I wasn't at all jealous of this. I was actually happy that he found someone else. So that was the end of Siggy and I.

Meanwhile, Uncle Adolf had a job making donuts in the bakery, starting at midnight until five in the morning, which he disliked from the very beginning. Adolf was very fastidious and neat. As a baker he had to really get his hands in the jam pot to make the jelly-filled donuts. He hated this. So one night the owner of the bakery and he did not agree on something, and Adolf just left the job in utter disgust, announcing to us as he opened the door at home, "No more baker."

At that time, doctors still made house calls, and our doctor really felt like he was a part of our family. I will never forget when my grandmother had a visit from her doctor. As he sat at her bedside she asked him, "Give me your word of honor as a doctor. Do I have cancer?" She knew very well that she did, but she still did not want it confirmed.

He knew that she did not want to know the truth, so he politely lied to her and said, "No, you do not." That was the answer she wanted to hear.

It was just as well that Adolf was no longer working at the bakery, as Grandma was to become very sick over the next several months and someone had to be with her all of the time. Uncle Adolf waited on her hand and foot and cooked for her—under her direction—and for all of us. At that point, Grandma had been operated on for colon cancer and had a colostomy bag, which my mother took care of for her. It was the first thing that she did in the morning before she left for work. And in the evening, it was the first thing she did when she returned home.

It was very sad for me to see Grandma in ill health as she was my great love and inspiration. My grandmother told me, "It is a shame that I didn't come to this country much sooner than I did in my life, as I could have accomplished many great things."

Meanwhile, my other grandmother, Grandma Mueller, remained in Germany. She lived with her daughter Hildegard and her husband, Alfred Eisemann, in Heidelberg. She died there in 1940, and was buried in Heidelberg.

I read in the newspaper that on September 4, 1940, German soldiers marched into Denmark and Norway. Denmark protected the Jews and helped many of them to use the bridge to flee to the neutral Sweden after the Nazis entered Denmark and wanted them to be extinguished. The Danish government advised the Jewish people not to be home at the specified day when the Nazis were searching for the Jews in their homes. Obviously the war was escalating even farther, and I was relieved that I was no longer in Europe.

I also saw in the newspaper that at that time, there was a three nation pact between Germany, Italy and Japan. Three other countries joined this triumvirate: Hungary, Romania and Slovakia. Several wartime alliances were made to fight them. At that time, as part of a 99 year agreement, America leased space for military bases in Newfoundland and the British West Indies. In exchange, the Americans provided the British marines with 50 naval destroyer ships.

While all of this was going on, I kept my job at Wollner & Klist until the end of the year. When December of 1940 rolled around, I attended my first company Christmas party. While I was there, the other workers decided that it would be fun to get me drunk. What a big mistake that turned into. Once I had several drinks in me it acted like "truth serum" or "liquid courage." Suddenly, I decided to confront the boss and give him a piece of my mind. I told him off, and let him know how miserly I thought he was. It would have been bad enough to just leave it at that, but the floodgates opened up and all the misgivings I had throughout the work year came spilling out of my mouth.

After I left the party I got on the Third Avenue El train and promptly threw up. So much for my first company Christmas party! Although I wasn't fired for speaking up, I felt that I could never show my face there again, and I never returned to work.

After the holidays, in January of 1941 I had to look for another job. Again, the people in the building helped me. I was assisted in getting into the The Amalgamated Garment Workers Union. After I received my union card, I found work at Howard Clothing in Long Island City. My first assignment there was sewing the sleeve linings together for the jackets to men's suits. It was such detail conscious work, and the supervisor didn't ever want to hear my sewing machine stop at any time.

At first I would stop the machine and cut the threads with a scissor. I had a tendency to sew one row of fabric and then stop the machine. I was instantly yelled at for not keeping my machine going at all times. "Never stop your machine for anything!" the supervisor would yell at me.

I distinctly remember him hollering at me, "Shake your leg! You won't earn enough salt for the soup."

"How am I supposed to cut the threads?" I asked, wondering how I could continue to sew without stopping.

"Instead of a scissor, you rip them in the back with your own two hands," he yelled.

So, I did as he said. And from that point on, I just kept the machine running.

I worked from 8:00 a.m. to 3:00 p.m. five days a week. I came home on the Third Avenue El, and there was a drug store there. Every day after work I would go to the soda fountain at the drug store and buy myself a strawberry sundae as a reward for making it through another trying day of work.

Finally I reached a point when I realized that I was not making enough money, so I confronted my boss at Howard Clothing and asked him for more money. He agreed to increase my pay, but only if I took on a more challenging work assignment. For the sake of more money, I took on the task of doing the binding for the inner arm at the armpit of men's suit jackets which was rather complicated. The binding was stiff, and the garment material was soft, so it wasn't easy to accomplish this. However, I had very nimble fingers, and I was able to keep up the demanding pace of the job.

Separate bins of pre-made jacket fronts and jacket backs would be placed on either side of me. I had to grab one of each, join them at the shoulder, and run them through the sewing machine one after another as fast as I could: grab, grab, and sew. It was the type of a job that a robot would be perfect for, and that was what I felt like in that job. All this was paid piecework. The more of these pieces I completed, the more money I received.

Over the next several months, I graduated from one job to another at Howard Clothing. Eventually I moved to sewing together the shoulders, which was even more detailed and better paid.

While we were in America and the war progressed, we didn't want to write to any of my mother's friends because we thought that it might be harmful to them to do so. And it could have potentially have been bad for ourselves as well. The authorities would give them trouble: "How come you have Jewish friends? Come on, we want details." You couldn't write to them, because you knew it could spell trouble for them. So, we lost contact with all of our friends and relatives whom we had left behind in Germany while the war proceeded and intensified.

After I had moved to America I became friends with a woman named Helene Fröhlicher. She was very benevolent and gave affidavits for over 80 people who immigrated to the United States. These affidavits meant that she had to show three year's worth of income tax returns, and verify that she had the funds to support these people if anything went wrong. She not only helped them come to the country, but she would give parties and invite them to come to her home. She also donated heavily to different charities and was an incredibly caring and generous woman.

In the affidavits she basically had to state, "I have so much income, and I have a place for them to live. If they need medical help, I will pay for everything." She did this gladly, and she legitimately had access to a great deal of money. She married a man, Dr. Victor Fröhlicher, who was a doctor of chemistry for Geigy.

Helene lived in Ridgefield, New Jersey, and she was very helpful to many people who came to this country. They could come to her house for a hot meal, and everyone soon discovered that she was very generous with both her time and her money. She was also a real strong and wonderful person. Both she and Dr. Victor Fröhlicher had come to the United States from Switzerland. After Helene was married to Victor they both became American citizens.

I always had a great time at her parties. If she invited someone who did not have any transportation, she would send them the bus fare to get there. Helene was a very intellectual woman, and she started out a Communist. Her parents were very, very rich and came from a wealthy Swiss family. They owned a big part of the silk industry in Switzerland. Her family name was Stehly, and they were a very well known family. She also became a Catholic, because she was raised as a Protestant. When she became a Catholic, she became a very fervent one—often acting "holier than thou." When she got behind a person or a cause, she really got on the warpath. I must give her credit. She was wonderful, and quite a philanthropist.

At these afternoon events at the Fröhlicher house in Ridgefield, New Jersey, we usually took a survey to find out who wanted to stay in America and who wanted to go back to their native country. This survey was primarily posed to the Swiss young men. We found that the criteria of the "point of no return" was two years. If they had been here less than two years, their reply was usually, "Yes, I would return to Switzerland." People who had been here more than two years, never wanted to go back.

On one occasion, Dr. Victor Fröhlicher went to Canada to sell the patents to the insecticide DDT to the Canadians. He didn't have his passport with him, but he had what he thought were the proper papers. When he got to the border, the Canadian border guard said to him, "You don't have a passport? We don't know who you are."

We have to remember that this was an era which was long before such things were computerized. Today, in the 21st Century, they could have just looked on a computer screen, or phoned somebody. Without the passport, the Canadian authorities wouldn't believe his story. So he called his son to go to the safe and open it and produce his passport number, but it was without avail. His son could not seem to open the safe. So, poor Victor spent the weekend in a Canadian jail. On Monday morning a call to Washington, D.C. resolved the problem, and Victor was free to have his meeting.

Back then, the borders in and out of this country were truly sealed. This is in direct contrast to what it is like today.

There are many things that people don't know today about the affidavit and quota system that existed back then with regard to immigration. If we had that system today, we would probably have less problems. Nowadays, it seems that anyone can come and go as they please. It is like a big free-for-all. I don't know exactly what should be done with the immigration system today in the 21st Century, but it sure needs corrections right and left. You cannot hide behind the Constitution. There seems to be no common sense today. It is the only thing that is fair to the people. I am very, very worried about this whole political situation today.

Helene Frölicher had three lovely daughters. Katie, was going to become a nun. Mayessa, whose nickname was "Assie," married a count who was working for Caritas, a Catholic charity. And, there was Madeline who later married a Wall Street stockbroker. When they were little girls, I taught them how to sew. I taught all three of them how to make the same dress for themselves. It was a red sleeveless jumper over a white blouse. But, between the three of them, they had to make six dresses, because each one of them had to make an extra dress which was to be donated to the local orphanage home. Only after completing the dress for charity could they finish their own dresses to wear.

Helene insisted on this. That was the type of woman Helene was. This exercise in selflessness was her idea. She said to me at one time, "I have raised my children in a manner in which I told them, 'If you fall in love with the lowest-paid blue collar worker in the country, you can be happy and have a fulfilling life.'"

I remember on one occasion, Assie was sitting in a nice soft chair. Her mother came by and said to her, "Have you sat in that nice soft chair long enough? I think that it's time for you to sit on a wooden chair and do some work!" That was Helene.

In addition to the three girls, Helene and Victor also had two sons, who were the oldest and youngest of their five children. Another demonstration of how strong and resilient the Fröelicher children were, was what I witnessed in the case of the oldest son, Bobby. He went to complete his military service in the United States. During the 1940s I went skiing with Bobby and a group of other friends. We were on our way to a ski area, and Bobby was driving the car.

The road conditions became icy, and we found ourselves sliding from one side of the road to the other. It was really quite treacherous.

I suggested, "Let's turn around and go home."

Instead, Bobby had a better idea, and announced, "Let's all pray for our safety."

I was rather surprised to hear a young man in his early 20's with such a strong religious resolve. Again, this reflected the way in which Helene brought up her children to be stoic and religious.

But the most harrowing thing that the family had to endure came in the 1950s when Bobby and his family returned to Lucerne, Switzerland. While there, he was working for the Viscose Company, translating English into German. He was still involved in the fashion and fabric industry. It was in Switzerland that his two children came home one day and announced that someone in their school had contracted Polio, and all of the children needed to be vaccinated. Since it was perceived as a disease which usually strikes children, Bobby took his two children for their vaccinations, never dreaming that he too was at risk, because he was 33 years old at that time.

However, Bobby came down with one of the worst cases of Polio in history. It effected his nervous system so badly, and it destroyed his diaphragm so severely, that he was left unable to breathe on his own. He was rendered an invalid. Thankfully he came from a very wealthy family who could afford to do everything possible to not only save his life, but to make certain that he received the best care available.

First he was flown from one country to another, where he met with specialists to try and help him. At that time, the prevailing mode of caring for patients who could not breathe on their own was to put them in an iron lung. Unfortunately, he had a strong case of claustrophobia, which made this impossible.

So, to ensure that he could still breathe, he was attached to electrical respirator that kept the air flowing to his lungs. I didn't think that I knew of a person whose faith was so strong that he could not only battle this condition, but had the resolve to continue his career. Although Bobby's body had deteriorated, his mind was fully intact.

In fact he suggested to his wife that she divorce him immediately, and go on with her own life. Coming from a very strong Italian Catholic family, and having a father who was an Ambassador from Italy in Switzerland, Bobby's wife would not hear of such a plan. She said to him, "I got married for better or for worse, and I will not even consider divorcing you."

Bobby was however, still considered the head of their family, and all decisions were to continue to be made by him. He even insisted on keeping his job—at reduced hours—which he maintained.

I visited them and was shocked to see such devotion, faith and stamina. Whereas lesser people might have just given up, Bobby worked even harder to live as normal a life as possible. The whole family behaved as if there was not a thing wrong or out of the ordinary as far as Bobby was concerned. They carried on and made believe that nothing had changed. I, however, was shocked at what I saw.

For instance, while visiting them, Bobby motioned to his wife that he had to go to the bathroom. At which time, one of his children came over to him, and assisted in putting Bobby's feet on top of his wife's feet. While she embraced and supported his weight with her arms around him, she walked the two of them to the elevator to accomplish this task. I was shown the "wankelbed," which is a bed that mechanically moves by itself to facilitate Bobby's breathing through the night. I will never forget the impression that witnessing all of this made upon me.

His sister Katie, who had become a Catholic nun, lived in the convent on 137th Street in Manhattan. She invited me and some additional family members to have brunch at the Essex House on Central Park South, with her and Bobby.

I volunteered to pick Bobby and Katie up at their hotel and take them to the Essex House. It took Katie and I, and the doorman to get Bobby into the car. He had to sit in the front seat of my car, and he required being accompanied by his personal breathing machine, which included a tube that went from his machine, into his mouth.

Although I found this to be a harrowing experience, he and his family all behaved as though nothing was out of the ordinary. After brunch I was emotionally destroyed to see the torture that this poor man had to go through. He lived to be 63 years old, out of which 30 years were—in my estimation—pure hell. This strong sense of survival determination was all a product of the strong sense of faith that Helene and Victor had instilled in all of their children.

Meanwhile, March 15, 1941 marked the first anniversary of my having moved to the United States. While my family and I avidly followed the news of what was going on in Europe, by now my day-to-day routine, and what was going on around me in my personal life, very much filled my mind.

I was a typical young girl, who was very much concerned with boys and relationships with them. My diary, which I regularly wrote in, reflects that fact.

Many of my thoughts were spent thinking about where I was going, who I was going to fall in love with, and the type of man he would be. Little did I know, but right around the next corner I was about to meet and fall in love with the most important man of my life. How could I have known that this mystery man was someone from my past, whom I already knew from Germany?

Chapter Six:
Enter: Francois Schwarz

Life is so full of odd coincidences. You can walk down one particular street, and your entire fate can change. I had been in New York City for one year at this point. One day in 1941, just by chance I was at 49th Street between Park and Madison Avenues, in front of The Barclay Hotel. And there, much to my surprise was a face in the crowd whom I recognized: it was Francois Schwarz!

"Oh, my God, what are you doing here?" I said to him with sheer surprise. He looked absolutely wonderful to me, and he was just as handsome as the last time I had seen him back in Germany.

Then I spotted Meta walking behind him. I warmly greeted her as well, like the long-lost friends that they were to me.

Come to find out, Francois and Meta had left France when the war started, moved to Manhattan, and were living in luxury in The Barclay Hotel. It was so wonderful to see them—especially Francois.

I explained how Mother and Uncle Adolf and I had escaped from Germany, through England. I also explained how we were living in the Bronx with Uncle Robert and his wife.

Then Meta asked me, "How is your grandmother?"

I replied, "Grandmother is fine. Oh, we must all get together and see each other."

After that chance meeting on the street, Francois and Meta came up and visited us in the Bronx, and we all had a nice time reuniting with them and catching up on all the news.

We had great conversations with them. Amidst our visit they wanted to know what everyone in the family was doing for work.

I explained to them, "I'm presently working for Howard Clothes in Queens at this time."

"Oh my God, piece work?" Meta said. "That is terrible work! Why don't you work for my husband? He is just starting his office here."

I said, "That would be great." So, we made plans for me to visit him at the office to discuss possible employment.

When I went to meet with Francois, I confessed to him that I didn't really have many office skills.

He said to me, "Why don't you go to school and learn? You can go to night school."

"Oh really?" I said.

Francois made it sound like such a logical solution, that I promised to do just that. After investigating I found out that there was a business school called the Interborough Institute, which was very good. I went there and enrolled, and as a business student I learned all sorts of things—stenography, typing, and bookkeeping—all skills to use in the office.

I continued with my job at Howard Clothing, paid for the schooling, and I was about to receive my diploma from the Interborough Institute. It took me a half of a year to do this.

In a conversation with Francois, he asked me, "How far are you in your business school courses?"

I said, "I'm graduating with these skills," and I proceeded to list what I had learned.

Then he said, "Well, why don't you start working for me now? I now have the office set up in Rockefeller Center. So, why don't you just quit your job at Howard Clothing and be done with it?"

"Okay," I agreed. We immediately set a date when I was to report to work for Francois.

My grasp of the English language had greatly improved, and I was getting quite good at this point. When I arrived in the United States I spoke English with a British accent. Everyone used to say to me, "Don't talk so affected."

I said, "That's all I know, I don't know how to change it." Well, after several months here, it changed anyhow. After that the British accent wore off very quickly.

When I reported for work at Francois' new 630 Rockefeller Center office. He said to me, "Okay, type." And so I did. That was how my business career officially began.

It was a very small office. One office was his private one, and there was one other small office in front where Alice, his secretary, sat. That was the entire company at that time—Alice, Francois, and myself—the boss and his two employees.

Francois had been very clever and foresighted with his finances. He had made a great deal of money from the sale of his company in Switzerland. When they sent him the money from Europe, he used it to start up his business here in the United States.

Before I began to work for Francois, my love affair with him was already underway as well. When I saw Francois for the first time in America, I immediately found that the attraction I felt for him in Germany—that he felt for me—was still very much alive. When I was still with Howard Clothes in Queens doing piecework, we began having an affair. He would phone me to find out what I was doing. He was really getting under my skin. Before we even physically started our affair, his enticing flirtation began.

We would meet at appointed times, in pre-determined rendezvous places. One of our favorite meeting spots was under the clock at The Astor Hotel.

This goes back to November of 1941. While Meta was in the hospital for some minor surgery, Francois and I went for a weekend to the Pocono Mountains. War with Japan and Germany had broken out, and we really began our love affair then. We were just inseparable from that point forward. We just gravitated towards each other.

That winter I went on a ski trip in upstate New York. I went with a couple of friends of mine. Grandma's health had been failing throughout the year, but she had suddenly taken a turn for the worse while I was on my skiing expedition. It seemed that she had held on until I returned to the city. I arrived back at the apartment to find I was to be with her during her last hours. I told her how much I loved her. She passed away, and it was a great loss to me.

In 1942 I had graduated from school, quit working for Howard Clothing, and was amidst a full time job working for Francois. It was at a very exciting point that I joined his company.

I soon found that Francois was an insightful marketing genius. As part of his company, we got into the ground floor of a new process for making quick frozen foods, and I typed up the papers known as a "know how," for Clarence Birdseye, and all of the patents for this process. My job at the beginning was just as the office typist.

By typing up these "know how" papers, it opened up a whole new business sense for me. I didn't just type the papers, I absorbed the information as well. Alice, his secretary, was very helpful too. She taught me what to do and where to go. She told me, "read this," and "go here," and "see this." I learned a lot from her as well.

It was a small office with only one window, in Francois' office. There were partitions, and then there was our office—Alice and I. Eventually it branched out to become a bigger and bigger operation. We moved to the ninth floor, then we moved to the seventeenth floor, each time gaining more space.

At that time Francois was just trying to utilize his knowledge in the food area. I am not sure what exactly he had in mind at the time, but it progressed from that point onward, and involved working with various food-oriented patents. He tried to get the license from General Foods to manufacture Birdseye frozen foods in Switzerland, as well as making pectin. There were agreements for me to copy, and then we had a contract with Unilever in England.

Since the war was underway, there wasn't much that could be done as far as trade agreements with Europe. So Francois bought a dairy farm in Bellmore, Long Island. Milk was produced, pasteurized, and sold. When he took over the company he was horrified to find that the cows and the farm were all very, very dirty. The first thing that he did as the owner of this farm was to whitewash the buildings. The cows had been living in dirt, and he upgraded their accommodations.

The guys who worked at the farm were non-Americans who spoke little English, and they were pretty dirty as well. They were all Mexican and Guatemalan refugees. Francois instructed them that the cows were to be cleaned up, the farm was to be cleaned up, and the workers were to wear white coats. They stared at him with a puzzled look, and asked, "What are we to do with white coats?"

He said, "You are going to do things differently from now on, and I am going to tell you how."

Francois hired a man from Germany who had once managed a German farm, and made him the manager. This man and his wife lived right at the farm, and ran it very nicely and very effectively.

He put a radio in the farm so that there was English language broadcasting and music all day on the farm, so the yelling and conversation ceased. Now the farm was clean—inside and out—and even the workers looked clean and orderly dressed in their new white uniforms. Where once there was nothing but dirt, it was all clean and sanitary—to the point that the cows were so happy that they now produced a lot more milk.

The milk had to go to a pasteurizing facility. One morning when I was there, the man who usually delivered the milk, didn't show up for work. Someone had to drive the truck to the pasteurization plant. I was there for the weekend, so I decided to take control of the situation.

The way the truck was set up, it was designed for a much larger man. But I got into the truck, and found that I couldn't even sit in the driver's seat. It was much too high for me, as I am a small person. So, I stepped in, and drove there standing up.

I arrived at the pasteurizing plant still standing, with the milk cans in the back of the truck. When I came to the plant the startled workers said to me, "What are you doing?"

I was just getting out of the pickup truck, and I was about to take the milk cans down from the back of the truck. They said, "Get off of there, the cans are bigger than you are!" So they unloaded the milk, and I drove the truck home.

The boys were sure startled. "What the heck is this?" they asked.

The milk from this particular farm was known to have the highest degree of butterfat. It was so good in fact that Francois received a commendation of honor from the Agricultural Deputy of the U.S.A. At that time the butterfat count was very important, as it was highly desirable for making butter. Francois was at that time "a dollar a year man" in Washington where he met a lot of interesting people.

The milk went off for pasteurization, and processing, and then there was a regular delivery route. That was something that we felt we were doing to keep the country running while the war raged onward. In that way, our efforts worked in everyone's benefit.

Although I was happy working for Francois, I still longed to use the education I had in dress designing. At one point, I was trying to get a job in the *Vogue* dress pattern department. Since I was trained quite differently from what I was doing, I was still trying to find a job more in my line. I had been trained in Germany as a fashion designer, and I kept applying to jobs in the garment business.

In the building in which we lived, was this very nice woman, Mrs. Goldsmith, who introduced us to another friend, and my mother had this friend who lived at 137th Street and Broadway on the river, and they had a son. Bobby Hirschkron was a tall and very nice fellow who was going to school. After that he went to college. After college he landed a job at General Electric as an engineer. He stayed there until he retired. He was very ambitious, and we knew each other very well.

About that time someone told me that they might have a job for me in the industry in which I wanted to work. That was in the pattern department at *Vogue*. I was told that I should prepare drawings and create a nice presentation. So, that's what I did.

On the Fourth of July I was home, and everyone had gone out to celebrate. I was sitting at home drawing, and sewing. After I completed several things, I thought I could finally present what I had made. I had the address of *Vogue*, and after the Fourth of July, I made plans to go to their offices, which was outside the city limits.

After I had worked all day on this project, Bobby called me and said, "Why don't you come over for a drink?"

So, I went over there, since he only lived five blocks away. We had a drink. And we had a great time together. There was nobody home at his place. There was nobody home at my place. So, hey, why not? So we decided to see if we would like each other. Now I was about ten years older than he, but it sort in intrigued me.

We were having sex, and all of a sudden the condom he was using busted. That was something that I had never experienced. I was immediately frightened. The only thing that I knew how to do was to call a gynecologist friend of mine, Dr. Bianca Steinhart. She lived at 40 East 83rd Street, and was a lovely, lovely woman.

She said to me, "How long ago was it?"

And I said, "About an hour ago."

She said, "Okay, no problem." So I immediately took a cab to her office. She evidently wiped it out with iodine or something like this, and said, "Everything is fine now." What a relief that was!

After the July fourth holiday, came my interview at *Vogue*. I was so excited, I even remember what I wore that day. It was a brown piqué blouse and white piqué skirt. Francois had sent me a brown pair of Gucci loafers. It was the first time I had seen loafers in brown suede. I was really put together in a very up-to-date fashion.

Well, as far as the job interview went, I was offered the job, but they offered me half of the pay I was making at my present job. At the moment I was in no position to accept anything less. I wanted to have more money, and be able to afford a better life than what I already had, not a lesser one. To take a cut in pay was an impossible idea.

So I thought to myself, "Well, maybe later on I can do something like this when the money isn't such a crucial issue."

Bobby wrote me a letter to tell me what a horrible mistake we had made, and he certainly didn't want my mother to know what we had done. He wrote this letter apologizing for our little sexual mishap, and he sent it to the office.

When Francois saw the envelope, he of course opened it, and all hell broke loose. It was unbelievable! Obviously, Francois was very jealous. After fighting, then discussing this, and crying over it, it all blew over. I promised that I would never see Bobby again, and Francois forgave me.

Fortunately, nothing happened. I didn't become pregnant by Bobby, and I was happy that everything returned to normal. So much for my experience with condoms.

Meanwhile the war in Europe continued to escalate. Finally, the United States could not stand idle without getting involved. In 1940, mandatory military service called for a term of one year. In 1941 it was extended to 18 months. That same year the U.S. extended a billion dollars in credit to Russia to fund its military efforts against the Nazis.

The war became even more complicated when the Japanese bombed Pearl Harbor on December 7, 1941. On December 11, 1941 Germany declared war against the United States, and everything escalated. I was now living in a country which was involved in a war that raged in the Pacific Ocean as well as across the Atlantic.

In 1942, in Germany came the *Wannsee Konferenz* which was the "final solution" to what Hitler referred to as "the Jewish question." It called for the systematic murder of the German Jews and anyone else who opposed the Nazi regime. They were rounded up, loaded into freight trains, and taken to a number of different concentration camps for systematic genocide. From that point until the end of the war, 4.2 to 5.7 million Jews were eliminated in these death camps.

Prior to the war, the majority of the German people had believed Hitler was successful in turning the German economy around, and that a rosy future for Germany was coming. However, everything turned bleak when Hitler started murdering everyone who opposed his ideas and ideals. He began to show his true colors in a most ruthless fashion.

Meanwhile in Europe, many of my relatives found themselves right in the middle of the war. One of them was Uncle Jub. I later found out that during the war, while Belgium was occupied by the Nazis, Jub was working for the government of Belgium where he became in charge of gasoline distribution, since it was being rationed. However he was found guilty of having given gasoline coupons to "the Resistance." When the Nazis—who had infiltrated the government—found out about it, he was scheduled to be executed by a firing squad for treason. Fortunately for him, his good friend Franz von Zealand intervened on his behalf, and narrowly saved his life.

From 1942 to 1945 we all avidly followed the developments of the Second World War. In 1944 Franklin D. Roosevelt was elected for his fourth term of office as President of the United States. The following year, Turkey was pressured by the allies to declare war against Germany. Then Russia declared war against Japan, and systematically marched troops into the Chinese Provence of Manchuria.

Ultimately it was too bad that Hitler killed himself in the end—on April 30, 1945. So many of us would have liked to have killed him ourselves. Suicide was too kind an ending for such a deplorable monster. On May 7, 1945, after massive bombing by the allies, a weakened Germany surrendered. Fortunately, many of the surviving German people had escaped the brainwashing by the Nazis.

On July 16, 1945 came a test of the first atom bomb. That signaled a turning point in the war in the Pacific. Finally, on September 2, 1945, the Second World War ended. What a huge sigh of relief we all breathed.

Occasionally on television you will see interviews with the woman who was Hitler's secretary. She was with him until the end, and she obviously escaped. I always wonder what she really did and felt. She must have seen and heard a lot from a very close vantage point.

After the war a lot of the ex-Nazi's migrated to Argentina and Chile, as it was easier for them to get into those countries. Some were arrested, and brought to judgment in Nuremberg.

After the war ended Francois sold the dairy farm, the cows, the milk route, and everything. He still owned some real estate on Long Island, having bought a house for his mother and her companion in Bellmore. With the war over, in 1946, Francois decided to go into the military representation of blue chip accounts to the PX's and commissary stores. This new business plan turned out to be a genius one. We would negotiate business deals for army bases around the world.

We started off with the army bases in post-war Europe. It began in Frankfurt. Our salesmen made representations to the head of the military bases over there. At this point Francois was in between selling the farm and starting up a new business. He went to Washington D.C. and made all of the contacts for this operation.

When I was a young girl, I had always grown up thinking that I wanted to keep my virginity for the man whom I was to marry. However, once Francois had entered my life in New York, all of the ideas that I had about this, and the boundaries and limits that I had set for myself, went out of the window.

I finally fell so in love with him that none of the good ideas which I had before, could possibly stand in my way. It is hard to explain this, but it was not merely for sex that I came to this decision. It was also for love. I enjoyed Francois' company so fully, even if we just went out for a walk, or for a heart-to-heart talk. Or perhaps my hand would touch him a little longer than necessary, and just knowing he was there, provided me enough strength to last me the whole day.

That was something that I kept deep inside of me. I didn't want anyone to know about it. It was my secret, so I kept it all within myself. And of course it became really hard to carry this around inside of me, this feeling of deep love for Francois.

So, one day—the 30th of March—it was a Friday, we went to The St. Moritz Hotel for lunch, a business meeting, and then to our secret little apartment on West 81st Street. It was a first floor little flat in a brownstone building between Columbus and Amsterdam Avenues, which was furnished very simply. I went to the 5 & 10 Cent store and bought cups and green glass saucers, a few pieces of flatware, and a pan in which we could heat water.

When Francois and I were in our secret apartment, we were there alone, and it was wonderful. We were there with our bodies alone, and with our thoughts. And it was just so wonderful.

At the time, there was no one I could really talk to about this. I certainly could not talk about this with my mother. I don't know why, but I was raised in a way that you would not show your emotions, and that you would not let anybody see what you really feel like. It was really sort of a strange existence. Whenever I felt blue, I had to keep it to myself as well. I was not raised in a way in which you would discuss your inner feelings. And, psychiatry was not in the cards for me either. That was not the common thing for affairs of the heart or emotional dilemmas. It was simply a different era.

Also, you must understand that this was a whole different era for women in general. Women were treated very differently. I was brought up in a middle class family, and it was not a family you could express your feelings freely within.

I found myself harboring feelings of jealousy for the time Francois spent away from me. Francois was married to Meta, and if anyone found out about our affair, this would be a huge scandal. These were close family friends. And divorcing Meta was not an option that Francois wanted to explore.

What should I do? Should I marry Siggy, a man whom I was not in love with? Should I just forget about Francois? What was I going to do? It was too much to ask the person you really love—and whom you would do anything for, to turn his back on his wife just so I could have him for myself. How was this ever going to have a happy ending?

Even though I loved him deeply, and he loved me, what were we going to do? I knew up front that I would probably never have him for myself. Should I simply be content with what I had with Francois, and just ignore the fact that he would never be mine exclusively?

To be the second woman to a man whom you love very much is very difficult. But there was no two ways about it. I didn't want him to get divorced, because I felt that was ridiculous. I didn't want to be the reason for Meta's unhappiness, but of course I was setting myself up to be the reason for her unhappiness.

At that point, I found myself at a crossroad. Maybe I should look for another job, and not work for him, and that way I could break this whole thing off. Maybe it would be different if I had been raised in a different environment. I found this all so confusing.

Finally I decided that—marriage or no marriage—I was in love with Francois, and I was willing to risk it all to have my relationship with him. All logic was thrown to the wind. How had this all started? When we finally consummated the sexual part of our love affair, the first time it took place right in Francois' office on top of his desk. Well— needless to say—there went my virginity! After we were finished, we went to some place and had a lovely filet of sole luncheon which lasted until 3:00 p.m. I had to steal a couple of big napkins to cover up what had happened between Francois and I before we got to the restaurant.

No one had ever explained to me what I should know about sex, or how the human body functions. And the only sex education that I had came from Erna Teufel, way back when I was about ten or twelve years old, in Mannheim. However Erna's knowledge of "the birds and the bees" never covered any of the finer details. All it covered was "how to make babies."

But, pregnancy was not something I had to worry about with Francois. He knew that medically he was sterile. Of course, in hindsight, I know that a lot of things could have been done to resolve this, and maybe I could have actually had a child with him—which at one point I would have loved to have done. However, as it was, nothing ever came up in that respect, because that would have even further complicated both of our lives.

At first we had sex in the office after Alice left for the day. That was to become our routine.

He told me that if I wanted, he would divorce Meta. I said to him, "No, I don't want that." I didn't want him to divorce her, because I felt I wanted to marry somebody else. I was waiting for my own Prince Charming to come along and ask me to marry him—eventually. I had in mind a husband of my own, children, and the whole works. I figured that would come later in my life.

I said to him, "No, no, no. Don't divorce Meta. It is fine as it is."

As time went on and on, I said, "If you were to get a divorce, it will just make a mess of the whole thing."

A lot of people live like that. Look at Europe. Everybody has a mistress there. Everybody has somebody on the side. Look at the British and the French—all the way back in history. It was no big deal to have a wife as well as a mistress.

I thought to myself, "It's much easier to say 'Goodnight' and then have my own bed and my own life, and enjoy what I wanted to do. This way I don't have to cook and clean for someone. I would be free, yet I would have all of the benefits as well."

And, I found that I still had a friendship with Meta as well. She was very sweet. She would call and invite me over for dinner. She had no idea in the beginning of my affair with Francois. Because of our age difference, she didn't think that my relationship with Francois was anything more than an old friendship, and now a business relationship.

Francois and Meta were always surrounded by a circle of friends. So my being part of their new American social circle was nothing out of the ordinary.

Francois did have other affairs while he was married to Meta, and she did acknowledge that this was going on. She just didn't know that this was going on with me as well.

At one time he told her, "Look, I'll tell you something. You get a divorce from me and you name the price. Whatever you want, you get."

"No." She didn't want a divorce.

He said, "Then you have to accept her. You have to accept that Ruth is my mistress. It is either, or. You have to either accept a divorce, or accept it the way it is. I will never, never retract from the relationship with Ruth. Not under any circumstances. So take it or leave it."

I was like his child, and in him I tried to find my father figure. He became not only my surrogate father, but my brother, my boss, my lover, and my idol. In my eyes he could do no wrong. He was a handsome man whom I simply and totally adored.

Although I originally thought he would help me to find my "Prince Charming," but soon I realized that Francois was my "Prince Charming!" After several futile attempts to break away from him, I made peace with myself and accepted the situation as it was.

Francois was a perfectionist and demanded the same of others— including me. But, he spoiled me in so many ways. Traveling with him was a unique experience. His generosity was legendary. His employees loved him, his wife loved him, and I loved him. On top of all of this, he made me financially independent. What more could I ask for? He was "the lord and master," and I was his willing slave, who lived a sheltered and protected life.

In 1947 the Truman Doctrine and the Marshall Plan were put into place to give financial and/or military support to any countries which were being threatened by Communism. This was the beginning of what was to be known as The Cold War between Russia and the United States.

When the Second World War ended, Russia was given jurisdiction over what was now called East Germany; and the United States,

England and France had jurisdiction over what was now known as West Germany. Likewise, the former capitol of Germany—Berlin—was also divided into East and West sectors. Again, the east side was Russian territory, and West Berlin was presided over by the Allies. Now that access to West Berlin was cut off from ground transportation, food and any supplies had to be flown in from Frankfurt to Berlin.

In the 1950s my mother and I went back to Germany for a visit. Francois Schwarz Company had an office in Frankfurt at that time. I heard for the first time in years, the sound of marching German feet again. However, this time it was not the sound of a well-dressed army. This time around it was the sound of a defeated people who had no decent clothes or anything. They were wearing whatever they could get their hands on at the time. The people were so poor that they had but one well-worn pair of shoes. Instead of having leather on the bottoms, they put nails on them to repair them.

While in Frankfurt I could hear them clomping on the sidewalk, and it was like the sound of the Nazi soldiers I had heard marching in the streets of Germany before the war. All at once I was horrified, mad, and frozen with terror. I had to talk to myself so as not to blow up or do something. I was furious to hear that sound again, going: clomp, clomp, clomp, clomp. The whole machinery of the Nazis came back to me in a wave of fear, when I heard this frightening sound of marching that day on the platform of the Frankfurt train station.

But it was not the sound of the marching Nazis, it was only the sound of the people's shoes on the platform at the railroad station. The sounds I heard were of the poor people who had lost everything in the war. For me, it was like I had seen a city full of living ghosts.

That was the first time I was back after the war and the terror I had felt when I left Germany—running for my life—all came back to me. I will always remember that day in Frankfurt as a chilling case of *deja vu.*

As I left the train station, I was amazed at what I saw. I had been to Frankfurt before the war, and was very familiar with its architecture and its charming streets. What I found there was a city in ruins. Like most of the German cities, it too had been severely battered in the war.

Here I am at five years old, in the dress I wore to the bank with my
Aunt Erna, the day of my impromptu performance.

Three generations of our family. Grandma Halfen, myself at the age of three, and my mother.

Uncle Adolf in the First World War.

As a teenager I danced at the wedding of Else Levy.

Uncle Adolf (bottom left) with his friends at the beach with the portable floating changing rooms behind them, in Holland before World War II.

At a hotel with my family. My father is in the white shirt in the forefront. At this point the swastikas of Nazi Germany were absolutely unavoidable.

The portrait of Francois I took from Erna and Jub's apartment. He was so incredibly handsome, I couldn't help but fall in love with him.

My dear Uncle Jub and Aunt Erna.

This was the front of my parent's bicycle shop after Krystalnacht, with the glass marked with the word "Juden" acid marked into the glass. It was the Nazi's way of keeping people away from our establishment.

In upstate New York in the 1940s, enjoying my new life in America.

With Francois at the Eden Roc Hotel in Miami Beach, Florida, in the 1950s.

The Convent of the Sisters of the Cross and Passion in England where I sought refuge in 1939 and early 1940. When I was in America, I sent Mother Superior regular "care packages."

With my mother at a wedding in the 1950s.

In 2009, I can still stand on my head, and everyday I practice yoga to keep me fit. At the age of 92, every day is still a new adventure!
(Photo: Sebastian Artz)

Wearing my Bob Mackie dress at the Waldorf Astoria with Raymond in 1985. The occasion was to honor Grace Fippinger. The dress was $5,000, and Raymond threatened that if I didn't buy it, he would buy it for me.

In the Hamptons in the 1990s.

My mother in Germany, before she met and married my father in the 1910s. This is one of my favorite photos of her.

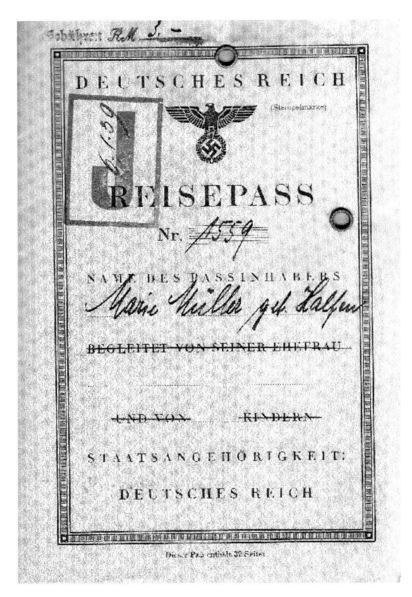

My mother's German passport with a red "J" stamped in it for
"Jewish." Note the swastika in the German emblem on the passport.

Most of the cities which were devastated had a similar look. In the middle of the city there would be a little trolley which the rubbish was put into and taken away. It was sad. This is what Hitler had brought to Germany.

Mannheim was awfully damaged. It was brutal, the destruction which took place. And then at the end they surrendered the city by telephone because there was not much left anymore. A few pieces, like the castle remained intact, as it was purposely not bombed. But, when I arrived there, it was utterly shocking to see. When I came to the apartment building where I used to live, which was a corner building, I saw nothing but rubble. And when I looked down and I saw pieces of about one inch square, and I said to myself, "This was our bathroom. These were our tiles in the bathroom. Thank God I was not here when this happened!"

When I looked over at friends' houses, I saw such amazing devastation that I took several photographs of it. Bathrooms which were once in apartments, were now lonely tiled walls with no floor below them. A bathtub was still there, however it was suspended in the air vertically—not horizontally. The structure was all gone, but the bathtub was left, hanging there almost as if in nowhere. All the rest of the building had disappeared into a pile of rubble. Things like that were really shocking to see.

When I had left Germany in 1939, our friend Hansy had remained in Frankfurt. Hansy had sent the message to me: "You are lucky that you get to leave the country. We have to stay here where the bombs will fall on our heads." Well, that is exactly what ended up happening. The ensuing war and the incendiary bombs were dropped on the building that she lived on, but she was spared. She told me of her harrowing experience, where a bucket brigade had to pour water on the fire before it consumed all of her belongings. After the war had ended I continued to send monthly care packages to Hansy and her mother. They would contain butter, honey, cocoa, and other things that they could not afford or obtain. She later wrote to tell me, "Your care packages saved my mother's life."

When I went to what used to be our apartment building in

Mannheim, I felt that I had to go to the basement. While there I relived the terrifying *Krystallnacht* evening when I accompanied the pro-Nazi students there to see whether or not we had been printing "illegal" anti-Nazi literature. As I looked around, I could only hope that the miserable neighbor who lived upstairs and tried to turn us in to the authorities, was here when the bombs fell. That guy was such a nasty and horrible person, I sincerely hoped that the bombs found him.

I didn't take any of the tiles from our building. I didn't want to have any part of it, but I took photographs of what I saw. I took pictures of a lot of things, like the bathtub standing in the middle of nowhere. These were such haunting images to witness.

Amid this trip I went to Frankfurt, Mannheim, and to Heidelberg. In Heidelberg I found that it was not bombed at all. One bomb fell by mistake. It was spared because the Allies had put Heidelberg down as their headquarters, and they didn't bomb it. That was all left intact. My cousin who lived outside of Heidelberg at that time, had their place all left intact as well.

Francois employed a man named Smitty who was stationed in the Frankfurt office of our company. Smitty had a car which he used to drive in Germany. However since he was an American, his car could only remain in Germany for a certain time period. To solve this logistical problem, his car had to be taken out of Germany, have his "trip-tic" validated, and brought back across the German border. On one such occasion he said to me, "Why don't you take the car, and go with your mother to her birthplace?"

That way we would get a little vacation out of it. So, I did as he suggested, and took his car, and loaded up myself, my mother and my aunt from Brussels. We all wanted to go back to see the birthplace of my mother and my aunt.

My mother used to say to me, "There is a huge mountain there. And, there is an ancient legend about the mountain, claiming that there was a virgin who jumped from one mountain to another, and was saved by a dashing hero."

We arrived there and I said, "Mother, where is this giant mountain? Is this the mountain you talked about?"

She said, "Yes, yes."

"Wait a minute," I said, "that's nothing more than a hill."

In her own defense she argued, "Well, when I was here I was very small. At the time it looked like a mountain to me! Now that I am tall and have been away for a long time, the mountain looks smaller." We had a good laugh over that.

When we were there Mother ran into some people who survived the war whom she recognized, but not very many. The majority of the population was the younger generation. It seemed that there were not many of the old people around whom she could recall from the old days. Between the war and the Nazi regime in Germany, things had changed a bit.

There was also the likelihood that many of them had been Nazi's or Nazi sympathizers, who fled the country after the war, or found an area where no one knew them.

We also went to Weisenborgh near the French border. There was a lovely inn where we stayed, and it was great fun. Many of the guests at this inn were part of a large hunting party. But it was so cold that even the people who lived there were all bundled up in coats and scarves. However, the hotel guests were all dressed up sharply.

At night when we went to bed it was so cold that we requested that they bring us hot water bottles that we could put in our beds to warm them up.

The lady of the house said to me, "Oh, I'm sorry, but we are all out of hot water bed warmers. Everybody has one who requested them earlier." So she put a brick in the oven and heated it up, and then put it in newspaper, and we used that as our bed warmer.

While driving around I asked one of the people in the street for directions where I should go. I constructed in my mind a very good French sentence to ask directions.

I spoke my sentence in French, and the man whom I addressed it to, replied to me in German, and vice versa.

I thought to myself, "What the heck is going on here?"

So I started speaking German to him, and he answered me in French.

I finally said to him, "What is happening? I thought we were in France."

He said to me, "Just look at the age of everyone here. We all learned either German or French in school here, depending upon when we were occupied by the Nazis."

In other words, while the area belonged to France, the official language taught in schools was French. When the area belonged to Germany, it was German which was taught and spoken there.

Following this explanation I realized that if I encountered older people there, I spoke in German. If I was addressing the younger people, I spoke in French. Knowing additional languages always comes in handy, and this was certainly confirmation of that.

Francois was always ahead of the times, especially in business. At one point, in the 1950s, he asked for me to get him Russian dictionaries, as he was learning to speak Russian. Throughout his life he taught himself a lot of things. He once learned Russian because he could see that this was going to be a much needed asset in the near future.

Not very long thereafter, however, he said to me, "Take those Russian books away. It's too late for that. I would have to learn Chinese, because China is becoming a mighty country to reckon with."

I said to him, "What are you talking about?"

He said, "Believe me, China is the coming power." He was that many steps ahead of everybody else.

Meanwhile, my affair with Francois continued, in spite of the fact that he was legally married to Meta. We became something of a threesome. Meta just looked in the opposite direction, ignoring the fact that I was Francois' mistress.

As per usual, Meta would always be there, but the two of us—Francois and I—would always find the time and space to do what we wanted to do together.

Then the three of us would go out to dinner together. When we were in New York City, Meta would invite me over to the house for dinner as though nothing out of the ordinary was going on. I was part of her household for years.

Francois and I would have long hours in the office, and then we had our *pied a terre* over on 81st Street between Amsterdam and Columbus Avenues.

We did a lot together, and of course we had the business as well. Often the business would require that we went together as well.

When Francois originally started the company, he wanted to change the name of it. However, everyone said to him, "No, keep Francois Schwarz, as everyone will remember that name, it is so unusual." And so he did. Thus, the firm of "Francois L. Schwarz, Inc.," was created.

I became the secretary of the corporation. I had the Number One share of stock in the company. That arrangement had been set up in 1946. One share had originally been offered to Hugo Loesch. Hugo had become friends with Francois and Meta in the '30s. He was a chemist for General Foods, and it was he who had given the affidavit for Francois and Meta to emigrate to this country.

When Francois offered Hugo a share of stock, Hugo got cold feet and said "no thank you" to this offer. His money was returned to him.

Francois and I traveled a lot together during this era—for business and for pleasure. For business we would travel without Meta. For pleasure, and on vacations, very often we would travel with Meta as well. Amidst this love triangle, I can't even believe some of the things that happened between us. Talk about a "comedy of errors!"

At one point we were at The Brenner Park Hotel in Baden-Baden, West Germany. It was a very nice place. Francois and Meta had their room there, and I had my room one flight down. One afternoon Meta went to the hairdresser, and Francois and I were spending some time alone. That was the day we really shocked the maid. While I having an intimate and sexual moment with Francois, the maid came in and surprised us. I was so embarrassed, but thinking back on it, it was really a riot. We had a good laugh over that. I can still remember the look on that poor maid's face as she got flustered and left the room—walking backwards.

I said to Francois, "What should we do?"

He said, "Nothing. We can't do anything. Whatever happened, has happened." I was horrified at the time, but in retrospective, it was really quite funny. I will never forget the look on the poor maid's face!

There was one time we went to Frankfurt where our office was, and then we flew over to France. When we were there, we stayed in a lovely hotel. We went downstairs, and there were so many people there, that we inquired as to what was going on. We were told, "This is a meeting held once a year: a pilot's convention. Everyone who has a private plane comes at this time to celebrate." Well, we had a great time with them, and we danced the night away. It was great. This took place in Deauville.

One time we were there, and Elizabeth Taylor was there too, dressed in dungarees and her big diamonds and a kerchief on her head. On her finger she wore a huge emerald cut diamond ring. I couldn't imagine at the time how anyone could wear such a huge diamond ring while wearing blue jeans. That goes to show you how provincial my fashion sense was at the time.

The occasion that time was the sale of the yearling horses. That was very interesting to me. I was fascinated with how they bid on the horses, since it was all new to me.

I also remember that Elizabeth was just a beautiful, beautiful girl. I did not meet her, although she sat only a few feet away from where I was. Maurice Chevalier was there as well.

I also remember that Count D'ornano gave a big gala of a party. I was wearing a long pink dress with an empire waist, a white fox fur over my shoulders, and long white gloves. The man who announced each new arrival was wearing a green silk jacket and white stockings—a very distinctive 18th century outfit.

As I made my entrance, he announced, "Madame Mueller of New York." And, with that I went down the staircase and made my entrance. I truly was part of High Society now, and I loved the excitement of it all.

I graciously said "hello" to Count D'ornano and his wife, who gave the party. And, there was Maurice Chevalier right next to me! I was frozen with fascination to be standing next to him. I will never forget that moment, or that exquisite party.

Francois was saying to me, "Don't stare at him! Don't look so intently at him!"

I couldn't help it, I found myself uncontrollably staring at Maurice Chevalier. It was hard not to look at him, but I did my best. That was just one of the trips we took together to Honfleur.

We went to Baden-Baden a lot, and then we would go down to Tegernsee. Tegernsee is near Munich. It's a beautiful area, and right now they even have a spa there. The hotel was managed by a lovely couple who have since passed away. She was always wearing the typical Bavarian looking Dirndl dresses, but it was made of silk and very beautiful lace.

We took two photographs there for the company's annual calendar. We would print a calendar every year, which was not only a wonderful calendar, it also had great recipes printed in it. There was a photo for every week of the year, and there was a special photo opposite the page that had Francois' birthday: June 26. We would create these calendars for all of our customers, and special leather bound ones for our principals.

To make this calendar, we had a woman whose job it was to put it together. She would travel all over the place taking photographs of international sites that we liked. Since Francois made his guest appearances in the calendar opposite every June 26, it was an excuse to run around the world, and take photos of him for that page. That was the perfect reason to go to Paris, or to Marseilles, or some other exotic setting to take his photo.

In the early 1950s, Francois and Meta lived at Number Five Riverside Drive. They wanted to get a larger apartment, and they had looked at a lot of available apartments, but couldn't find a suitable one.

Meta and Francois were in Paris at the time, and I heard of an apartment that was still under construction. Somebody had purchased it, but changed their mind.

A famous designer used to live there on the second floor. It was a very fine, fine building. The Frick Museum was right next door, so they had no obstructions, and they had a beautiful view from the 15th Floor. They had a view over the park, and south down Fifth Avenue. It was just exquisite.

What happened was that the original couple who bought it were newlyweds. And, the new wife said, "You expect me to move into the apartment that was built for your former wife? No way."

I wired Francois a telegram that read: "Call me."

So, he called me, and I told him that no real estate agent was involved, which made for a better financial deal.

I said to him, "Do you want an apartment? There is something on the market that is so perfect for you. It is located on Fifth Avenue...*and so and so.*"

I explained to him what the apartment looked like, and I told him that it was still a raw space, but I was shown one of the finished apartments, and was very impressed.

Francois told me, "Let Jack look into the financing, fax me back, and maybe I can even get some photographs of the place. Let me know what you think."

Jack got all of the paperwork together, we faxed it to Francois, and he said, "Okay."

I went there with Jack and got a good look at it. We basically looked at the concrete, since there were no finished floors in it yet, or anything else for that matter. But we looked at the space and the view, and together we agreed, "This is perfect."

It was the last apartment that could be purchased in the building, so we had to act on this immediately or risk losing it.

I said to Francois, "Give me your 'okay' and I will close the deal for you."

Francois and Meta were in Paris while all of this was taking place. Jack, the accountant, and I were in New York City at the time, and we spent the Fourth of July in the lawyer's office, wrote up the contract, arranged for payments, and called up Francois in Paris and told him, "You have a new apartment in which to live, located at 900 Fifth Avenue."

That was quite something. But that was the way Francois did business. Everything was "Yes, no, go." There was no dilly-dallying over getting something in motion once Francois made up his mind about anything.

While Meta was still in Europe, we informed her, "Oh, we have a brand new apartment for you."

Meta said to Francois, "Well, I didn't appreciate that you didn't consult me."

Francois said to her, "If you don't like it, you don't have to live in it." There was no nonsense when it came to making a decision.

Francois would always say of Meta, "My wife has the horizon of a scrubbing pail." It was a phrase in German: *"Meine Frau hat einen Scheuereimer Horizont."*

He would give her money to run the household, but she never wanted more than a thousand dollars at a time. Anything more than a thousand dollars she did not want to deal with.

He would say to her, "You want something? Here's some cash. You want to buy something? So, do it. Whatever you want to do with the money, do it. Just don't bother me." And she accepted that.

Meta was a very pretty woman. She was a charming young girl at the age of 19 when she married Francois in 1923. Meta's mother was an American, who was from Texas. Her father was a typical Prussian, and didn't want his younger girl to marry, because he had an older daughter, Erna, who was an oddball and couldn't find a husband.

So, Meta's parents had asked my grandmother if she maybe had somebody in the family or knew of somebody who would marry their older daughter Erna. Unfortunately, Grandma couldn't find anybody.

Meta also had two brothers. One was a very good tennis player, but neither of them were great brains. Since, Meta was the youngest, according to tradition she shouldn't marry first.

She met Francois, and she said to her parents, "Hey, if you don't like it, you can lump it, because I am going to do this."

Of course, the man was not Jewish, that was another obstacle. The father didn't want her to marry anybody but a Jewish boy—not for his daughter.

Francois was in a dilemma around this era, because he lived with his grandmother. When his grandmother died, that was the greatest tragedy that happened to him in his life, because he was raised by his grandmother. He treated her like royalty, and carried her on a silver platter.

She loved him, and took really good care of him. The situation in Germany at that time was such that you couldn't get an apartment unless you had a family. So, he married in a hurry, as to not lose the apartment that he had lived in with Grandma.

That's how they married. Meta loved Francois dearly, and he loved her too. There was nothing there not to love. She was a very pretty girl. Not the smartest girl, but she was a very pretty girl, and she was always a very comfortable person to be around.

In their marriage, whatever Francois said, went. He was the Lord around the house. She was used to this way of doing things from the home in which she grew up. Her father was a real Prussian, and he dictated the way things were going to be in their household. Nobody said, "No" to him. It was strictly, "Aye, aye, Sir," and that was it.

So Meta had tried to work as a young girl, in a winery. She found a job in the office there, but that was very short-lived. She didn't have much experience in the business world. But she learned to cook. She was an excellent cook and told her cooks how to prepare food very well. She was an excellent hostess, and of course when Francois called from the office and said, "We are coming home at 8:00 for dinner," the "we" meant that I was coming along too. She wasn't always happy about this situation, but she made the best of it. She tried to be very good to me. Occasionally she would take my side and stick up for me. If Francois was wrong, she would tell him, "You are wrong." She was very fair in that way.

At this point, she didn't make us dinner by herself. She had a maid and a cook to do that. All her life she had cooks. In America she didn't have a chauffeur, but she did always have cooks and maids.

She taught them how to cook things the way she and Francois wanted them. Their table was always set in a princely fashion. The linen and dinnerware was really in the old German tradition, and very high class. It was really a pleasure to sit down at her table. She knew what I personally liked to eat. For instance, she often had the cook make potato pancakes with apple sauce for me. This was always one of my very favorites.

She realized that I was helping Francois. And he told her, "You have to thank Ruth very much, because she works for you too. If it wasn't for her, you wouldn't have a lot the of things that you have. Now, hush."

She realized that too. For both Meta and I, it was an arrangement.

In other words, I was a very necessary part of this whole operation. He told Meta, "I need Ruth, and you must accept her."

And she did so very graciously. We were an odd and unconventional trio, but somehow it worked.

Meanwhile, back on Fifth Avenue the architects and contractors were working on the construction of the new apartment. A lot of the construction took place while Meta was on a trip to South America. She went with a friend of hers named Irmgard. Francois always wanted her to go and travel with her girlfriend, so they went to South America where Irmgard had family.

Francois hired someone to come in and decorate the apartment and pick out the furnishings. When Meta came back from South America, she took one look at the fully-decorated apartment, and she said, "Oh God, this looks like a Miami hotel lobby!"

The seating arrangement for the living room was uncommonly huge, so much so that the massive sofa had to be brought up through the window with a special crane. It was so big that using the conventional elevator was impossible.

Francois said to her, "If you want to change it, change it, but leave me alone." So she changed everything. Jane Anderson was her interior decorator, who worked for Macy's at the time. She was of Norwegian descent, and Jane became very good friends with Meta.

Jane later helped to get me into the Knollwood Country Club as a member in 1977. She was a wonderful person. She not only decorated Meta's home, and our offices, but she also did many things for me as well. We worked very well together. Jane had excellent taste and a good sense of color.

That was in the early 1950s. So, life went on, and I always wanted to travel, but I couldn't do so extensively. We always traveled to Germany or France. I would go on weekend trips like that, and I would still be back in the office on Monday morning.

Often, I couldn't afford to be away any longer, so Francois and I would take off for weekends together to Paris and other destinations. We were always doing things together, and finagling time out together.

Meta had a great time during her trip to South America, so she continued to go off on her own travels. On one occasion she was in Europe with Irmgard, while Francois and I went to Palm Beach, Florida together. We stayed at a lovely hotel called The Majestic for that particular vacation.

It was so classy, and wonderful. Francois said to me, "You know, this is my 25th wedding anniversary. But *we* celebrated it."

I said, "Really? We haven't been married 25 years yet!"

He said, "No, but we are as good as married!"

We had lot of fun together in Palm Beach. There was a swimming pool there. I understand that nowadays, that same building is a condominium. We had a beautiful time. Here it was, his actual 25th wedding anniversary with Meta in 1948, and I celebrated it with him. Meta never forgave him for not spending it with her. She was furious. She was in Paris expecting his arrival and he told her, "I can't come."

She never forgave him for this and always brought it up. I didn't understand how Meta didn't scratch his eyes out for that. But, they had a very civilized arrangement together.

One day from The Barclay Hotel, Clarence Birdseye telephoned me, asking me to buy the nicest, biggest pair of sunglasses I could find. Conveniently, there was an eyeglass store next to our office at 500 Fifth Avenue called Meyrowitz. He requested that I bring them over to The Barclay Hotel immediately. According to him, "I got poison ivy in my eyes, and I can't see." So, I had to take him from the Barclay to our office. I had to lead him by the arm and walk every step of the way with him.

Francois had business meetings with several powerful men during this era including: Bill Mennen from the Mennen Corporation, Mr. Moss from Clorex, Mr. Clauson from Brach Candies, and several other manufacturers of food and related products—including Pillsbury, Green Giant Foods, and many others. Later he negotiated exclusive contracts with the government and these companies. These were exclusive contracts with these companies for the representation and resale of their goods to the military commissary stores and exchanges around the world. These firms would pay us a commission for the orders, and we would work with the military department of each firm.

One might ask, "Why do these big companies need another company to sell to the armed forces?" But the regular sales departments of these companies gave various sales persons specific territories in which to sell. For instance the salesmen did not like to go to an army installation which was 100 miles outside of their main territory base. While they could reach many buyers nearby, our salesmen came in and made various appointments with the representatives of the military bases, with products to sell from numerous companies. It became more cost efficient to let our Francois L. Schwarz [FLS] sales representative go there and sell a multitude of products in one visit. In addition to the geographical advantage, there was also a good reason to pay Francois / FLS a commission which came out of their advertising department. And, in the exclusive contracts with the government, the contracts stated that the price given would be the absolute lowest available anywhere. If the government found these goods cheaper anywhere else, the government could purchase against the manufacturer.

There was a supply bulletin between the armed forces and the manufacturer, guaranteeing that we were getting the lowest prices anywhere. This became the key to our company's success.

The prices were very enticing for the government. FLS Inc. was appointed the exclusive representative to the armed forces for the manufacturers. There was quite a bit of red tape to establish these contracts, and keeping up on the prices and presentation. We had our own computer, and we were actually the first representatives that had computers available to us. IBM picked up the invoices from us, after we had coded the items on there they did all of the punchcards for this, and we would end up with a mountain of paper at the end of the month, which was sent to our sales people, so that they were informed of up-to-the-minute lists of their sales.

The sales force of FLS visited the various installations to make presentations of the items FLS wanted to sell. The orders were received and processed and delivery instructions were mailed out, with instructions as to where to make the deliveries. So we never took title of any merchandise, as the government had their own transportation.

And the manufacturer delivered according to our instructions, and our activities ceased there. Our greatest assets were our people. We had to have top notch and very intelligent people as our employees. Francois was a very well known figure in the industry, and everyone knew that the ethics of the company were beyond reproach in every aspect.

At one time after the Second World War, we had hired some salesmen who had flying experience having been in the Air Force. They said, "Why use our cars and get stuck in traffic when planes would be much more efficient? That way we can land right at the bases." It seemed like a logical solution, so we purchased three Piper Cubs, which we named "Everywhere I," "Everywhere II" and "Everywhere III."

Potentially this plan could work out very well, as it would cut down on the traveling time of our salesmen. We also made it very clear that no passengers were allowed to ride in the planes. For a while, everything went smoothly without mishaps. This was a fine plan for our three sales people, who each had previous flight experience.

Then, we had another salesman who also wanted a plane. He took flying lessons. We were reluctant to buy a fourth plane.

However, when he went up on his solo flight to receive his license, something horrifying occurred. While amidst his first solo flight he was instantly killed in a crash, which occurred in front of his wife and son. This was such a shock to us that afterward, we felt very uneasy about having our other three sales people flying the planes at all. Although we were stunned by the fourth salesperson's death, we continued to use the other three planes.

The straw that finally broke the camel's back suddenly came one morning, when one of the three pilots was using his plane and flying on his normal course. However, he did not read his mail in the morning and landed on what he thought was his usual landing field. The unread letter to him contained the fact that the field had been given back to the farmer who now planted potatoes on the former flying field. Very lucky, the plane only turned over with no further mishap. The sales person was shaken up, but that was the end of FLS Inc. operating their own planes. From that time forward, all of our transportation was to be via commercial flights, trains or cars.

There was one other incident which is still another sad memory. It involved Alice Leopold who was Francois' secretary. She was a lovely, very well read and educated person. I always looked up to her, because she had gone to college and received her undergraduate degree, which I personally would have loved to have had. I found that in spite of my accomplishments, I felt absolutely inferior because of this lack of education.

Alice was German by birth, but had a wonderful grasp of the English language, as well as German and French. She was also a top-notch secretary with great office skills, and a lot of useful business knowledge. She always had something interesting to tell because the *Wall Street Journal* and *New York Times* were "must read" material for her in the morning as well as several other publications. We were all very sorry to hear that a tragic accident had occurred during on one of her vacation trips. She had asked for one of the managers of our Swiss office to give her a ride to Germany from Switzerland. It was our manager who drove with her in the passenger's seat, via Colmar, Switzerland. It was fall, and the harvest of sugar beets, combined with the rain, left the streets very slippery, and the car slipped. Unfortunately, the passenger's side of the car hit a tree, and Alice was instantly killed. The driver had nothing but a small scratch and a very heavy heart over the fact that this would happen while he was driving. We were devastated when we received the news.

It was at that time I became the Office Manager at FLS. I had to try a lot of different secretaries before we were able to find the proper replacement for Alice.

When FLS started its operation, at first we covered only overseas Military Bases. But in the mid-'50s we added the domestic area, so we had it globally—domestically as well as exporting internationally.

One day Francois said to me, "As long as I am alive you never have to worry, and even if I die, you never have to worry either." And I must say, he kept to his promise. My friend Smitty, who was our Senior Vice President, said to me, "You are putty in Francois' hands. You are his Galatea."

My Uncle Jub and Aunt Erna would very often stay in touch with us. I remember one amusing story from this era. Having lived through the war, Aunt Erna became something of a "pack rat," in that she saved everything just in case it might become useful again. Even a worn out pair of men's pants could be taken apart and made into a lady's skirt if you knew what you were doing.

Apparently their apartment in Brussels was stockpiled with all sorts of things that Aunt Erna was saving. One day Uncle Jub had finally had it with living in a sea of possessions. He opened a closet and saw a wall of large round hat boxes, and he came to the decision that Erna would never miss them. So, he grabbed two arms-full of them, and hauled them down to the area of their apartment building where garbage was to be brought. That evening they went out together, and were walking home. When they reached their apartment building, Erna spotted a stack of hat boxes, and commented, "Those look like my hat boxes!" Well they were. She took the lid off of one of them, and to her horror, there was one of her prize hats. Needless to say, she hauled them back upstairs, and she never let Jub forget what he had done to her precious hats.

In the 1950s, Mother and Uncle Adolf and I had moved from the Bronx to 617 West 141st Street and Riverside Drive in Manhattan. Eventually I decided that we needed to move out of there, as the neighborhood was changing—and not for the better. A friend of mine told me that there was a nice four and a half room apartment at York Avenue and 85th Street, off of East End Avenue. I thought this would be perfect for us, but I wanted Uncle Adolf to take a look at it first. He agreed, and went down to inspect the area. When he came to York Avenue and 85th Street, what he saw there was garbage stacked up on the sidewalk, and people sitting outside on the stoops—in other words, it was a very undesirable area. He took one look at this, and didn't even walk the extra block to East End Avenue, which would have shown him a different view of the East Side and made all the difference in the world. He found the area before York Avenue really below par; so he turned around and came home. When I arrived home, I asked him what he thought, and he informed me that it was a terrible area.

"Where did you go? Explain to me," I asked.

He told me what he had done, and I said to him, "You have to go the extra block, to see what it really is."

Then we went together, and he realized that in New York City, one block makes a hell of a lot of difference between a good neighborhood and a bad one. When we finally got there, he saw the difference with his own eyes, and naturally agreed to my plan and we moved. Now we paid three times the rent we had paid before. But, now we would live on the more prestigious East Side of Manhattan.

Mother and Uncle Adolf and I had apartments in the same building. Mother and Uncle Adolf were on the fifth floor, and I lived in an apartment on the fourth floor. Mother constantly wanted to know why I was not planning on getting married. I said to her, "I am very sorry Mother, but I will not change my life, and you can either accept it or lose your daughter."

My apartment on the fourth floor was a lovely one bedroom, with a kitchen and dining area, and a dressing room. One day Francois decided to buy me a Vespa motor bike, and he had it shipped to me in New York City from Italy. I kept it in the garage in the apartment building across the street. Then I had it uncrated and brought up into my apartment.

To me, the Vespa was truly a beautiful sight. I wanted to have proper insurance for it and it was my intention to drive it every day to work. But when the insurance agent told me that he could not get me insurance for it, my mother pleaded with me not to ride it. She then showed me a story on the front page of the newspaper, in which a man had been driving a Vespa like mine, was hit by a car from the back, and his life was snuffed out instantly. After reading that sad account in the newspaper, I began to change my mind about the safety of my motor bike.

With disappointment and resignation, I finally had to give up my idea of whizzing through the streets of Manhattan on my beautiful beige Vespa motorbike. Sadly, I never did ride the Vespa. I put an ad in the newspapers, and within 48 hours a young Italian couple came to see it. They took it out for a test drive and loved it. That was the end of the Vespa!

Whenever someone telephoned for me, they called me at my mother's apartment. Mom told everyone, "Ruth is in the shower, and she will be right with you." Then, she called me on the intercom to come upstairs to the phone, which I did. In the eyes of my friends who called, I must have seemed to have been the cleanest person on Earth, because I was always seemed to be in the shower!

In 1954 Uncle Jub was operated on for a brain tumor. I received the telegram that everything went well, but I had a dream two days later that I lost my two front teeth. That is usually a premonition of death. Sure enough, two days later I received another telegram that informed me of his death. Some people say I am psychic, but in this case I wish it was not so. We all have to live with the cards that are dealt to us, and there is nothing that can be done.

My cousin Rose and her husband Larry Friedman had a daughter named Audrey. Audrey and I kept in contact for a while, but we lived so far apart. Larry was a good provider and a very sunny individual. One night after he drove home from his "night out with the boys," his car slipped on an icy spot, five minutes from his home, and he was killed instantly. It seems the best have to go early. Audrey and I still correspond with each other through birthday and holiday cards.

During this era, I bought a beautiful and very expensive cognac colored silk dress at Bergdorf Goodman, which I loved to wear. I gave it to the cleaners, and when it was returned, the imprint of a hot iron was right on the left breast of the front of the solid-colored dress. It was absolutely ruined. I was horrified that they had done this. So, I marched it back to the cleaners.

I got there and I told them that I expected their insurance company to fully replace my ruined dress. The owner of the dry cleaners wouldn't submit the claim to the insurance company, or make any restoration what-so-ever. Whereupon I marched to the Small Claims Court and registered my complaint.

When the court date came around, much to my surprise, the ombudsman who was handling my case, turned out to be the councilman who had wanted me to be his mistress several years before. What a small world it is indeed!

The facts of the case were quite clear, and instead of it becoming an uncomfortable situation, he dealt with my case in a very professional way. The dry cleaner was legally forced to settle the case, and reimburse me for my loss. I have always been someone who stands up for her rights, and I was not about to quietly accept the destruction of my beautiful dress!

I have a distant relative who had stayed in Germany while we had fled the country. His name was Heinz Novak. He was only one half Jewish, and he was living in Wiesbaden. He was in the *Arbeitsdienst,* which was a non-military entity to build roads or other civic projects. I have always suspected that during the war he had someone who protected him. He was to remain in Germany until 1956, when he came to this country. He was one of the few relatives in Germany with whom we got back in contact with after the war. When he arrived in the United States, he and his wife and their three sons, who were aged three, five, and seven at that time, came to stay with us for three days.

When they arrived in New York City, we were living on 85th Street, and they came to stay with us. We clearly had no room for them all to sleep comfortably when they came to live with us. The youngest one slept on a chair. The others slept on a blow-up raft on the floor. After three days with us in our cramped apartment, they went to stay with relatives in Louisiana.

Heinz was a hard worker and a very good engineer, whose invention in the hydraulic field secured his family a good living and an education for all three boys.

On one occasion I visited them in California. Since that time, both Heinz and his wife have passed away, but I am still in contact with their three boys. They are all grown up with children of their own. The youngest one, Andrew, bought his father's business. He married a Chinese girl named Terry. Her father is Chinese, and her mother is Russian. She is a very pretty girl, and they have two children. They are still amongst the few relatives with whom I have maintained constant contact throughout all of these years.

One day in the late 1950s, I was at work when I received a phone call from Uncle Adolf at the local police station. I couldn't imagine what had happened. He informed me that he had been arrested in the men's room of a subway station, and I should come down and arrange for bail for him. He was booked on a charge of "disorderly conduct" with an undercover police officer.

He obviously made a pass at the wrong guy, and it was a police officer who was there looking for any gay activity in that bathroom. It was a matter of being at the wrong place at the wrong time.

Adolf had caught me at the office at the end of the day, and I could only arrange for bail the next morning, so he had to spend that night in jail. I had to inform Saks Fifth Avenue that he would not be in for work the next day.

The next morning, after I talked to Saks, I went downtown, while I arranged for the bail to be paid. Francois did not want me to go down there alone, and he said to me, "You have no experience in this at all, and I will go down there and help you arrange for bail." He figured that the City Hall / Police Headquarters area was a part of town which I was not familiar with, so we went down there together.

This was not considered a criminal offense, so Uncle Adolf was not prosecuted beyond a hearing and a fine. Although he was not happy to be spending a night in jail, my mother and I were happy that he did spend one night there. That way he would think twice before doing this again. From then on, my mother always wanted to chaperone him wherever he went. When they went out together, she would tell him not to look at men who passed by on the street, but she told him he was free to bring all of his friends home with him. After that incident, we had wonderful canasta games with all of his gay male friends.

One of Adolf's gay friends was a man named Otto who was from Switzerland, and worked with him at Saks Fifth Avenue. Since Otto was younger than Adolf and had just arrived in America, Adolf had an opportunity to help Otto get acquainted with the way of doing things in the United States.

Otto became a good family friend to all of us. As I came to know him better, he told me a little bit about his own life story, and how he decided to move from Zurich to America. He told me that in Switzerland, he had worked for a very prestigious and exclusive ladies and men's haberdashery there, and was very much in love with a Swiss girl. However, she broke off their relationship suddenly. Otto was so distraught, that he sought the aid of a psychologist. The psychologist told him that he needed to make a change in his life.

"Why don't you move to America, and start all over again? That would be a positive change," the psychologist suggested.

Otto decided to take the psychologist's advice, and he saved up $20,000, which was a very large sum of money at that time. A friend of his told him that he would invest the money for him, and make Otto even more money with it. However, the money was lost in this risky venture. So, Otto simply continued to work until he made another $20,000, to come to America. At that time it was necessary to have that exact amount of money in the bank to emigrate to the U.S.

Before he left Switzerland, Otto came to the root of his unhappiness, he discovered he was gay. After he had saved the second $20,000, he came to America in 1956, where he landed a job at Saks, and became close friends with Adolf. Uncle Adolf became Otto's mentor.

On one of his vacations back to Europe, Otto went to Amsterdam, where he met a man by the name of Buzzie. They fell in love, and Buzzie asked him if he would relocate from New York City, and move with him to Miami, which he did.

In later years when my mother and Adolf came down to Florida to stay for the winter in Miami, Otto and Buzzie were very helpful to them in chauffeuring them around. Otto is still a friend of mine to this very day.

In the 1950s I had invited my Aunt Erna to come to New York City to visit. After she arrived, she complained about a pain in her stomach, so I made an appointment for her at a cancer clinic on 34th Street, where I went for my annual check-ups. After Aunt Erna was examined, the doctor informed me that she had cancer of the stomach, was terribly anemic, and should be admitted to the hospital immediately.

I spoke to this doctor's superior and explained to him that it was impossible for me to personally care for my aunt, who was a citizen of Brussels. I said that it would be more proper if her own son and daughter-in-law cared for her instead of me. So we agreed not to tell her of the findings, for fear she would become sicker with worry. I went with her on the S.S. Flandre, which took us from New York, back to Brussels. All the way, during the cruise I continued to keep her diagnosis a secret.

I had purchased an apartment for her a year before, right around the corner from where her son, Francois, lived. She told me how much she enjoyed the two-bedroom apartment. It had a balcony and a fireplace, and she decorated it beautifully with her own exquisite taste. She said to me, "I hope that I can enjoy it for many years to come."

By this point I had explained Erna's condition to her son and daughter-in-law. In fact, her daughter-in-law, Micheline, ran three operating rooms at one of the hospitals in Brussels. The three of us discussed the situation, and came to the conclusion that it was best not to tell her, and not to have her operated on, because this would only give her a sense of doom, and would cause her only a lot of mental and physical misery. We consulted with a doctor there and he agreed with our plan, realizing that her cancer was inoperable.

My aunt very often said, "I am relieved that I do not have cancer, or they would have operated on me." She had the best care there was, her son and daughter-in-law took excellent care of her, and she was spared much pain and discomfort by being kept in the dark about her prognosis. In that way, she was able to live an additional two years, and did not know of the severity of her disease until the very end.

Also around this era, Uncle Adolf was diagnosed as having colon cancer, and he was operated on. Everything went well, and he was sitting up and walking. His health seemed fine, and then suddenly peritonitis set in. The doctors explained to me that unfortunately, the seam where they had removed a piece of his colon, had come apart and infection had set in. He died that same night. On one hand I felt that the doctors were at fault, yet on the other hand there was nothing to be said or done. He was gone.

This was a true tragedy for me. All through my life Uncle Adolf had been an important part of it. I was so very sorry when he died, because he had really been my surrogate father for all these years.

In the late 1950s, Francois and Meta and I all went on vacation in Lyford Key together in the Bahamas. We stayed at a beautiful resort which is very exclusive. I had my own room there, and they had their room next to mine. Several times Francois and I went out swimming together, and we would have a good time. The three of us would travel together—everywhere.

Lyford Key is a club in the Bahamas. There is a guarded club area where very well-known people have beautiful villas. The main building has a number of rooms that you can rent. These rooms are very large, and each one has a balcony. It is just beautiful. You can eat breakfast on your terrace, and the setting is very lovely. When we were there—Meta, Francois and I—Dr. Bruno, Francois' doctor went along as well.

On one occasion my three traveling companions were all in the cabana at the pool, when I came in from having water skied. However, my return that day was marred by a painful injury I sustained. While water skiing the rope had slid down the inside of my thigh, and I was bleeding from the rope burn. When I came in from the ocean, I put a towel on it and rested in the cabana. It was a horribly painful rope burn. And, it all happened so fast. It bled, and I took off several layers of flesh with that one very quick misjudgment of where the rope was at the wrong moment.

Luckily Dr. Bruno was there with us, and he took care of my wounded thigh. I was fortunate to have him there that day. It was the end of my career as a water skier. I never wanted to do that ever again. It was so awfully painful.

Lyford Key is such a stunning place, with its beautiful villas, and still is lovely. There were French chefs there to cook for us, and we had lovely accommodations. There was dancing under the sky. They have a roof that rolls back so that you can see the stars and the moon in the night sky. Everything was very formal and everyone was very well dressed.

They have what they call The Golf Club on one side, and they have the Marina area on the other side where there are huge yachts which come from Canada and other ports. Money is no object there, and they have exquisite parties all over the beautiful property.

The scenery was intoxicating and so were the cocktail parties. I remember one night I got so incredibly drunk in the golf club. There were twelve of us at the table that night, and I drank a lot, and didn't eat much. All of a sudden it caught up with me, and I had to throw up and I didn't know what to do. So, I saw the ice-filled champagne bucket next to my seat at the table, and I ended up vomiting into the ice bucket. Then I put my napkin over it so that no one could see what I had just done. That was really a ghastly event. Fortunately the Maître'D saw it and removed the ice bucket at once!

Other than that one occurrence, I always had a wonderful time there. It was really a lovely arrangement that they had there, and we all had a wonderful time. Everything was beautifully located and appointed. There was a bar outside, and inside everything was truly elegant. It was just beautiful to be down there. But that sure taught me a lesson about drinking too much without eating.

Around this same era Francois and I took a trip to the Hawaiian Islands at stayed at The Mauna Kea Beach Hotel, which was located on the large island of Hawaii. This resort is known as being the height of luxury in every respect. It was financed by noted hotelier Laurence S. Rockefeller, and the site is known for the beach it is located on, which is reputed to be one of Hawaii's most beautiful.

There were wonderful activities, and we would go on beautiful sunset cruises. I was impressed to find that all of the amenities were completely "top drawer." It was so popular and plush, that all of the restaurants were filled with hotel guests every day. You had to make advance reservations for all of its dining areas.

While we were there, Francois and I had a wonderful time. In fact we were having so much fun that we took several nude photographs of each other. When we returned to New York, I sent the rolls of film to Kodak headquarters in Rochester, New York for developing and printing. However, much to my surprise, I did not receive copies of our photos in the mail like I had expected. Instead I received a very formal and business-like letter informing me that "these were indecent photographs," and as such they could not legally be sent to me through the U.S. Postal Service. Furthermore, they confiscated my roll of film.

I was so incensed by this invasion of privacy that I wrote to Kodak to complain. Thinking that I was being very clever, I claimed that I needed these photos returned to me immediately, as they were necessary evidence for a pending divorce settlement. Naturally I made that up in order to get my photos back. However, I never did receive them, and they refused to budge. So we lost the negatives and the nude photos of ourselves.

Can you imagine this happening today? I am certain that in the meantime, Kodak has seen pictures of just about everything, to the point where these photos of Francois and I without clothes would be considered pretty tame. Actually, I have to admit that I was amused to think that Francois and I had caused a scandal at Kodak.

With regard to our Hawaiian vacation, I was so impressed by The Mauna Kea Hotel facilities and the location of this wonderful resort, that I later revisited it. However, I will come back to the second chapter of Mauna Kea later.

Meanwhile, back at the office, I was still receiving some opposition from some of our employees who had difficulties to accept me—a woman—as their boss. Anyone who complained or questioned my position in the company, quickly found out the score.

One of Francois' secretaries had once said to him, "Mr. Schwarz, it's Miss Mueller or I."

And he said, "Is there a question?"

"What?"

"What are you saying? You are quitting? Is this correct?"

"Oh."

She thought she was going to pull a fast one, and write me out of the picture. That was not even an option—at any point.

At one time, I created a new department in the '50's, to deal with business between our company and all of the American Embassies around the world. This was based on an idea of mine. When I told him about it, Francois was wholeheartedly behind me seeing it to fruition.

Francois said to me, "Well, maybe when I am gone, you will not be able to carry on this business. Who knows, maybe the business will fall apart. But who knows, if you have the idea, why don't you pursue it, and maybe later on this will be your livelihood."

I had this idea to go to all of the American Embassies and provide food and sundries, whatever they needed in their small little isolated places. So I went to the suppliers, and I said, "Look, we are representatives for all of the military bases all around the world. What if we supplied the Embassy's with the same services?" I proposed it in that simple a fashion.

John Connolly came to us from Washington D.C. to inquire about our business. He wanted to know what our "mark-up" was for the embassies. I explained to him that we had no mark-up and we sold at the same prices that armed forces would purchase through us. After I had everything explained to him, he went back to Washington, and all of the embassies received a telegram stating that they should all buy through us, because they could not buy things anywhere which were better or cheaper.

The embassies had previously paid exorbitant prices for their deliveries from the U.S. via wholesalers. A nice young man came from Washington D.C. to check our activities, and he explained our situation to Washington, whereupon Mr. Clark signed a telegram from Washington D.C. to all U.S. Embassies around the world to buy from us at regular supply bulletin prices.

We first sent out a query letter to the Embassies and asked them what kinds of goods and food they would want if we were to launch such a service. When we received their replies, we went back to the individual suppliers and told them about this idea, and indeed we ended up getting the same reduced prices that we had given to the military. Furthermore, there would be no additional charges to us or the recipients.

From that point forward, we ordered directly from all of our accounts we represented. Sometimes we learned that they previously paid as much as 100 percent over the prices that we could obtain for them. So, we finally did put this deal together, and it turned out to be a very profitable service that we provided. Sometimes we would receive all sorts of extra business from the ambassadors as well. Perhaps the ambassador's wife wanted something special, or something in exactly this size and color, or whatever it may be.

They would say to me, "Could I get this particular cream?" or "Could I get *such-and-such*?"

And I would say, "Sure, we can do that." So I went out and bought it for them. It was kind of an extra bit of business service for them. And everyone loved it, because we would send it to them, and they would pay no extra mark-up. I would get the same kind of price breaks that I would get if the Army was buying it. I was very pleased that my idea was not only useful, but it also made everyone happy.

At one point the son of Baron Revon, Claude, was sent to me from Paris to work in our office as an apprentice. That way he would improve his English speaking, and he would learn some valuable business skills.

He was working in our mail room at the time. One day I called him to my office and said to him, "I have an errand for you to run."

He said to me, "Certainly, what is it?"

"You are to go downstairs to Stern's Department Store on 42nd Street, and go to the ladies department, and purchase for the wife of one of the ambassadors, a brassiere."

"What?" he asked me with a look of horror in his eyes. "I can't do that!"

"Oh yes you can. You work here don't you?"

"Yes," he said with a degree of resignation in his voice.

"Now get downstairs, and go buy her the brassiere that she wants!"

He did exactly what I told him to do. After he returned from New York, he told his friends in Paris that he had to buy a *sutien-gorge*—which meant "bra" in French. Assuredly, this was not one of the valuable skills he was expecting to learn while working for FLS! According to him, they all had a good laugh over that. And, so did I!

Chapter Seven:
The Exciting Sixties

One day in 1961, quite out of the blue, Meta asked me over to meet with her for lunch. This was highly out of the ordinary for her. I sensed trouble and immediately thought, "Oh no, here we go."

When I arrived for our luncheon, I was certain that she wanted to tell me that she knew all about Francois and I. However, we ended up just having lunch, and we talked about everything that was on her mind BUT what I knew she wanted to talk with me about.

I sensed that she was obviously afraid that if she had done it, she would have to take a position regarding our unconventional trio. It could lead to a huge argument with Francois, and possibly a divorce from him. This was clearly something that she didn't want. In the final analysis, she simply didn't have the nerve to do it, so she never came out with it. She was not someone who enjoyed confrontation at all. It was like that old saying: "Let sleeping dogs lie."

Meta and I were quite polite to each other during lunch. When we parted, everything continued just as before.

Everyone—including Meta—knew what was happening between Francois and I at this point. Meta had a very beautiful home, with all of the best and most wonderful luxuries. Their marriage had long since become a comfortable arrangement. But they were no longer lovers. They simply shared a portion of their lives together. The rest of Francois' time was divided between his work, and his affair with me. And so, Meta continued to have her comfortable life as Mrs. Schwarz of Fifth Avenue, and Francois and I continued to have our relationship.

Working for FLS, there was nothing that we did that wasn't done with style. In 1961 we hosted a gala golf tournament just outside of Paris, which was a perfect illustration of this fact. It was held in the spring, and it was a very elaborate event held at a great course called St. Non de la Bretech Golf Club. Francois booked the golf club, and I was very impressed with the place, since everything there was very posh and First Class.

It was to be a fun and friendly game of golf in France for several our valued business associates. All of the arrangements for the event were organized by one of our directors, Ed Lane. The people who were invited to golf that day were either industry big-wigs or high-ranking military people. Amongst them were manufacturers and corporate big shots we dealt with during the business year. The Army was represented by Generals and Majors, the Navy was represented by Admirals and several other high-ranking officials, all of whom enjoyed golfing together.

Unfortunately, the outing also caused us to lose one of our very big accounts, due to a huge misunderstanding. One of our principals was Jewish, and he was not sent an invitation by Ed. Now, Francois didn't realize that there was a problem like this afoot until afterwards, because it was up to Ed to take care of the planning of it. Well, Ed certainly took care of it, and not in a good way. He simply left this man off of the invitation list, which was the ultimate reason the big problem.

I don't know if it was a personal thing, or what it was. I am not sure if that particular French golf club had a policy of prohibiting Jewish members, or if there was some sort of personal conflict on Ed's part, but it certainly created a real mess for us. I won't mention the man's name here, but he represented one of our huge accounts. He was very hurt to be excluded, and the bottom line is that we completely lost the account because of this misunderstanding. All I know is that several weeks after the tournament, the account was abruptly canceled on us.

Francois was furious with Ed for causing this problem. He demanded to know, "What the hell did you do?"

In his defense Ed replied, "Well, I left him off of the invitation list because I knew there would be a problem because he is Jewish."

"Well now it is a bigger problem for us!" I said. "Now it is a financial problem."

Those were the times when everyone was really concerned about religion. Now it is not such a big issue. Nowadays something like this wouldn't happen. But back then, everyone was very sensitive to things like that.

Aside from that one *faux pas*, the tournament was a huge success. It started off with the actual golf event, then right afterwards a lovely party took place. It was a delightful day, and I was impressed to find that all of the arrangements were wonderfully organized. The grounds there were gorgeous, and the people who attended were all very happy. Everyone took a leave from work to attend this event. There was also great camaraderie between the people who attended.

The arrangements that were made were all lovely and typically French. Everything there was wonderfully appointed. The gentleman who ran the golf club was a great golfer himself, so he genuinely loved making certain that all of these arrangements ran smoothly for us.

There was a big beautiful car as a prize for anyone who got a hole-in-one. However, in the end, no one won the hole-in-one competition. In the country club's main dining room there were long tables with fantastic French food displayed. I very much enjoyed the elaborate buffet which was a feast for the eye as well as for the stomach. At the climax of the evening there was a fireworks display, which spelled out the words "Au revoir Chez Francois." I have never seen anything like that, and it was quite breathtaking to witness.

The year 1961 also turned out to be a good year for purchasing apartments. The real estate market was down, so there were some great bargains to be had. When my limousine driver, Henry, picked me up on East 85th Street, we would drive across East 79th Street. On the corner of Madison Avenue I kept seeing a brand new building that was being constructed where brownstones had previously been. It was built as a rental building with the option to buy. The party who occupied 15B, opted not to buy their apartment. So, with the encouragement of Francois, I looked at it.

There was another apartment with the same layout, on the 9th Floor, that was going to be available as well. But, Francois convinced me that I should take the apartment on the 15th floor because its height cleared the buildings to the west of it, giving it an unencumbered view of Central Park.

The view of the park was so lovely from this building, and it is protected by the historic society. None of the blocks between Madison Avenue and Fifth Avenue can have any gigantic high rise apartment buildings constructed on them, so the view from my apartment would forever be unobstructed. Of course, that made for an even bigger selling point.

I couldn't seem to make up my mind until Francois emphatically said, "Look, this is a one-time expense that you are talking about. Do not settle for the apartment on the ninth floor with no view, take 15B." And so I did it. With that, mother and I moved into the beautiful one bedroom apartment in that very building.

Very shortly thereafter, 14F became available in the building, which was a smaller one bedroom apartment with a tiny kitchen, facing south to The Carlisle Hotel. Its southern exposure afforded beautiful sunlight streaming through the windows.

Harry Riker was the selling agent, who had sold me both of these apartments. Only six months later, he met an unfortunate end very shortly after selling them to me. It seemed that he had absconded with some of the money which he had collected from the sale of the apartments, and invested it in the West Hampton Tennis and Beach Club. He was caught in this embezzlement scheme, and rather than face the music, he committed suicide instead.

That same year, a new arrangement at FLS was put into place. Jack Gill and I bought the business from Francois. We paid Francois out of our earnings, and I subsequently took a loan from the bank to pay him off.

It was Jack and I who purchased his stock, and made contracts with him which provided us with great remunerations. From this point forward, Jack and I were the owners of FLS. That was the best kept secret you can ever imagine. Neither our clients nor our employees had any idea that Francois was no longer the owner of his own company. We treated him like nothing ever happened. He was the boss, and we were his employees. Although, behind the scenes the tables had turned, but we never treated him any differently.

Jack and I paid for all of Francois' amenities, his apartment, his car payments, everything. Without Francois there was no business, but in this way he could draw a great income for which Jack and I were accountable—with him as our "employee." It was a brilliant plan which was ultimately advantageous to everyone.

Francois was the real leader of our company, and no one had any clue how we had our business arranged. When I had to take out that massive personal loan to pay for this, it made me absolutely crazy. Never before had I taken a loan out of the bank for that astronomical amount, which I had to pay back.

The way I was raised, you first had the money, then you put it in the bank, and when you had enough to buy something, you buy it then, and not before. I would never think of buying anything on credit. Well, this was really like buying on credit.

But, Jack and I knew we could do it, and we followed through with it very nicely. And the business was very successfully run this way until 1977. It was a new era for FLS, and I was now one of its owners.

The apartment Francois owned in Paris was located on Rue Raynouard. It is in the Passy district, on a very busy street. The apartment was facing the Troccadaro.

I knew this apartment well, having visited it much later in 1961. I remember a wonderful party there at Francois and Meta's beautiful Parisian apartment. It was very tastefully decorated. They had three rooms leading into each other: a library, living room, and dining area, connected or divided with sliding pocket doors which opened from one room to the next.

There was a singer who sang a song called "Minuche." I still have the record to this day. The entertainer was a good looking gay man. Francois and I met him in a casino where he had been performing. He was a wonderful singer and we loved him when we saw him at the casino. A secretary of Francois' booked the singer for Francois' forthcoming party.

As a performer and as a gentleman, the singer was marvelous. Since he was gay, Francois encouraged me to flirt with him, knowing that I could never have him as a lover—no matter what. Francois bought me a copy of his record, and we had a lot of fun with him at the party.

Francois was a great gambler. Anytime Francois made a little money at the Baccarat table, I came by and I got the money or the chips. He would say to me, "Okay, those are your chips, go and play them on one table or another. Go."

One evening, after I had learned how to play a bit, I passed by the Baccarat table. As per usual there were lots of people surrounding the table. From the back of the crowd I just said the word "Banco."

Francois turned around in amazement at my courage, as I could have lost $1,000. I was scared of my own courage, as "Banco" in Baccarat means that you challenge the whole amount that is on the table. Francois sat at the table and was stunned. He later explained to me what I had done.

So, after that, I never did say "Banco" again.

It is at a Baccarat table where you place your bets on the table, and actually wager against the bank. Before this incident I had played at Atlantic City in New Jersey. I kept losing, and each time I lost, I doubled my bet. I went from betting $5.00, to betting $10.00, in other words, doubling whatever I had lost. Finally I came to my last doubling bet, as there was a $2,000 maximum on the table and finally I came to a bet of nearly that amount, and I won!

When I counted up all that I had gambled, and all that I had won, I found that all totaled, I had a profit of $5.00. All of that time and all of that effort in a smoke-filled room for a profit of $5.00!!! That was the end of my gambling days. I figured, "This is not worth it. There must be an easier way to make money than that!"

After that incident, I would gamble a little amount of money. I would just hold onto the money that Francois gave me. One time, when we were in Las Vegas, and we were gambling, I said to him, "Francois, you just gambled away one Cadillac!"

He said, "Is it your Cadillac?"

I said, "No."

"So don't worry about it," he said.

When I came back and saw how much money he was losing at this point, I said, "Three Cadillacs!!! Oh my God!"

At that time a Cadillac cost $5,000. "Three Cadillacs!?"

He said, "Yes. Now you go and wire to Uncle Ed." He was a guy who worked for Nestle Company, and who came to work for us as a director in the firm. So, I had to go and wire him, and have Ed send Francois more money. I had to go to the bank to pick up the money because he didn't want his name involved in any form, shape or manner in a way that the bank would think that he was a gambler.

So, Ed wired the money, and sent it to me via Western Union, or some such transfer method. I had to pick it up and bring it to him, and he had to pay off his gambling debts. So everything was fine.

He was determined that before he left, he made it all back. I don't know if he actually did or didn't. But it was a lot of fun. That was our Las Vegas adventure. And, in the long run, he knew what he was doing, and he was never out of control with it. "A certain amount of it, I know I can lose," he said, "and after that, no more."

He claimed that he always made money in the long run. And, it could be. One time in Paris, a guy we encountered—a real gambler—was out of money. All that he had left was a pair of diamond earrings. And he begged Francois to buy them from him.

He said, "I don't want to buy them, because I don't want to encourage you to play more. This is not healthy what you are doing."

But, the guy begged him even more: "I don't want to gamble. I want to pay my debts."

So, Francois said, "Okay, okay," and he gave him the money to pay off his debts in exchange for the earrings.

I have those earrings to this very day. They are beautiful diamond earrings with a number of stones in them, and they were beautifully done in white gold. I still have them. They are very, very fine and expensive earrings, although they spend most of the time in the safe.

One time when we went to Las Vegas, my mother came along. She was a gambler at heart. She didn't gamble a lot on that trip, but she still loved it. Francois was playing all night long, and so was she. Mother was playing the slot machines—the one armed bandit—until she had blisters on her hand from pulling the lever so much. But, "It is fun!" she said.

That week was a very wonderful trip to Vegas. However, on another occasion a robber came, and nobody noticed him. He was obviously very clever, and took our money and jewelry out of the suite where we were staying. Fortunately, he dropped our credit cards on the way out when he ran away, and the hotel found them in the hallway and returned them to us.

When someone from the hotel gave me the credit cards back I said, "What is this?" I didn't even know they were missing!

We also realized that nobody else in the hotel noticed the intruder either. He was so clever how he opened the doors and did so without making any noise as he took everything. Not expecting to be robbed, we had laid everything out on the desk and table there in the suite. Our jewelry, our money, and all of our valuables we had right there in plain sight.

We weren't in the suite at the time of the robbery, and naturally the hotel wasn't insured for it. If there was a robbery, you are simply out of your belongings, your jewelry, and your money. Back then there weren't any individual safes in the room. We certainly had the option of taking our valuables down to the front desk to have them locked up, but that seemed like such a bother at the time. Besides, I had never been robbed in a hotel before. How could I have predicted that this might happen?

One time I was at the Hilton in San Francisco, I had gone there alone on business. I thought to myself, "I'm going downstairs to take a quick swim in the swimming pool." I left my luggage in the room, and put it on the floor. I stuck my jewelry in a pocket inside of the suitcase, and off I went for my swim. When I came back, my bed was turned up, so I knew the maid had come in. I looked in the suitcase— only to find that all of my jewelry was missing. Somebody had opened the bag very nicely when I was gone, ransacked it, and took my jewelry. It was all gone.

These were a couple of unhappy situations, but what can you do? These are only things of material value, you can't take it with you anyhow. Now, I don't have to bother thinking about to whom to leave it. When something is suddenly gone, what are you going to do? That's the only way to think about it: it's gone and that's it.

Without a doubt, some of our most amusing adventures occurred in hotels. Francois and I were once staying in Los Angeles at The Beverly Hills Hotel on Sunset Boulevard, and a friend of ours came in from Europe and couldn't seem to find us on the premises. When the front desk attendants were unable to locate us for her, she resorted to her own instincts.

She tracked us down and found us in our private little bungalow. When she unexpectedly arrived I asked her, "How did you find us? How did you know we were here?"

She very logically explained, "I went along the row of cottages, until I caught a smell of something familiar. It was Chanel No. 5, and I know that was Francois' perfume. As soon as I got a whiff of Chanel No. 5: I knew he was here!"

Well, she was right! Francois used Chanel No. 5 all of the time. Sure enough, she resourcefully used her own nose to find him. We all had a good laugh over that, and had a great time together!

I used to say that when people where hired to work for our company, the new people were all beer drinkers. But when they joined our firm they suddenly switched from beer, and now they only drank vintage wine. Everything we did at FLS was done with a great sense of style, and everyone who worked for the company soon emulated it.

We would always have such beautiful Christmas parties. I would be the one who would make all of the arrangements for them. I also bought everybody a Christmas gift. Usually I went to Brooks Brothers, Tiffany's, and Saks Fifth Avenue to shop for them. Mostly, I knew— or was able to find out—everyone's size or their favorite color. I would know the length of their sleeves, or what it was that was each individual's personal style. I would pick everything out, have them gift wrapped and shipped over. Big boxes would arrive all nicely packed and wrapped with bows.

I would often throw our Christmas parties at The St. Regis Hotel on Fifth Avenue. On the Mezzanine they have these wonderful baroque and Renaissance rooms. We would go there for lunch and drinks, and then Santa Claus would arrive. I usually played Santa Claus myself. I would give all of the packages out, and I loved to do that. They were all wrapped the same way, and they all had labels on them.

I would spend a lot of time and energy preparing for these Christmas events. It was always such a lovely affair, and everyone just raved about it. That beautiful Renaissance Room at the St. Regis was such a lovely setting for this every year. We would arrive there in time for lunch, and we would stay there until six or seven o'clock in the evening.

We would have lunch, which was followed by a big presentation, and then to finish it off we would distribute all of the gifts. We would also give out Christmas bonuses too, of course.

Throughout the proceedings Francois would make toasts as well. He always had a quiz. He would ask questions, and if you had the right answer you won a $50 gold coin. He loved to give out prizes. People always enjoyed that very much.

His questions would be things like: "Who knows who is the king of *such-and-such* a country?" And people loved playing that game.

As part of the presentation, sometimes things that were not of general knowledge would be revealed. Francois would get up and say, "We understand that this person is in the process of buying a new house," or "We want to congratulate so-and-so on his new grandchild…" or whatever the latest office gossip was. I made a list during the year of all noteworthy happenings and spilled them in a very congenial way later on. Everyone was surprised how I came to know all the little scraps of gossip and news.

Our Christmas parties were always elaborate productions that were really fun. In addition to the holiday presents, there were also other presentations as well. Francois would get up in the middle of the party and announce things like: "I understand that this person has had an accident with their bicycle. So, we are buying them a new bike." Such acts of good will and generosity are always wonderful, especially when it comes unexpectedly.

It was always a very uplifting event. We didn't always hold our Christmas parties at The St. Regis Hotel, but that spot was certainly amongst my favorite places to plan our annual holiday event. They were always great parties to look forward to, and they were very much appreciated by everybody. This is a great era that I look back upon with a lot of fondness, because I always had so much fun planning these events.

By now, most of the wounds of World War II had healed. It took years for financial restitution to be made to many of the German survivors of the Second World War—my mother included. After the Nazis labeled all Jewish shops in Germany and cut off the income to their shop owners, my mother had been forced to sell her bicycle shop to a Mr. Fricke at a ridiculously low price. He had been introduced to Mother by Mr. Heidemann. It was Mr. Heidemann from whom we had purchased the bicycles. Finally, in the 1960s Mother received an adjusted payment for the sale of the store. In fact, I too, received a $5,000 check from the German government for the loss of my post-graduation career.

In 1966, the American Federation of Art planned an interesting trip to North Africa. It was a cultural trip that would have us journeying from Casablanca to Cairo. I went along for this incredible trip. It was truly a grand adventure unlike any other I had ever experienced.

Bill Lieberman was at that time in charge of the print department at the Museum of Modern Art (MOMA). He was the tour guide who went with us, and he was accompanied by a painter named Moyer, who was also partly responsible for guiding us on this trip. Moyer handled the commercial end of the trip, and Bill handled the artistic aspects of the tour.

Our grand adventure in Northern Africa started at Idlewilde Airport, which was later to be renamed Kennedy Airport. The first stop on our agenda was Casablanca, which I found to be both fascinating and exotic. We also had with us several of the people who were the organizers of the trip. Amongst them was the man who was in charge of the Egyptian department at the Metropolitan Museum of Art. He did excavations in the area that we visited.

He explained to us, "In the 1920s where we are now standing, I was excavating with a German expedition. And, we had excavated to a certain point to this level," he said pointing—to a certain level of what was exposed. "All of this which you see now, is newly excavated," he would tell us in great detail. Then he explained to us what was done from one place to another, and how this differed from what we were going to see the next day.

It was a beautifully, well-prepared trip. Francois didn't go with me, so he insisted that I take Irmgard along with me, as my chaperone. "Ah, ha!" I thought, "Not my chaperone!"

However, we all had a good time. We went all through Morocco and all over North Africa: from Casablanca, through Tunisia, on our way to Egypt. Since the United States was not on speaking terms with Libya, we were forced to skip that country—or so we originally thought.

At one point we were in Rabat, Morocco, all of the guys were going out somewhere in the evening. I said to them, "I want to go with you boys." They said, "No, we don't want to take you along." I figured that they were going out to see belly dancers or something like that, and I didn't want to miss it.

I said to Bill Lieberman, "Bill, I will be no trouble. I won't make any noise. Take me along, please." I swore, "You won't see me, I will be quiet as a mouse, I promise."

He finally said, "Oh, okay."

What they were up to didn't involve belly dancers at all, they were going to buy hashish! It was very funny. We had to go here, and then we had to go there, and we had to wait for someone, and then the guys had to go somewhere else. We seemed to be going all over the place, and I still didn't know exactly what they were up to, but I kept my promise to be quiet and just come along for the ride.

Finally we came to the end of this Wild Goose Chase: purchasing hashish! We arrived at a place that looked a little like an American 1950s diner with an off-white floor. We ended up having to wait for someone to come. It seemed to take a long time, but finally they arrived with the hashish. It was all very much fun and quite an amusing adventure. We smoked it and had a silly time. At one point I went and climbed up on one of the pedestals which held statues in a public place and made a "proclamation" for everyone to hear. So much for being quiet!

In Morocco hashish was all very legal, so this was not a big deal. But we sure had lot of laughs that evening. It was one of the most fun escapades that we had on the trip. And, thanks to the hashish, everyone who passed by us that evening was lucky enough to hear my very important public proclamation.

Other than that, I was very quiet—as promised. I didn't create too big a problem, for fear that I wouldn't be invited on the next "boys' night out."

While we were on this North African tour we only stayed at First Class hotels, so the trip was very nice from start to finish. At the time Alice Kaplan was the president of the AFA—the American Federation of Art. She was a great friend, and she was along on this trip as well.

Ingeborg ten Haff was also there. Her daughter married a South American aristocrat. Ingeborg was a real bookworm. She knew a lot, and she was fascinated with my ability to dive right into all of the different situations that confronted us. She later became well known as a painter, and she married a man much younger than herself.

She once said to me, "You're so athletic and outgoing, and so active. I was never that way. I was never athletic like you. I was always the type to sit and read."

I responded, "I never liked to read."

In other words, we were two opposite ends of the spectrum. But, we got along very well together.

Peter Fink was invited to the home of the American Ambassador to Morocco, where he had arrangements to photograph the man and his wife. As he was preparing to leave, I asked him, "Can I go along with you? I will pretend that I am your photographer's assistant. I will hand you your rolls of film and I will do whatever I can to assist you. I would love to see the Ambassador, and this just sounds like a fantastic event to be present at. Can I come along?"

Finally, he agreed that I could assist him. He put a camera around my neck, and I went along with him as his assistant.

The home of the American Ambassador to Morocco was a nicely decorated apartment with a lot of American memorabilia. It was traditional and very American looking. It seemed sort of like an oasis of United States-styled decor, in the Moroccan desert. I remember sitting outside where the ocean could be seen. They had lovely quarters there, and it was just a beautiful sight.

It was also fascinating for me to watch Peter while he worked. He took some gorgeous photographs of the Ambassador's wife and her lovely home. She was a lovely woman, and I was absolutely in admiration of this whole ambiance and what she had done with her home. She was a delightfully charming person.

At one point she clapped her hands twice very loudly, and all of a sudden one little black boy came out to serve us coffee. He wore a little traditional Moroccan outfit with a turban on the his head. I recall a little ceramic stand that was next to the chair that I sat in. As he set down a tray with a cup of very dark espresso-like coffee that is the tradition in Morocco, I felt as if I was on a Moroccan movie set. The coffee was so strong that I could barely drink it. I took several sips of the coffee just to be polite, but it was so intense and bitter that it tasted awful to me.

Peter was on this trip taking a lot of photos specifically for Eastman Kodak in Rochester, New York, among other assignments. The Kodak photos were specifically for the Eastman Kodak galleries.

On one of the outings, we were in the governor's tent, and we found that they had a specific event which Peter photographed. As we looked down, we watched as ten traditional Moroccan riders in very colorful garb rode by on horseback. The photograph that Peter took of the ten riders was fully choreographed so that when they came to an end mark, they simultaneously shot their rifles into the air. Peter took a breathtaking photo of this event. It was so tightly planned that the intention was to have all ten rifles fire at exactly the same time, just as the horses came to a sudden stop, also exactly at the same moment they kicked up a cloud of sand. It was really a dramatic sight to behold.

After the trip, I visited Peter in his apartment in the famed Dakota building in New York City, to see that he had made a huge blow-up print of this scene which literally went from floor to ceiling in full color. In the photograph, every detail, from the colorful clothing, to the desert sand blowing, was larger than life to view.

Our whole group was invited by the Moroccan governor to come to the garden of his palace where carpets were put on the grass for us to sit on, and bolsters to lean against. Men in Moroccan outfits came by with water in small basins for us to wash our hands with. Across from where we sat was a lamb turning on a spit, over a fire. A big bowl of couscous was passed around, which we ate with our hands. A platter of lamb was passed around which everyone likewise ate with their hands. Several other platters contained fresh fruits. After we had finished eating, water and basins were passed around again so we could rinse off our hands. Observing our hosts, they were rather in contrast to the Moroccan hosts who were wearing Madison Avenue suits, white shirts and ties. This was in deference to the fact that we were Americans, and they wanted to make us feel comfortable. However, the hosts in Brooks Brothers attire looked as ridiculously out of place since they were dressed as American businessmen.

After Morocco, our next stop on the trip was Tunisia. I was quite fascinated by the light green color of the ocean there and the white sand, with very few people swimming. I surmised that the waters were better for boating, since there was the beautiful sight of several sailboats anchored there.

The architecture was different from the other places we had been and the museum there had wonderful pieces of the history of Tunisia, as well as artifacts and art from other countries. I was deeply occupied viewing the exhibits and all of the items that they had on display. Then I started speaking to a German couple who were also visiting Tunisia. We got into the middle of a conversation, and I was so engrossed that I forgot that the bus was leaving at a certain time, and I missed it. The German people graciously took me in their car, and drove me to a nearby police station. From there I called the hotel and someone came to get me. Needless to say, I got a lecture requesting that I never do that again, as everyone was worried about my whereabouts. The speculation was that I had been abducted and was now behind the carved stone screen windows of a harem. Fortunately, this was not the case, and everyone was relieved when I was safely returned.

In found that the food was very good in Tunisia. In some of our other destinations, the food was so spicy that I could barely eat it, but in Tunisia I very much enjoyed the cuisine. I found the country as being a very quiet place. The next day I bought an authentic caftan in a real Tunisian shop in the marketplace. It was very comfortable to wear. I still have that same caftan today. Every time I wear it, people marvel at its simplicity, and its great cut of the cloth.

I would like to visit Tunisia again to see what it is like now—after so many years. Maybe not so much has changed. The people there were all very nice—especially when I got lost one day. The police were very polite and helpful. Also, I found that my being able to speak French was of great assistance to me while in Tunisia.

Our next stop was supposed to be Cairo, but we made a sudden and unexpected stop in Libya. We were not supposed to land there at all, but for some reason the authorities insisted we go there, because we had to transport two American workers from the oil riggers in Benghazi. Therefore, we had no choice but to make this unplanned stop. As we landed, we found that the authorities had all sorts of surprises in store for us. Since Libya had just gotten their freedom as a country, the men who were in charge there were of course acting in a very "macho, macho" way. After years of not having any individual rights, they now wanted everyone to know that they had power and authority and they insisted we all get out of the plane.

A big obstacle came when the Libyan guards demanded that we give them our passports. Peter refused to cooperate, and I found myself interceding for the sake of our safety.

They had already obtained everyone else's passports on the plane. But he insisted, "I am not giving them my passport."

Then, Peter didn't want to get out of the plane. I said to him, "You have to. Peter you cannot start a stink here. We are in Libya, and we absolutely have to get out of the plane like they are requesting."

"No," he replied.

I said to him in a scolding tone of voice, "You absolutely cannot behave like a child. We are in the wrong country for this kind of behavior. I am going to have to take you over my knee and spank you like a child if I have to." Finally I talked him into getting out of the plane as we had been commanded by these gun-toting men.

At the time, Libya was one of the most volatile places for Americans to be, and we were all very well aware of this. I tried to talk some sense into Peter, so that he wouldn't cause any problems for himself or for us as a group. I explained to him, "Libya is not somewhere where you question what the government is doing. This is crazy to create problems here. So, stop it, and do what they say."

He was still very argumentative towards all of this, and he said very loudly, "They are damn lucky I complied."

Trying to calm him down I said, "Please just do as you are asked, and let's proceed with our trip."

Finally I talked him into cooperating.

At that point they unloaded all of our luggage from the plane, and we had no idea what the reasoning for that was. Were they going to confiscate it? Were they going to search it? As they took our luggage out, Peter again argued, "What is all this about?"

In a very dimly lit area, we stood quietly as we watched as all of our luggage being brought in, and it was piled up on the side.

Then came our next surprise of the day. Two very intimidating Libyan government officials with guns tried to play the "big shot" and insisted that we get vaccinated. They didn't explain to us what this vaccination was all about, which was rather frightening in itself.

This was a major dilemma to find ourselves in—while in a potentially hostile foreign country. We had no idea what they intended to inject us with—or if they had clean needles. The two gun-toting Libyan men were most unfriendly about all of this, and none of us knew what to do. We certainly didn't want to be injected with anything. Thinking quickly, our guide, Bill Lieberman, got hold of one of the passengers who was a labor lawyer. Knowing that this man was used to negotiating difficult deals, Bill asked him if he could please intervene on our behalf. Unfortunately, that did not immediately produce the favorable results we hoped for. The labor lawyer was absolutely furious that he couldn't deal with them logically, and they refused to listen to him.

At that point, Bill telephoned one of our foreign Ambassadors with whom he was acquainted. By now it was 2:00 in the morning, but he somehow reached the Ambassador, and he explained our precarious situation. Finally the Ambassador somehow arranged to settle the problem.

While all of this was going on, we sat in this airport building for what seemed like an eternity, and waited and waited until this was all resolved. We spent several long and tedious hours of sitting on the floor next to our luggage, in this miserable area—a country we did not want to be in at all.

We were relieved when Bill Lieberman agreed to the Ambassador's solution: pay the Libyans some amount of money to set us free. Finally, this frustrating situation was resolved and we were given our luggage back. We were also given back our passports, and we were allowed to re-board our plane with the two oil rig workers who were the reason for this unplanned stop. We got the hell out of there. We were especially relieved when we were allowed to leave without the vaccination. In the end, it was the American dollar that obtained us our freedom, which was probably their objective to begin with.

Once we were safely back on the plane and in the air, we all breathed a sigh of relief that nothing bad happened to us. With that, we were gladly on our way to Cairo, and Bill Lieberman was hailed by us as the "hero of the day."

The next stop on our adventure was exotic Egypt. Compared to some of the places where we found ourselves along the way, Cairo was a very civilized destination indeed. Due to our unexpected trip to Libya, when we finally arrived at the Cairo airport it was 3:00 a.m. Needless to say, we were in a state of exhaustion, frustrated anger, and ultimately relief.

Egypt's historical and archeological riches are too great for brief descriptions of everything we saw and experienced and studied while there. They included the Cairo Museum, the pyramids at Giza, the

Sphinx, the beautiful elaborate mosques, the great Temple at Amour, the Avenue of the Sphinxes, Hypostyle Hall in Karnak with its 134 gigantic columns, the Temple of Ramses III, and the Obelisks of Queen Hatshepsut. The sense of history is so incredibly exciting in these surroundings. We owe an eternal debt of gratitude for the dry and benevolent climate that has kept these artifacts and monuments of historical significance and extreme antiquity intact for us to admire and study.

We went to see the majestic pyramids, which I very much admired from the outside. Then I tried to go inside, where one would have to ascend a very steep incline of steps. The passageway was so small that only one person had space to go upward at a time. Very shortly, not more than about 10 steps up, I got such a bad attack of claustrophobia, that all I wanted to do is get the hell out of there—immediately. So I had to go backwards, and all of the people behind me had to back down the passageway as well. There was no way I was going any further. So much for my romantic vision of ascending the inside of the pyramids. From that point on, I was content with admiring them from the outside.

What was even more dazzling was going to the famed Cairo Museum and seeing the incredible mummies and all the riches and treasures of the pharaohs. What impressed me the most were the ancient Egyptians' artistic techniques and agility to create all of these beautiful sculptures, jewelry and artifacts.

Peter had some friends who lived on a houseboat on the Nile River, and we went there and visited with them. I was very surprised to see that people could live like that for any length of time, as opposed to having a house or an apartment. The boat itself was very "boxy," and the rooms were very small. They weren't divided by doors, but instead had curtains. I couldn't see how anyone could live there, as it wasn't at all comfortable. In the way of furnishings, it was very sparse. I surmised that one must have to be really in love with the sea and the water to even consider living that way.

A few of us took a breathtaking flight to Luxor. I remember a fantastic yellow marble bust there. They were shooting a film called *Khartoum* at the time, and we watched them filming some of the scenes from it.

While we were in Egypt, Peter had to go and photograph some of the ancient ruins, and I went with him on that shoot as well. Along the way we became very friendly with each other.

One of the other people in our group was a man by the name of Robert C. Scull. He was well known for owning a fleet of taxi cabs in New York City in the 1970's. He was known in social circles as "the taxi tycoon," and he was also a great art collector.

Robert was very polite to me, and he often helped me on and off of our tour busses while on our many excursions. I often found him saving me a seat on the tour bus, or carrying my bag, or assisting me in some other way.

While we were on a particular tour bus in Egypt, and he said to me, "I am performing all the duties of a husband, but I am getting none of the 'benefits.'"

I knew exactly where this was leading. So I turned to him, and replied, "And the situation will remain that way, and it will never change."

He later came to one of my cocktail parties in New York City, and we had a great time reminiscing about our fantastic tour of Northern Africa. However, the affair he wanted with me never happened.

On another occasion in Egypt, Peter was trying to send a telegram, and he had a problem with the Cairo wire office. Knowing the protocol of sending things in and out of the country, I helped him to straighten things out with this particular wire telegram.

I told him, "Do this, do that…" and "Don't do it that way, I would do it this way…" I just helped him to make proper business arrangements. He had a business call with a woman who was causing some sort of problem, and he didn't know what to do, so I helped him to iron out everything.

I told him, "Let's sit down and organize this together." Between the two of us, we came up with a logical solution.

He was impressed that I had successfully solved the problem. Whatever the dilemma was, I was able to work it out.

Then later on, we decided to try something else together.

We went home to our hotel. We had a great time that day, so he said,

"That was so fabulous of you to help me. The photos I took are going to be great, and I really appreciated your assistance. Let's have a drink together."

So we went back to his room to celebrate. We had a drink together. And then we had another drink, and another drink, and then we *really* had some great fun together.

Afterwards he said to me, "You know, you aren't only better in business, you are better in bed!"

I couldn't have agreed with him more.

My logic for sleeping with Peter was the fact that Francois always told me to do whatever I pleased, and—surely—he would not care if I had my own "foreign affair," as long as I was honest and up front, and told Francois everything that I did. So, when the opportunity presented itself, I figured: "Why not? Francois knows where I am, and whom I am with." I didn't think that there would be any consequences from my actions.

The night that I had sex with Peter, I had told Irmgard—my chaperone, "I will be going out tonight, and don't mind me, I will be home late."

Fortunately for me, she was very naive. I came up with some sort of a cockamamie story which I told her. And somehow, she bought it, and was none-the-wiser as to what really happened between Peter and I that fun night in Cairo.

So we finished our leg of the North African trip, and I went up to Frankfurt to meet Francois. He knew that Irmgard was with me, so he knew that I wasn't going to do anything that wasn't right, or that was improper. Well, he was sure in for a surprise.

Francois met me at the Frankfurt Airport, and he asked me how my trip was. I said, "It was absolutely wonderful! I had a great time."

"How was everything along the way?"

"Wonderful, wonderful!"

We got back to the hotel room at the Frankfurter Hof. It was a very lovely room, and we had a drink together. We had nice dinner plans, and a fun evening scheduled.

So we were sipping our cocktails in the room, and I decided that I would reveal to him in greater detail all that had happened on my tour of Northern Africa. He was most entertained by all my stories. Then I came to the part about my night with Peter in Cairo, and nonchalantly told him I had indeed had sex with Peter during the trip. I didn't look upon it as an "indiscretion," but as a fun mid-trip conquest on my part.

Little did I know, but he was not to see this revelation with the same sense of amusement with which I viewed it.

His eyes got big, and he went absolutely nuts on me. He had a horrified look on his face.

"What!?!" he said.

"Well, you told me to tell you if I ever did anything," I replied.

"You stupid..." and with that he grabbed me by the neck with his two hands, and began to strangle me!

I thought that he was literally going to kill me! His hands were so tight on my throat that I couldn't breathe anymore. I heard myself gasping for air. He was absolutely furious with jealousy and rage, and much to my horror he went completely ballistic on me.

He ranted and raved, "How could you do this to me? How dare you?"

Finally, after several terrifying moments I felt his hands loosening their grip on me.

As I gasped to regain my full consciousness, I found that I was dumbstruck. That was really something. I couldn't believe it: he almost killed me that night! I was nearly strangled to death.

He admitted afterwards, "I was really close to killing you."

But at the last minute, he regained his senses and decided against it.

So many things were going on in my head. "Why is he doing this to me?" I asked myself while he was trying to strangle me. "How dare he do this to me!"

Finally, when I had recovered, I asked him, "What on Earth was wrong with you?"

He acted like it was he who was wounded, and mad. He said to me, "Why did you do this? Don't you know that you don't do things like this! Don't you know that?"

I said, "No, I don't know. You told me different, and I believed you! You told me that I could do anything that I wanted to do, as long as I told you what I had been up to."

I tried to tell him that I was right and he was wrong. I was so mad at him, I wanted nothing to do with him the whole rest of the evening.

It is funny how the passage of time can change your entire perspective. The next day we made up with each other, and continued on to Berlin.

That night, we went out in Berlin and the bar we went to was a striptease place. I watched these girls in awe, as it seemed that they could do just about anything with their bodies. They could do a striptease like nothing I had seen in my life. They were gorgeous to look at, and presented themselves as really First Class girls.

Francois told me that I was a "First Class girl," however as I looked at these voluptuous girls, contorting their bodies to the music I thought to myself, "Compared to these girls I don't feel First Class."

From beginning to end, that trip was definitely something memorable. After our stay in Berlin, Francois and I came back to New York together. All in all, that trip was unforgettable on many levels. Northern Africa was incredible to see and experience. And what had happened between Francois and I was also unforgettable. I knew that Francois was possessive, and capable of jealousy, but now I really had an idea of just how intense his possessive sense of jealousy could become.

Clearly, Francois was putting a "double standard" on me, which I felt was totally unfair. He could have a wife at home, and have me as his girlfriend. Yet, if I wanted to take a lover on the side, this was strictly forbidden. Instead of blaming him, what I finally surmised was that I was wrong in what I did, and in trying to strangle me—he was clearly wrong in what he did. When we returned to New York City, I was resolved to just forget the whole thing, and continue our lives as they had been. I wanted to forget about it, or write it off as a huge misunderstanding. This however, was not the last time that I ran up against the jealousy of Francois.

That was the one and only time that I had an affair with anyone else during all of our years together. However, there were several times when Francois suspected me of infidelities. He was so jealous. In the 1950s I had already seen the signs of his possessive nature.

In New York one day, a friend of our family took me home in his car from a dinner party at the home of a mutual friend. Afterward, Francois called me in a jealous rage.

He yelled at me accusingly, "Where were you? You weren't at home. Were you with that man? Did you betray me *again?*"

I told him, "No, I told you I would not do that again. And, I have stuck to my word! You can trust me."

"How can I trust you?" he proclaimed.

"Because I told you that you can trust me," I argued back. "If something happened, I would tell you about it."

But that was not enough. Francois phoned the young man who had given me a ride home. He asked him to come to the office, and forced him to sign a statement. At the time, I knew nothing of this. It wasn't until Francois' death that this document came to my attention. The statement on the signed piece of paper read:

State of New York
County of New York
Walter Lynn
Being duly sworn to deposes and says: that I reside at 89 Wadsworth Terrace, New York City, New York. That I own a Buick four door sedan, New York City registration number [no number filled in] that Miss Ruth Mueller and I have known each other for more than ten years past. That on June 25th 1958 while I was visiting at the home of Mrs. Rose Schacker at 4580 Broadway, New York City, where I had traveled in my mentioned automobile. I was the guest for dinner as was Miss Mueller, who arrived there alone at 9:00 p.m. on the evening of that day. After dinner Miss Mueller and I visited with Mrs. Schacker in whose home we remained until approximately 11:30 to 12:00 p.m. When we, Miss Muller and I, left together, I was anxious to return home that evening in time to enable me to complete certain clerical work consisting of the typewriting of invoices because I was scheduled to leave the following day, June 26th by plane to Europe.

Accordingly, when Miss Mueller and I arrived in my automobile in front of the apartment house, 529 East 85th Street, New York City, I did not even enter the building as I was in a hurry to return to my home as stated. And, in addition, there was no place to park my car. All I did was to come around to the side of the car where Miss Mueller was sitting, escort her to the entrance doorway to the building and immediately left. Neither on the night of June 25th to June 26th, 1958, nor on any other day or night in all the ten years or so that I have known Miss Mueller, have we ever been intimate with each other. Nor have we ever done anything or been anywhere as a result of which anyone could by any stretch of the imagination construe that we had been guilty of any misconduct or intimacy. That the foregoing statement is voluntarily made by me at the request of Miss Mueller, who has asked me to describe the events of the evening of June 25th from the time that she arrived at the home of Mrs. Schacker, until the time she arrived in front of her building at about 12:15 on June 26th, 1958.

Walter Lynn
Sworn to before me this day of November 1958

I found out about this letter much later. I couldn't believe that Francois had done this. I was furious for what Francois put Walter through, all for the sake of his jealousy. I couldn't believe how jealous he was of me.

When Francois made Walter Lynn sign that letter in November of 1958, he did not have any reason not to sign such a document. There was absolutely no "hanky panky" between us what-so-ever. Nothing happened. Francois was absolutely outraged that day, and he didn't go home at all that night. Meta was in Europe. So he went to a bar on Broadway called The Jack Dempsey Bar. I still have a photo of him that next day. He looked terrible. He was talking himself into a real rage. Despondent, he sat at the bar and really drank himself into oblivion.

The next morning he arrived at the office unshaven, and I was absolutely appalled to see him looking that way. I said to him, "You had better get home and shave and shower if you are going to show your face at this office."

He went home, and he wasn't seen until the next day.

The next day he came back, and he was all right again. I don't understand how anybody could have done that. He must have talked himself into thinking that I was having sex with every man I encountered. I don't know what he had going on in his mind. He was just so jealous that there was no talking any sense into him.

There was no basis in reality to his rage. But he somehow saw every man around me in the business world as a potential lover of mine.

And there was still another one.

Every morning at East End Avenue came Henry Cowings with his limousine, which he used to transport seven people to work. Henry bought the limousine when the taxis were on strike and he created a needed service. He liked doing it so much that he kept up the habit after the taxi strike was over. The passengers were all very friendly on this morning run, and it was a very enjoyable way for me to get to work as well.

One day when I was putting my make-up on in the car, there was another fellow who was also a passenger in this limousine. While I did my make-up, I was startled to see him pull out his electric shaver, and he started shaving in the car. I started to laugh at this, but he said to me, "What is right for the goose, is good for the gander." We all had a good laugh over this. Needless to say, I never applied my make-up in the car again after that.

This particular gentleman was the publisher of a Spanish-speaking newspaper. One day he had a friend with him from Latin America by the name of Mr. Roca. He and I had a great conversation in the car.

I was even more startled to find that this man sent me a dozen dark red roses to the office, and that he asked me out on a dinner date. Needless to say Francois demonstrated his extreme jealousy again. He literally blew his top when he saw the roses and the attached note. So at Francois' insistence, I had to send Mr. Roca a letter which Francois wrote for me to sign and send. It read:

Dear Mr. Roca:
Many thanks for the nice flowers and your telephone call. For personal reasons, would you please not call me again, neither in my

office or in my home. I certainly would appreciate it.

Sincerely yours,

RM

It was in Francois' handwriting. I had to copy exactly what he had written down, deliver the note, and make sure I broke this off immediately. It was an ironic double standard to which I was held accountable.

It infuriated me that Francois was above being questioned. He could do anything he wanted to do. I, on the other hand, had to do as I was told.

The same thing went for Meta. If she ever had an affair on the side, that would be reason enough for him to divorce her on the spot.

In Francois' mind, what women do is completely different from what women are allowed to do. Both Meta and I were judged by this double standard of acceptable behavior. That was quite something to witness.

It was a shame about this affair that never took place. Mr. Roca was really a charming man, and I actually would have loved to have gone out with him. But, the way that Francois was, and as possessive as he was, this was an impossible situation.

It reminded me of a Hildegarde Knef song in which she sang about wanting to be free—but not alone, and not in a love affair that was suffocating. In many ways that was what my affair with Francois was like. To maintain a fine balance between being free, and not ending up alone, is a difficult dilemma.

In a way, this is how I lived my life. I was rarely all alone, and I certainly had my freedom for the most part.

Before that, Francois was in Paris with Meta and I met a very nice man. This was in the early 1950s. I was really taken by him. His name was Ozzie. He had a slim face, and stood six feet tall. He weighted about 170 pounds. He was well-built, well-educated, and possessed a lot of charm. We had met in school somehow, when I had taken a class.

I had to go to Francois' home on Riverside Drive, to drop something off, while Francois and Meta were in Europe. I took Ozzie along with me.

I was talking to Francois later on the telephone, and when he asked what I had done that day, I told him, "I ran up to your apartment, and Ozzie came along with me." It was an innocent statement, and just the up-front truth.

"What? You took Ozzie to my apartment?" Francois said in an accusatory tone. "What did you do?"

"Oh we read the newspaper," I said.

"Come on, that wasn't all," he replied.

"Yes, that was all," I told him, and it was true. It was a very wonderful friendship that I had with Ozzie. He was studying singing, and he had a beautiful voice, and he was from upstate New York. He lived in a coldwater flat on Avenue A or Avenue B in Greenwich Village.

As friends, Ozzie and I had great times together. But he sent me these letters:

Tuesday the 8th

Dearest Ruth:

Because you have already read the letter which I had intended to send you, or a section thereof, it is better that I start anew.

I called an old pal while I was in Boston and he told me a good excuse to make another ski trip, so we came from Boston by car—somewhat more pleasant than the train. There were no accidents and we arrived sans mishap Saturday evening.

Sunday we went skiing at Cannon Mountain. The day was exceedingly warm and fair, so even though the skiing was not good, I enjoyed myself very much and you can be sure.

Yesterday I fear naught was accomplished. I only fooled around and imported what I had seen and done in the big city to the folks and townspeople. Come evening though, my brother and I attended the Easter ball. It was rather dull and we didn't stay very late. I wished that you might have been there to liven it up a bit.

Today, dear Ruth, is bright and clear, with a warm southern breeze to melt away the snow which has remained so late. The birds, who were hearty enough to come here earlier, are singing their gratitude for sun and coming summer. I had forgotten that here the arrival of spring is such a great event with everyone marveling at each successive change while you in the city are only aware of the change in temperature and clothing. I am sorry that you could not have been with me at Cannon Mountain Inn. But I know you enjoyed the Easter Parade and I know that many envious and admiring eyes were cast upon you. Had it not been for vacation, be assured that there would have been two more.

I'd best close now in order that this may be sent on the morning bus. All my love,
Ozzie

Wednesday the 9th
Dearest Ruth:
Everyone has gone to bed except the dog and I, which leaves me free to write you. I'm hoping at the same time that you don't mind me writing to you two days in a row. Please don't be angry, because I've been wishing all day that people would retire so that I might set down some of my thoughts to you, of you.

But first allow me to rid myself of the feeling that I must pass on the amusing incident following. About an hour ago, my mother stated that she detected the aroma of an American skunk, and called me in. We brought the dog inside, for fear she might attempt to engage the skunk in combat. We had about settled again when there was a knock upon the door. Upon opening same, we found my brother Ralph, and his family, the children being wrapped in blankets and born in arms. It appeared to be some sort of emergency, so I allowed them to enter. This is their story. They had a dog also who had five pups about a week old, and whose name is Mitzi. Well, Mitzi is no different than any other mother in her desire, instinct if you wish, to protect her young, and upon hearing the odd noise outside the door asked permission to investigate. Ralph's wife Evelyn obligated by opening the door and Mitzi actually flew at the intruder too late for anyone or dog to realize it was the same skunk we had smelled 200 yards away. Poor Mitzi caught the full effect of the skunk's protection square upon the eyes and dashed back into the house before Evelyn could close the door. At close range the aroma of the woods pussy is almost unbearable. It causes nausea and smarting of the eyes as well as taking away all desire to breathe. And Ralph's house was completely filled. So he had no choice but to wrap the children and seek temporary refuge here.

They are now bundled safely off to bed. So ends our saga, but not without a moral. It being of course never to trust a bitch in heat.

I'd like to apologize for yesterday's letter, I fear it wasn't up to par. The house was in confusion and my mind only seemed to concentrate on the fact that the mail has left at 11:00. Tonight though, I have more time. It's only midnight and I have no lessons tomorrow, or subway ride, damn it. So you'll really learn how I can fowl up a number of sheets of stationery.

What a lovely week you must be having with not so many phone calls to mar your day's work, and lots of sleep in which to rest. I do hope you don't find out how much better off you are without me around to upset you. And I always also hope that you never learn how better off you are sans Ozzie or that I'll ever want you to. Just think also that when I'm away you don't have as many messes to clean up. I, since the last mess I made, resolved not to allow any more accumulate that could not be cleaned up on the spot. I trust that by now the apartment on Riverside Drive is just gleaming with its cleanliness and that all sox are darned and that Freddie is happy about the whole thing. I hope there isn't enough time as I return to have it become the disgraceful disorder it was at my parting. It is a dreadful shame that you could not come with me. There is plenty of room and the days have been fair so we could have gone on nice long walks in the wilderness which is always with or without the well known flask of wine, a great adventure.

And so dearest Ruth, I hope that you've had an enjoyable week and I also hope you've found time to dream a wee bit of what may well be our future. Lord knows I've done wee else but dream since coming home and shouldn't have been, there was too much for me to do. I still would have dreamed a good deal of you which you may think is bad, but which I think is the only thing I do. Ah well, if I don't stop writing, neither you nor I will have any rest. As it is, you'll be tired before you've deciphered this in its entirety.

I love you,

Laddie, Ozzie, Osgood, Skunk, Dog, Rat and Stinker

At the time, Ozzie was taking singing lessons to perfect his beautiful and deep baritone voice. This letter just illustrates the fact that I had a lot of admirers chasing me during this era. It was actually a lot of fun to feel so desirable to other men.

It also shows off the fact that Francois had reason to be jealous of the men I attracted. If we were out in public together, he was always instructing me not to look at anyone who passed by and gave me the eye.

"Don't look!" he would insist.

"Why don't you just put blinders on me?" I would argue back. "What are you doing to me?"

But he was that jealous, and he was that threatened that someone might steal me away from him. I had to make sure that I was always looking straight ahead.

In the case of Ozzie, I managed to keep his infatuation with me a secret from Francois. Ozzie came from a blue collar working class family in upstate New York. He had a scholarship to go to the Julliard Music School to study voice. And, I am sure, with some financial help from somebody, he could have made a great professional singer.

But, in the end, I had to tell him that I didn't think our relationship could ever lead to anything, as I was pretty much occupied. Who knows: maybe it was wrong. Maybe it was right. But that's the way it was.

It was a long way from Riverside Drive—a beautiful apartment, and my apartment on 85th Street and the east side, down to Ozzie's coldwater flat on Avenue B. It was unfortunate, but it played a role in my finally breaking things off with Ozzie. But, that was the way it was.

In retrospect, you see things quite differently. But when you are amidst something, you don't always see clearly. And you sometimes want something, but you don't want to go through with it. You debate with yourself in your own mind. You end up putting up barriers within yourself, and making comparisons and choices in life.

Maybe I should have gone to a psychiatrist at that point? Maybe that would have helped? Maybe that would have helped me to decipher myself and put myself in the right context? But I've always thought if you have a good friend, and you talk to that good friend, it's as good as any psychological therapy session.

Another one of our most memorable parties also took place at The St. Regis Hotel. On this particular occasion the directors of the corporation gave a beautiful party in the honor of the 50th anniversary of Francois and Meta. We put it all together, and for this event we booked the rooftop at the St. Regis.

My good friend Smitty was a co-worker whom I loved dearly. He was in charge of this spectacular party. That night the rooftop was immaculately decorated. It was absolutely beautiful to behold. Smitty had mimosa flowers flown in from Cannes which had such a beautiful and unforgettable scent. At the entrance to the elevators that took you upstairs to the roof, we had a little round kiosk and a copy of Henri de Toulouse-Lautrec's "Avril"—the famous painting of the Can-Can dancer. That way, when people arrived, they knew they were in the right place. As if that was not enough of a sign to signify where the party was, they could locate the beautiful mimosa blossoms and follow the scent of their perfume to the event.

The guest list was very impressive as well. We had invited one of the governmental ministers from Germany, Helmut Schmitt. Herr Schmitt was a very wonderful man. He was the Defense Minister, and he was a very erudite talker. He was very well liked in Germany, and he is now the publisher for the Hamburg weekly newspaper *Die Welt*.

He came from Hamburg, and he was very friendly with a friend of mine from Karlsruhe who was his dinner partner. He sat at the dais, along with Francois and Meta, Helmut and Christine, and Ambassador Paul and his wife. Now, Ambassador Paul had only one arm. He lost the other arm in the Second World War. He was the Ambassador to Israel at the time. When he arrived in Israel, people "booed," and when he left they cried.

Just for a little background: when the Olympics occurred in Munich,

Germany in September of 1972, and the terrorists took the Israeli athletes hostage, it was Ambassador Paul who was called upon to negotiate with them for the release of the hostages.

He went there and very bravely proclaimed, "Let the hostages go, and take me instead."

But they didn't. They took the hostages and shot and killed a lot of wonderful Israeli athletes. That was one of the first acts of international terrorism. It was later termed "The Munich Massacre," and it was the worst tragedy in modern Olympic history. It involved the Israeli Special Forces Counter Terrorism unit, and Heritage Rescue. It was a horrific event.

Anyway, that evening's party at The St. Regis Hotel was a very memorable event. It was an elaborate dinner party, and we took over the entire roof. With its fragrant mimosa blossoms arranged all over the place, it was truly a beautiful affair. Since the directors of the firm hosted the party for Francois and Meta, we made certain that we invited a lot of important people, including several key business personnel. Usually you have big bouquets of flowers in the middle of dining room tables, but unfortunately the blossoms of the flowers often obstruct your view across the table. Smitty came up with a clever idea in which the long stemmed flowers were in elongated vases that were so high they were above the guests' sight line while they were seated. I had never seen this done before, and it was a very clever way to arrange the tables. Also, he had gold mesh table cloths placed over solid pink table cloths, to really give the dining room a unique and glamorous look. To top it off, Smitty came up with the idea of printing the evening's menu, on everyone's pink cloth napkin with gold printing. He even included the names of the wines we were drinking.

We had dancing to a big band orchestra, door prizes of fine Steuben glasses, and the nicest Tiffany presents you could think of having. There were about 200 guests that night, and each of them left with gifts. A lot of money was spent on this event, but it was really worthwhile. In fact, that event was talked about for weeks afterward.

That was not the end of the parties for Francois that month. We also celebrated 50 years of Meta and Francois' marriage in Paris at The

Meridian Hotel. And then again in The Brenner's Park Hotel in Baden-Baden, Germany. So that way they had three different celebrations to commemorate their 50th wedding anniversary.

In 1970 I organized a very nice luncheon for my mother's 75th birthday, at The St. Regis Hotel. I invited all of her friends. She was at that time diagnosed with Parkinson's disease. I had collected all of the information on the new drug on the market: L-Dopa. At the time doctors thought that it might be the cure for Parkinson's. I took my information to the doctor who was experimenting with L-Dopa at Presbyterian Hospital. He was quite fascinated with my collected file on L-Dopa, from newspapers and magazines..

I went there with my mother, and I asked him if L-Dopa would be appropriate for my mother. He informed me, "I am not certain whether or not L-Dopa would be right for her. It might make her symptoms even worse."

I gave my mother all of the information, and let her make the decision as to whether or not she wanted to submit to this treatment, which had been approved by the F.D.A. She decided to go ahead with it. So, I checked her in to Lennox Hill Hospital, where the L-Dopa was administered to her in an increasing daily dosage. After about a week, it was decided that it didn't work for her.

At one point she was so agitated that they had to tie her down to her chair, and a special nurse had to be assigned to watch her, because she was determined to get out of the hospital. It was the decision of the doctors at the hospital, that she had to remain there while they administered decreasing dosages of the drug, to wean her off of it.

After that I hired somebody to be with her all of the time. The person whom I hired to watch her during the day, also agreed to go with Mother on a vacation to the Catskill Mountains. There were a lot of other German people there, and she would not feel alone that way.

Mother didn't have a tremor in her hand, she only had a slight staccato walk at this point, and she was beginning to have problems saying things that she wanted to say. Someone explained to me that people who have Parkinson's disease often feel buried alive in their own bodies. They have a thought in their brain that they want to verbalize, but they are somehow unable to transport the thought to their vocal cords.

At the vacation spot she had a very comfortable cottage, which she shared with her hired companion. At one point she wanted to go to the hairdresser. Her companion let her stand on the lawn for a moment, as it had started to rain. During those brief moments when the companion went inside to retrieve an umbrella and raincoat for Mother, she slipped on the wet grass, and broke her hip.

This could have been avoided if the companion had only asked someone to watch her. She took my mother into her room and kept her there for two days, hoping that nothing serious had happened. Since my mother was not a big complainer, she never expressed properly the pain she obviously was experiencing. When things did not seem to be right, the companion finally took her to the hospital, where they indeed discovered a break.

I was furious to find this out. I was in Brussels at the time, and I received a telegram that I was to come home immediately. I took the next plane home. I traveled with our doctor in his car, from Manhattan to the hospital in Monroe, New York, to check out the situation.

There was nothing that I could do for her, except find space for her in the DeWitt Nursing Home. Fortunately it was just two blocks from my apartment.

After all these years in America, she spoke better English than I did. However, once her health started to deteriorate, she suddenly reverted back to speaking only German. The doctor said the anesthesia that was used in the upstate hospital had "thrown her over the brink," and it took a toll on her brain.

From now on I had to hire nurses for her who could speak German with her. For the next and last three years of her life, she was given the best of care. There was not a day that went by that her nurses did not dress her up, and take her out on walking excursions in her wheelchair. They would take her to the stores, or to Central Park, and Mother just loved that. There was nothing else that could be done about her health, but she had a fantastic life within her physical limitations.

Not only did I love her dearly, but the girls whom I hired to take care of her, came to love her just as much. She was treated so well, that her nickname in the nursing home became "The Princess."

My mother had a wonderful disposition, and was generous to these care givers. Finally, one of the nurses said to me, "Please do not give your mother any more cash. She hands out dollars to everyone who is kind to her, and she is going through all of her money." Since she was always a generous woman, as she got older, she only intensified her generosity.

This was a very stressful time for me, knowing that Mother was slowly losing her health. I not only had to take care of her, but my full time job was very demanding as well. It seemed that during this era I was destined to become the caregiver and the problem solver for some of the most important people in my life. However, I was up for the task. As I have done all of my life: whenever I have to tackle problems, I face them head-on and deal with them directly.

Chapter Eight:
A Life in Transition

In late 1973 I had no idea that Francois was very ill. How would I know, since he seemed completely unchanged to me. In fact, right up to the end, my sexual relationship with Francois continued. I used to be able to do a handstand—and sexually that made it very easy for him. I will never forget the last time we did that—it was in a hotel room. There I was, standing on my head, so that he did not have to bend down too far. It was really quite amusing! I never regret anything that I did, because I really loved that man without any hesitations.

We were in Miami at the time and on vacation. We were staying at The Kenilworth Hotel, when Francois became very ill. Both his heart and his lungs were giving out. He was admitted to a special heart hospital there so he could receive the best possible care. I remember sitting there with him, and Meta was with us.

At that point, Meta and I had a pretty good understanding regarding Francois, how to take care of him and how to give him anything and everything he wanted.

He had sent Meta back home to New York to take care of the house and things, while I stayed with him in Miami. When he was there at first, it didn't seem like he was terminally ill. I expected him to get better and leave the hospital. Then his health suddenly took a turn for the worse.

While we were in the hospital, Meta was back in New York City. So, I did my best to keep his spirits up, and to make him laugh.

Then he sent me home to take care of business, and Meta came back to Miami to stay with him. It was sad to see a man with such a sense for business, who was so smart, fading away before my very eyes.

When he wrote some of our business contracts, people who saw them would be so impressed that they would ask, "Which lawyer drew this up for you?"

And, I would say, "No, no, it was just Francois drawing it up off of the top of his head." He was that good at it. He had such a great grasp of the English language, and he had such an incredible business sense, that he was absolutely the top in his field. He was able to draw up these contracts, and negotiate deals with such finesse. He was second to none.

In business people either locked horns with Francois, or they absolutely loved him. For him there was no middle ground: he inspired either extreme love or extreme hate. He was that strong a personality. He had an impeccable style about him, and he was always very beautifully dressed to "the nines"—all of the time. Whenever he entered a room, everyone in it noticed him.

Francois died on January, 12, 1974. Before he died, Meta and I were there at the hospital, and we were both able to say "goodbye" to him.

In the last couple of decades, my life was very structured, business-like and male oriented. I wasn't the kind of woman to took time to cry or let her emotions rule her. However, the pattern of my life was suddenly interrupted by Francois' death. His demise was a terrible shock to me, even though his health had been fading over the last two years. When he was suddenly gone, it took an emotional toll on me. Looking back on this period of time, it took me three years to get over his death. With Francois gone from my life, I also had to confront the decision as to which path I was now going to take.

Meanwhile, my mother was still in the DeWitt nursing home. Just after Francois died, she suddenly took a turn for the worse. I had arranged with the owner of the nursing home, Dr. Lichtman, that under no circumstances would my mother be taken out of there, and taken to a hospital to be submitted to inserted tubes and any other "life saving" devices. He agreed, and wrote in her chart in red ink, "She is not to be transferred to any hospital without my written consent."

Mother had developed pneumonia, and the night nurse who was on duty proclaimed that she should be admitted to the hospital immediately. I went to nursing home, and proceeded to get into a huge argument with Mother's youngest brother, Walter.

He said to me, "What are you doing? She should be in a hospital!"

I argued with him, "To what avail? She will be hooked up to all sorts of machines and tubes, and then she will live through two weeks of absolute misery, I will not permit it!"

I stood my ground, and Uncle Walter later admitted that he was in such shock that he didn't see my logic at the time. Later he fully agreed that I was right in my decision. Oddly enough, Francois had passed away in January of 1974, and Mother died one month later. It was an emotionally draining time for me.

I continued my work at FLS, and slowly pieced together my new life. In 1975 I went on a trip to Europe as part of an organized tour. It was a trip which took me from Scandinavia to Italy. It was a joy from start to finish, and just what I needed at that time in my life. Seeing Norway gave me a much better understanding of Grieg's music and Munch's paintings—including the famous *The Scream*. Both artists knew and portrayed the distinctive and subtle beauty of their wonderful Northern European country. Norway's history and traditions are still preserved in such interesting things such as the 28 remaining stave churches there and the Viking ships museum.

Next on our itinerary was Stockholm, Sweden. I saw the extreme beauty of that historic city of islands and canals. At the Garden Museum I saw an impressive painting by Carl Mille called *The Hand of God*, which I will always remember.

Finland surprised me with it's similarities to Russia. The Art Museum of the Atheneum is in no way comparable with The Hermitage, but its Impressionist painting collection is of great quality, variety, and it is well displayed. Watteau's *The Swing* was one painting which appealed to me particularly.

A short trip took us from the cold of Helsinki to the sunny warmth of Venice, Italy. I have long since lost track off the number of times I have been drawn back to this unique cultural center. Each time I saw something that had been missed before. This trip was more rewarding than ever. I had the good fortune to be the guest of friends who own the Palazzo Barbaro on the Grand Canal. It is one of the few palazzos that has not become a museum. It was a treat to have cocktails under a Tiepolo ceiling in perfect condition, and not feel that I had to leave at closing time. In fact, the Gardener Museum in Boston was built from the blueprints of the Palazzo Barbaro.

Quite by coincidence, the day before, my friend Sandra who was traveling with me, was sketching the beautiful gate at the back entrance of that very Palazzo, when she realized where we were going that evening. The next day she brought Mrs. Curtis, the owner of the Palazzo, the drawing she had done of the gates and presented it to her. Mrs. Curtis was greatly impressed with the sketch.

From Italy, we took a quick trip to Zermatt, Switzerland, which was our last destination. Simply gazing at the majestic Matterhorn in the Alps is a great antidote to almost any problems or troubles that might be in one's mind. How can any of our human activities seem important after a few hours spent at the foot of this awesome phenomenon of nature?

While in the Alps I was fascinated to see a tall, handsome, bearded man in a bright red ski jacket skiing on one of the glaciers.

"How could someone do that?" I wondered to myself. And another one had his very small baby in a nap-sack strapped to him. He too was skiing the glacier!

The next thing that I knew, the man in the red jacket skied over to me, and we started a conversation. I told him that I was fascinated to see him ski in such a beautiful, but potentially dangerous icy setting.

He said to me, "Let's get you some skis, and you come ski with me. You would love it."

"I can't do that," I argued.

"Yes, you can," he insisted.

He was so convincing, but there was absolutely no way I was about to do that, and finish my trip in a leg cast. You really have to be an expert skier to ski a glacier.

Although I opted out of the skiing, the scenery that I saw in the Alps was breathtaking. And, what a wonderful setting to finish off this fantastic trip through Europe. I had a great time, and it gave me the clarity to look at my life and where I was heading.

Looking back on my affair with Francois, it was a wonderful relationship. When he died I felt a great loss and I also felt lost. I had to change my life and my pace, because the pattern was broken. I found it extremely difficult to function, but I managed somehow. I needed the warmth and comfort from another human being to replace my loss.

Francois and I really had something great, aside from the fact that occasionally he drove me insane. First of all was his jealousy.

From time to time, one of the interesting things that Francois would do, was to ask me, "Who of our business associates would you really like to be with, after I am gone?"

And I said, "The only one would be Bob Grosjean." This was because Bob was my type of person, and he was really interesting: good looking, impeccably dressed, excellent manners, and had a fine reputation.

Well, after Francois died, I got together with Bob and we went to Puerto Rico together. We had a wonderful time there, and it was a lovely week. We went swimming and bicycled. We also went to Brussels together. His parents had a big house there, which was of course taken over during the Nazi occupation of Belgium. We went there, and had a wonderful time.

The beautiful white villa his parents lived in was majestic and was located in the most desirable area of Brussels. The backyard butted up against a great park. During the Nazi occupation, the butler made sure that the Nazis didn't get the truly great wines, so he built a wall over the entrance to the wine cellar, which was removed after the war.

I thought everything was going fine between Bob and I. But when he didn't introduce me to his brother, I realized that somehow he viewed me as not being of the social standing of the Grosjean's, because they are one of the first families of Brussels. For whatever reason, I didn't come up to his expectations.

He went alone with his brother to Persia to some huge shindig given by the Shah of Persia, which was given for all members of the Rossiers School in Switzerland. They had attended that school, and the Shah was one of their classmates.

He later told me that this was the most elaborate party that I could imagine, complete with tents, and tables full of food and liquor. The way he described it, it must have been "out of this world."

When he returned he brought me a nice souvenir from it, two little cloisonné dishes with a lid, and another dish without one. But I had wanted so badly to go with him.

"No," he said. "No one is to bring a date, or a fiancé, only wives."

"But I could be your fiancé," I said.

"No, no, no," he claimed. "It can't be done."

I still have the two little cloisonné pieces that were my souvenirs from the party I was not permitted to go to. But, listening to all of Bob's stories of the party's pomp and circumstance, was certainly fun. And I am still of the opinion that we should have let the Shah rule his country in any way he saw fit. Eventually, he would have brought his people into the 21st century.

It is so strange how important things seem at the time, and how unimportant they are now. Time passes, and things take a different perspective.

I had a great time with Bob, but he told me later on that he didn't feel we could be together. He said, "I could not be what you expect me to be, because you would expect me to step into Francois' shoes. And, I couldn't do that. I don't want a child, and you were treated like a child by Francois. And, I couldn't do that with you. I want a woman."

From the beginning, I somehow realized that this affair with Bob was more of a fantasy in my mind than a reality. I guess that I instinctively knew it would never work. There was a big difference between Francois and Bob. Francois had been generous to me—almost to the point of it being a fault. Bob was very frugal on the other hand. He was a lot of fun, but at that point I was still comparing every man I met to Francois. As it turned out, Bob ended up married to a very lovely woman in Australia, and he died there later on.

At the time that Francois died, the employees of FLS Inc. thought that they would now own the business, and that everyone would get a share. That was something that was always hinted about by Francois. And, that was actually his original idea. There were 125 to 135 employees at that point in the office, and the number of high ranking employees who were expecting a piece of the business were around 20.

But Jack and I had already decided that we would not entertain such thoughts, because we could envision nothing but trouble. Everyone who had a share of the business would lose their incentive to work hard, and they would all want to draw a large salary. Nothing would ever get done that way.

From 1961 until Francois' death in 1974, we had to keep up the facade that Francois was the owner of the company, and that everyone would share in the profits after he passed away or retired.

When he died, we had a big meeting, and Jack and I informed everyone of what the true story was. We informed them that we had been the actual owners since 1961. They were in shock to discover this fact, because we had never acted as owners. We behaved like two employees just like everyone else, and we had made the payments and had paid off our bank loans. These were the facts.

I had an arrangement with Jack. If anything was to happen to Jack, or to me, the other party had to pay book value to buy the other one out. As soon as Francois died, I had a big fight with Jack. He wanted to dictate to me, and I set him straight.

I told him, "You cannot replace Francois. Don't even try!" So we had a big fight over this.

We were to have a meeting with all of our suppliers and all of our own people in Litchfield, Arizona. Smitty and I went on Thanksgiving week of 1976, and made all of the arrangements.

The meeting in Litchfield took place the following May. At the meeting Jack became a prima donna. He was not speaking to some people, and then I had to jump in and be the pacifier. He called me at 5:00 a.m. one morning in Litchfield and argued with me. I had to show up in the morning for coffee, and I had to pretend to everyone that everything was fine and wonderful.

I was very happy when all the events in Litchfield finished with tennis and golf, and all of the activities. Finally, all of our business associates left for their respective homes. I breathed a sigh of relief that nothing happened as a consequence of Jack's behavior, and everyone went home.

After that, Jack went on to spend most of the time in his newly acquired condominium in Palm Beach, Florida. Whereas I had to head the New York office, and to deal with the employees and try to smooth out the rough edges that Jack had created.

In September 1976, I decided to study for my Bachelor's degree at Fordham University. At the time, Fordham offered a course which they called "Life Experience." By enrolling in this course, I could earn up to 40 credits for successfully completing this program. As part of the requirements, you had to spell out what you considered you main life experiences and your accomplishments. We had a fine instructor for this course.

As students of this course, we all had to prove that our life experiences gave us a proficiency in several fields of study, which brought us up to university level. We had to write essays, and complete reports which proved that we had a grasp of several different skills.

There was also a non-credit course in which we had to attend in which we learned how to study again. Most of us in that Life Experience course were people who had foregone their formal educations because we had gone directly into the business world. Or others, for one reason or another, had attended college but were forced to quit without earning their degrees.

In this "studying" course we had to learn how to write papers, and there was an area in which we could use the school's typewriters. When I had originally gone to school, we didn't have typewriters to work on. We were not permitted to use them. Our schoolwork all had to be completed in our own handwriting. And, that handwriting had to be very legible and precise. People laugh when I tell them this nowadays. In fact, during my first school years, all of our work was done in chalk on a small blackboard. I remember crying on one occasion, when my teacher had not liked what I had written, and took a damp sponge to my blackboard and made me start all over again.

Attending Fordham University five decades later was a totally different experience. I remember the first time that I heard of the concept of cutting and pasting a document together. In those days, before computers came along, you could take a pair of scissors and cut one paragraph from one page, and paste it onto another one, then photocopy them onto a single sheet of paper as part of your editing. This was the pre-computer way of "cutting and pasting"—as it was done with actual scissors and paste.

In our "studying" class, they not only taught us how to study, but where to go to find research material as well. We had a counselor whom we could go to and ask questions if we got stuck on something. She would then guide us: "Oh you can go here for that," or, "You can find that over there." There was a very specific outline as to what you had to produce.

We had to write it, produce it, and document it. It was just like a thesis. This "Life Experience" degree was not given on a silver platter. It was especially hard because we really had to look back at our lives again, and draw strong conclusions. It was really a case of reliving our past experiences. In many ways it was a really wonderful thing to have been able to do.

In one of the classes there was a lovely girl from Iceland. She was a stewardess. It seemed like she was never there, because she was so busy flying around the world. She made up for it with all of the work that she put into her project. And another student who never seemed to be present was a 19-year-old. He never showed up either, so the professor did not let him pass. I was glad about that.

The other students all took the class very seriously. They did their essays on time, they were there on time, and they did the work. It was the older people who were there who really wanted to do the work, as that's what they came there for.

I sat up one night in the kitchen until 4:00 in the morning, typing up the pieces that I had to turn in the next morning. But, I did it. It was hard work, but it was a very happy time for me.

For my final presentation for the "Life Experience" class, I had to write a thesis explaining all of the things that I had learned on my own unique path in life. I also had to explain my purpose for returning to school. Part of what I wrote included:

By any criteria, I have achieved more than moderate success in business, and obviously, I have learned much in the three decades that marked my progress from the status of immigrant to the comforts and position held today. But no amount of on-the-job training and trial-and-error learning can take the place of formal, academic study. No material wealth can satisfy the hunger for knowledge.

As part of the class requirements, someone I knew in a business capacity had to read my "Life Experience" essay and presentation and confirm that it was all accurate and true. To do this for me, I chose our employee and good friend, Lindley M. Smith, also known as "Smitty." In his November 7, 1977 letter to my Fordham instructor, Smitty graciously wrote:

For 28 years I have worked more closely with Miss Mueller and the late Mr. Schwarz than any other member of our executive staff…I hasten to confirm that all statements made by Miss Mueller in her essay are true and correct…[however] she is guilty of gross understatement of her role in the management, development and success of Francois L. Schwarz, Inc. Miss Mueller was Francois' alter ego, and much of the credit heaped upon him by associates, competitors and top executives of large manufacturing firms is rightfully hers.

It was in this "Life Experience" course of classes that I first met my famous, wonderful friend, Raymond Griffis. Part of our course of studies included a painting class, and that's where I first met him. Raymond helped me to put my easel in a good position, as well as arranging the still life we both had to paint. As I watched him arrange the still life, I thought to myself, "That is exactly how I would have done it." It was neat, attractive, orderly, and pleasant to look at.

I was immediately impressed with him. He was tall, with thick dark hair, and he had a warm and pleasant smile.

At one point, he asked me, "What is the building down there?"

At the time we were standing in the Fordham University building, facing the Opera House at Lincoln Center. For me, it was unthinkable that anyone could ask a question about the Metropolitan Opera House, which was so famous.

So I asked him, "Are you pulling my leg?"

And, he was very nice, and said, "No, not at all. It is only my second day in New York."

At that point I offered my services as his tour guide to show him my beloved New York City. That was the beginning of a great friendship.

He invited me to lunch the next day, and thought that this little old gal in the very everyday looking clothes had probably scrounged her last pennies together to pay the tuition for the university. At school I didn't wear any jewelry, and wore little make-up, so I am certain that he felt sorry for me, and just wanted to be nice to me.

One of the first times we went out together was to listen to a concert at the Frick Museum. We met each other there. He was late, and the rotunda was closed, so we had to sit in the Frick atrium to listen to the music. It was a wonderful experience. We met several times thereafter for lunch, or for a drink at the Tavern on the Green, which was close to Fordham.

I will never forget, about six months later, when he came to my apartment to go to the Frick Museum where I invited him to the Fellows of the Frick Gala Dance. When I opened my front door and he saw me all dressed up, and saw my apartment, his opinion instantly changed. The amazed look on his face told me that he was surprised to see that I was not the simple little sparrow he expected to meet him at the door.

Whether Raymond was "the flint" or "the iron" is not important. The wonderful thing is that we did find each other and a cascade of colorful sparks has followed since our first encounter. The typical experience in "serendipity" is probably the collector who finds a Stradivarius violin in an unlikely pawn shop. The collector is looking for something of value, but I found something upon which no value can be placed. Who can appraise a beautiful human relationship?

Raymond was a personable young man, and I was strangely drawn to him. The idea of spending time with him was very appealing to me. One day, when he asked me to join him for lunch at Cleo's, I jumped at the chance. On the way to the restaurant, his many little acts of kindness stirred emotions in me, which I didn't know I had, or at least thought to be dead. I enjoyed his masculine protectiveness when we were crossing the street, holding my arm or hand, and generally treating me with the tenderness usually reserved for a teenaged girlfriend. I felt so young and alive in his company.

At the restaurant that day, he told me his life story. I was not prepared for such revealing confidences, but was flattered by the complete trust he had in me. We repeated our lunches together each Thursday. I soon found myself looking forward to that day with such excitement that it scared me. We both were aware that we cared for each other very much. Emotions run high!

What was I going to do with these feelings I was now having? I knew that I had to make up my mind as to exactly what I wanted from this relationship with Raymond. Later, when I took inventory of the situation, and I became frightened.

I mentally made a list. First, on the negative side:

1.

I was old enough to be Raymond's mother.

2.

He had admitted homosexual experiences.

3.

My friends and peers would certainly be shocked and tell me I am a damned fool.

4.

Raymond's friends would react in the same way to him.

Second, on the positive side:

1.

We were attracted to each other, without a doubt, and—why avoid the word—we were in "love."

2.

In some way, which neither of us understood, our "normal" feelings for each other took precedence over his homosexual tendencies.

Why was I, in advanced middle age, having an experience for the first time that is commonplace to the vast majority of girls in their teens?

I thought to myself, "I should have met Raymond in Germany. I should have known the excitement of being tossed in the air and caught by strong arms and pressed against a manly chest, with my heart beating wildly and my face snuggled under his chin. And all of this in the open for the world to see, and perhaps smile about.

Why did I not know the wonders of young love? Was it because Mr. Hitler cast a sinister shadow on all frivolities? Was I frigid because of the incomprehensible time in history that substituted "hate" for "love?" I guess I will never know for sure. I made my decision to live for today, for this hour, for this minute.

Childlike thoughts of Cinderella often came to my mind. On one occasion, we were out to dinner, and I had to come home to prepare to leave town for a business trip to Phoenix. When I got home, it was 2:00 a.m.—which would have be ruin for Cinderella. However, hearing Raymond's voice on the phone at 4:25 a.m., just to let me know that he was thinking of me, and wishing me "Bon Voyage," made my Cinderella dream worthwhile!

Meanwhile, at that point, I was taking a biology course. The instructor was a doctor at Mt. Sinai Medical Center.

He said to me, "Look, you don't want to become a doctor. You don't want to be a chemist or anything like that, why don't I tell you something about your body? You should know how your body functions, what it's supposed to do, and what it is not supposed to do."

It was really a fantastic class. He taught us everything everyone should know about a body, and I have found that much of the information he taught us has been useful in some other form, shape or manner. It is wonderful to know how your own body works.

While I continued to work in the New York office, Jack chose to be in his condominium in Palm Beach. On occasion he would come to the

Tampa office of our company. However, things were not going well down there. Jack had a great flair for antagonizing and irritating everyone. If he was mad or upset with someone, and at the office that person said "good morning" or "hello" to him, he would just ignore it.

Another way that he would show his displeasure to anyone who worked for us, was by not signing their paychecks. Since Jack and I were equal owners in the company, the payroll checks—and every check for that matter—had to be signed by both of us. This was a protocol that dated back to when Francois was the sole owner of the company.

When it came to my attention that Jack was using this ploy on one of our Tampa employees, I said to him, "What are you trying to do? Our greatest assets are our people." We had no machinery, no samples, no manufactured "product," we had only our employees.

His reply to me was, "I don't care, I am not signing it."

He left me in a position where I had to negotiate with him to get him to do things. Here I was being blackmailed by my own business partner.

When Jack suddenly became extremely sick he said to me, "I am very grateful for all that you do and have done." He would have never said anything like that to me if he were healthy. That's when I knew that he knew he was really sick.

As Jack's illness progressed, I realized that our business had to all be in order, in the inevitability of his death. I called people for a 9:00 a.m. meeting at the airport hotel in Tampa. It lasted until 6:00 p.m. with only a half hour break to grab a sandwich and a cup of coffee.

I requested in the meeting that everyone who had problems with Jack, write it in a letter to me, which I would keep. However I would only produce it if I should get into a lawsuit with Jack. I received two and three page letters from all of the men who were there, with the exception of one. The one who did not promise that he would write me a letter, was the same person who once wrote a letter of complaint to Francois about Jack. Francois in turn showed the letter to Jack. So, you can say that he felt like, "The burned child who fears not only the fire, but the water as well." So, I understood his behavior.

At a time when everyone at the company seemed to be taking sides and shifting loyalties, I always knew that I could count on Smitty. In a personal note to me dated January 28, 1979, he wrote:

I feel the need to write two letters; one for "on the record" and one that is more personal. I meant what I said in the letter addressed to you at the office, but couldn't single you out in it as a very special friend, whose loyalty, understanding and Integrity sets you apart in my memory of the past 28 years. I know that only you can understand the continued affection and respect I feel for Francois. And I believe you know that I feel no resentment toward either you or Jack. Oddly as it might sound to some, I'm glad for both of you. God knows you worked hard, contributed much of your lives, and earned the right to ownership. Retired I am, but not yet senile or dead, and I hope you will always think of me as a friend who is ready to be helpful in any way…With love, Smitty.

At the meeting we had agreed that all employees should not contact Jack directly, but that they should come to me instead, and that I would deal with Jack. That way, many potential collisions could be avoided. One young man came to me when it was all over and said, "In the morning, I thought that I was going to 'jump ship.' But now, after today's meeting, I feel that I want to stay here and do the best I can." This was very encouraging for me to hear.

The unfortunate situation was that Jack and I had a 50/50 partnership, and that is something that nobody should have. Someone should have 51 and someone should have 49. Hindsight is always 20/20 vision. Obviously, I had several new challenges ahead of me.

Chapter Nine
New Adventures

In May of 1979, Raymond and I graduated together from Fordham University with Liberal Arts degrees. I decided to offer Raymond a job at FLS as my assistant. His first job was to produce our 1980 calendar and help me wherever it was necessary.

At this point I was such good friends with Raymond that I would tell him of some of my business frustrations. One of my prime irritations was Jack and having to deal with him.

I said to Raymond, "I think he must be dying. He is suddenly acting very nice to me."

Raymond replied, "I can tell you when he is going to die, I am that certain of it."

He predicted the date Jack would die, and he was correct: February 21, 1980.

After Jack died, I had to settle with his estate for his half ownership of the company. That was actually no problem because our standing agreement stated that either of us could buy the other one out at the "book" value of the company.

However, from Francois' death until Jack's death, it was a very rough time for me. I ran the company myself, and that was quite difficult.

When Francois was alive he always provided a buffer zone for me. I was very secure in my position within the company, as was Jack.

A woman in an executive position of power in those days was not the norm, and definitely not in our kind of business. A secretary?

"Yes." A receptionist? "Yes." But, the owner of a corporation? "No." It was a tough time to always be between two roles: being a lady, and being a boss, without showing preference.

It was difficult to be appreciated and to be accepted. It was not an easy time, yet I still had to produce. People had to see that I was producing, and they had to respect me for that. When I went to hire employees, I always had to ask, "Can you work for a woman? Do you have any problems with that? Let's deal with this right now. Because if you do, we won't get along together, because I will be your boss."

This would also be a problem with some of our customers. Routinely, I would sign any correspondence "R. Mueller." Then they would call and want to speak to "Mr. Mueller." I would say them, "There is no 'Mr. Mueller.' I am 'R. Mueller.' And, I am not changing my sex for you. So, you have to deal with me 'as is.' Sorry."

We did it all very nicely, and ultimately it came out very well. But, it was very often very hard. It was especially difficult to get things done in an authoritative way. Some of the various departments—the shipping department, or the accounting department, or whoever it was, might think, "Who is she? She is just a woman." They would like to dismiss you. They were not trained in a way that could look beyond my gender. Whether they liked it or not, they had to deal with me as an authority figure. I would tell them, "This was the way it was going to be from now on. You had better change your attitude."

Finally, in the end it was okay. But, in the beginning it was very tough for me. After Jack's death I continued to run the company myself.

During this era I sold the "embassy supplying" part of the business for one dollar, to the woman who worked with me. Her name was Ann Metz. For a long time we had made a nice profit with this line of business. But in time I found that I had enough demands running the military end of the business. Ann opened up an office on Broadway, and for several years made a nice business out of it. For a long time she would stay in touch and write me about how wonderful the business was, and how she was doing.

Around this same time, I hired a new president for my company. His name was Charlie Bridges, and he had previously worked for Scott Paper. Charlie was a good golfer, and I found people asking me, "Did you hire him so you could improve your golf game?"

In the beginning of our working relationship, Charlie was willing to follow my advice when making business decisions. Then he suddenly decided that he wanted to move down to Tampa to work out of that office. Slowly he showed me that he in fact wanted to control everything.

Raymond went down to Tampa with me. The Tampa office was in a rental space at the time. I told Raymond that I wanted to move our office to a particular brick building in the industrial park. So Raymond investigated it, and found that it was for sale. So, I bought it, and I created a special company for that purpose, Mueller Realty. After Raymond designed the interior, including the computer room, elevator situation, and other important items, we moved into that space.

I also purchased a condominium in Innesbrook, Florida, because I decided that I wanted to spend more time in the Tampa office.

Now that I owned the brick building which Raymond had redesigned and furnished to meet our needs, I in turn rented the space to FLS, Inc.

I continued to run the company for a couple of years while Charlie was the president. But, after a while, I saw no reason to be involved in the daily trials and tribulations of running the company. Besides, Charlie was constantly trying to get more and more power away from me.

Francois used to say to me, "Don't become the richest woman in the cemetery. Know when to close up and say, 'Goodbye.'"

He had a lot of good advice for me. He would tell me, "Don't stay in the business so long that you are there to the point where all of your business contacts are being let go and replaced by younger ones. Leave the business when everyone can still say, 'Why are you leaving the business so soon? You could stay with us for a long time!'"

Also Francois would say to me, "If you sell your business and you get a great deal of money, be careful. People will come to you with all sorts of schemes and ideas. Don't fall into that trap and take good money, and invest it in a business where you have to work twice as hard just to not lose it. If you do, you will just lose all of your hard earned money. Don't do that. Don't be so greedy. Relax, let somebody else work for the money. Have somebody else invest it. Relax and enjoy it."

My principals wanted to know, "Who will be your successor?"

At first Raymond expressed interest in continuing to run the company with Charlie. However, while Raymond began to negotiate with Charlie, he realized what a headache it would be. I was very happy that it did not work out because now my friend Raymond could follow his true calling. He had a chance to earn two Masters degrees, which would permit him to work in an area in which he would not only be competent, but it was also his great love: art and design.

Not too many people have that luxury and enjoy their work. If you can find that situation, it is not a chore, but a pleasant situation to wake up every morning, knowing that the day holds for you a career that you really love.

In 1986 when I sold the company to Charlie, the billing that year was for over $180 million. We agreed on a settlement, and it all seemed fine. Everything seemed to be right on track.

But, whenever I asked Charlie Bridges for the "numbers" as to our expenses and profitability margin, I never received a straight answer. He had an accounting firm which supplied us with the balance sheets. However, when I saw these balance sheets, I had a sneaking suspicion that they had somehow "cooked the books."

Charlie very skillfully kept me away from talking directly with the man who ran our computers. That way I knew that I was not getting a true picture of the situation. The payments that I received were so much smaller than what I knew they should be, that I had to start a lawsuit against the company.

My accountant went to the bank and the bank would not let him see the memorandums in the files. But he advised the bank officials that he would subpoena them unless they showed them to him right then and there. They had no choice but to agreed to this. When the accountant got hold of the files, and he saw a memorandum from one of the officers of the bank. Apparently Charlie Bridges tried to take out a bank loan. However, analyzing the figures, the bank said to Charlie, "You don't have enough collateral to secure this loan." Charlie told him, "If I give you the right numbers, I will have to pay Miss Mueller a lot of money." There it was in black & white.

My accountant and my lawyer instantly realized that someone had indeed "cooked the books" to reflect the numbers that Charlie wanted everyone to see. That was all the evidence they needed to unravel this mystery.

My lawyer told me that I could put Charlie's accountant and lawyer both behind bars if I wanted to do so, and have them barred from ever working in their respective fields again. But I didn't want to do that because they had families, and why deprive the lawyer or the accountant of their livelihood?

I let them know that I could have prosecuted both of them. I told them that I was horrified that they would do such a thing, and for such a small amount of money. My lawyer insisted that they both be required to pay a fine to the company. And they received a warning that we had documented everything they did, and if they were ever caught doing anything illegal again, we would make these documents public.

Both of these men were outside workers whom Charlie had hired. They were Charlie's accountant and Charlie's lawyer.

I ended up having to sue Charlie Bridges for the money. The lawsuit ended up being very costly for me. I sued him for delivering a crooked balance sheet, and payment that was due to me. I sued to make sure that he corrected this attempted theft.

It was legally awarded to me with no questions asked. They had to give it to me. And they knew that if it wasn't paid back, I would have taken further legal action which would have proven devastating to them. I would have them indicted.

In my mind, justice came in the corrected payment. I just wanted what they owed me, nothing more. It amounted to hundreds of thousands of dollars that were at stake.

I felt that now was the time that I could do all of the traveling that I had always wanted to do, but never seemed to have the time for. And, since Raymond was free of the company as well, he was available to accompany me.

I once read an article in *Reader's Digest* magazine, which was based on a true story. It concerned a blind man, and the woman who loved him. The man was dependant upon this woman for everything, and loved her for her kindness towards him. One day a doctor told the blind man that there was a way of restoring his sight to him. He was so excited about the prospect of finally being able to see the woman who loved him so much, and that he agreed to the operation. But, the woman was horrified at the prospect of him finally seeing her with his own eyes. She considered herself to be quite unattractive, and was certain that once the man laid eyes on her, that would be the end of their marriage. In the story, the man's eyesight was indeed restored, but instead of seeing his wife like other people saw her, in his eyes he saw only the beauty of her goodness, and the love she had for him. In his eyes she was beautiful, and because of the love she felt for him. In fact, he saw her as being even more beautiful than she was.

This story reminded me of my relationship with Raymond. Like the blind man gaining his sight, I feared that once FLS, Inc. was gone, Raymond would only see our two decade age difference, and that would be the end of it. I wanted to make sure that Raymond saw me for the person I was, and not for how much older I was than him. Somehow, just like the charming story I had read in *Reader's Digest*, my friendship and relationship with Raymond only continued to grow and blossom once FLS, Inc. was no longer part of my life.

From that point onward we have remained the closest of friends, who are also wonderful travel partners. I was with Raymond in Germany on one occasion, and we were driving a car on the Autobahn. For anyone who isn't familiar with Germany's most famous freeway, it is known for not having a speed limit at all. You can drive as fast as you want, as long as you drive safely.

I was in the car with Raymond, and all of the other cars were whizzing by at top speeds. We discovered that we had gone too far in one direction. The next thing I knew, he turned into the island that was between the lanes, and pulled a "U" turn in the opposite direction. I couldn't believe he had done that! That is not something you do on the Autobahn!

I thought I would die! I felt my heart stand still.

I said to him, "What do you think you are doing? Can you imagine what the fee would be if the police saw you doing that?"

He still tells the story about how he almost made my heart stop on the Autobahn!

Meanwhile Raymond and I were visiting the sites of the concentration camps in Germany. I had never been to them before, partially because I was terrified of seeing them. I was astonished that Raymond knew exactly the way to get there. Yet, he had never been to these places in this lifetime.

I was trying to tell him what turns to make to get to the concentration camp, and he said to me, "You don't have to tell me. I know exactly where it is."

I said, "How is that possible? You have never been here before in your life!"

He explained to me that he had a feeling that he had been there in a former life. His birth date aligns with the operation of the concentration camps. It is not impossible to believe that he was a reincarnated victim of someone who had been killed in one of the death camps.

Raymond was so accurate at the way in which we arrived right there at the concentration camp it astonished me. I had told him to make a turn in the opposite direction, and he said to me, "No, no, no, trust me. I know precisely where it is located."

It was hauntingly odd.

The concentration camp which we visited was near Munich, in Dachau.

Those who did know what was going on with the concentration camps, pretended that they knew nothing, for their own safety. The general public heard rumors, but most of them just shook their heads and said, "Oh, no. That couldn't really happen."

To see the concentration camp in person is very devastating. When you see films like

Schindler's List, which are about what was done there, and then you see with your own eyes the place where these horrible things took place, it is terrifying.

It is unbelievable to stand there in the walls of these places and see how one group of people literally exterminated another group of people. It was just overwhelming to witness.

And then there were sadistic doctors who performed gruesome experiments on the people. It was horrifying to see where these events took place.

The Holocaust Museum and Jewish Museums have recorded all sorts of stories about what people went through during the war. It is rather unbelievable to hear these accounts. History is full of stories about one group of people doing awful things to each other. But, bar none, what the Nazis did during their reign of terror is one of the worst accounts ever recorded.

So many German people tried to come to the United States during the Third Reich. However, most of them were not allowed to emigrate here. You had to have the right visa, and there were quota systems back then to restrict an overflow of immigrants to be allowed in the country, or I am sure that millions would have made the journey. Following the war, Germany was left devastated—both physically and economically. One of the ways that the United States tried to help Germany to get back on its feet was the Marshall Plan.

Dr. Alex Möeller, General Director of the Karlsruher Lebensversicherung, who was at one time the Minister of Finances for Germany, was a good friend of mine. He asked me to accompany him as his guest to a luncheon given by General McCloy, who was the architect of the Marshall Plan.

The luncheon was given at the River Club in New York City. Alex was a very interesting person. He was part of the Weimar Republic and was imprisoned by the Germans for his activities. He rebuilt his career after the war. He was a very prolific writer, and he wrote several books about his life and his personal adventures. One of the books he wrote was entitled, *General Director/Genosse*.

Möeller came to that luncheon hosted by McCloy, where he handed a check from the Singer Sewing Machine Company in Germany to McCloy for the amount of $200,000. It was very heartwarming to hear him at that luncheon as McCloy stood up and told us, "We Germans are so appreciative of America's Marshall Plan, and what it did for us. As a small token of our appreciation for what your country has done for Germany and the German people, here is a small repayment of $200,000 towards the American goodwill."

It was very wonderful to be in that room and to see and hear all of the signs of true goodwill and the great diplomatic relationship between Germany and the United States. Now, from the perspective of 2009, I wish that these two countries would come back to this kind of understanding for each other.

In the summer of 1985 I went down to Key West with two friends: Willi and Dory. Willi Völler was a very good friend of mine. He worked for Tiffany & Company, and he started the Elsa Peretti counter for them. The first sale he made of the Elsa Peretti line, was her "Diamonds By The Yard," and I bought them, in the gold and diamond chain. He was also the front man on the main floor, and he loved what he was doing, and he charmed all of the people to whom he sold items. He was even sent to Germany to start up the Tiffany stores in Munich, Frankfurt, and Berlin. He stayed with Tiffany's until he retired.

On his vacation, I said to him, "We are going to Key West." He hadn't been there, so we went down with Dory, a good young friend of mine, to explore. We had a lovely time. One day I said to Dory, "Let's go to the museum, and see what's there."

Well, Willi didn't want to come to the museum, so we went alone. And what did we find? An explorer named Mel Fisher had just come into the museum, and we met him and had our picture taken with him. Mel Fisher was a dreamer and a wonderful person who went out to sea in search of treasure from the shipwrecked Spanish galleons, which had sunk with over $300 million in gold, silver, and emeralds. It took him 16 years of searching. But in 1985, Fisher found the remains of the Atocha, which sank in 1622 due to a hurricane, just off the shore of Key West.

We proceeded in going through the museum with him, and he showed us all of the beautiful pieces of jewelry which he found there, and brought out of the sea. Although he did retrieve over $300 million in treasure it was not without tragedy, because he lost his son in a diving accident down there. And since that time, there wasn't anything so great in his private life. But he fulfilled his long time dream of going after the bounty that was deep in the water. It was quite something, to see all of the coins and jewelry intended for Queen Isabella which he had brought up from the sea. We had a great time hearing all of Fisher's tales. Mel had gone bankrupt a couple of times before discovering this ship. However, his problems only escalated afterward. He was hit with several lawsuits from the state of Florida, which wanted part of his finds. Then to top it off, his wife sued him for divorce, which cost him a lot of his money. It was as though the treasure was cursed.

When we arrived at the museum, in the entrance hall was a display of many of the recovered silver coins. They were arranged in a pile, which was visible under a protective mesh net. On a subsequent visit, I found that the museum has lost a lot of its charm and flavor. The coins are no longer there. When Mel was still alive, the exhibit seemed alive. After his death, it seems that his joyous sense of adventure is missing.

Willi told me a story about the ship that I originally taken to American in 1940, the S.S. Lancaster. It had been used during the war, and unfortunately had struck a mine, and sunk with 4,000 refugees on board. Hearing this made me realize how lucky I had been all those years ago. Willi also informed me that he was supposed to be on that ship during its fatal voyage. However, he was not properly dressed, and was held up by the German authorities, and missed the ship. That mishap ended up saving his life!

It was through my friend Willi Völler, that I met and became friends with famed actress Hedy Lamarr. Hedy was the film star who was seen naked in *Ecstasy* in the 1930's. Her appearance in this film at the time was considered risqué. Of course by today's film standards this was nothing shocking. We see much more today.

Willi was funny, and a really good looking guy. I was with him once on vacation. We went to Qui si Sana Hotel in Italy. At the time I was feuding with Francois a little bit. I went out with Willi for the evening. As I left the hotel, I told the concierge, "There might be a phone call for me. And if the person asks where I have gone and what I am doing, would you tell the person that I went with an elderly lady for tea? And, for doing that, here's $20.00."

Naturally, when I handed him the $20.00, he said, "Absolutely. No question."

So, Willi and I went out sightseeing. We went to the Upper Capri. We got back to the hotel, and of course there were messages from Francois. He was so jealous that it was ridiculous. He wanted to know what I was doing every second of the day.

Willi was not at all interested in having sex with women. He was gay, except when it came to Hedy. I don't know about bisexuality personally, but it seemed to work for Willi. He claimed that he had a great sexual relationship with Hedy, but according to him, marriage was totally out of the question.

One day, when I was at The Plaza Hotel with Hedy, waiting for Willi to join us, the violinist who was playing in Palm Court along with a pianist, recognized her. He came over to our table and asked for an autograph, which she happily gave to him. Then he told us that he was in the orchestra, playing the soundtrack music to accompany the film *Ecstasy*—which had made her an international star. According to him, during the recording session, the musicians seemed to have trouble concentrating on their instruments. Finally, the conductor stopped everyone from playing and said, "Look at the film, and afterwards we will play the music and you can give me your undivided attention." And that's exactly what they did.

Hedy was more than just an actress. She actually had the original idea for what turned out to be the beginnings of the wireless telephones. She always said to me, "Oh, they stole my invention. I had that idea first, and nobody believed me."

Now, years later, it turns out that she was right. One of the New York newspapers ran an article which gave her credit on the subject, and confirmed that she was indeed the first. She and a friend of hers had actually come up with the idea of sending a signal to what we now know as "cellular" or "handy" phones.

Hedy was a very outgoing person throughout her life. However, she had reached a certain age when she did not want to be seen in public any longer. She had a lot of face lifts, hand lifts, and all sorts of procedures to prolong her beauty.

In fact, she was one of the first of the famous actresses in Hollywood to prescribe to all sorts of plastic surgery. She was nipped and tucked, but her beautiful face was never severely altered. And, she would always get her plastic surgery done for free, because she was Hedy Lamarr. All of the doctors were thrilled to be able to say, "I worked on Hedy Lamarr." At the height of her fame, Hedy was a true "sexpot."

Unfortunately, at the end of her life, she decided that age had caught up with her, and she wanted people to remember her as a beauty queen. After that she would only go into public with huge sunglasses on, so that she could travel incognito. She decided that she would rather people remembered her the way she looked in her films like *Samson and Delilah* and *Ecstasy*. This way, she could maintain her "legend" status.

At one point, Hedy received an offer to do a high-profile TV project in her native city of Vienna, Austria. She was offered the task of hostessing a special broadcast in which she would give a guided tour of Schöenbrun, and other Austrian castles, like Jackie Kennedy did on television at the White House in the 1960s.

I remember sitting with Hedy one day, and she said to me, "What am I going to do? They offered me a million dollars."

I said to her, "Do it! What are you crazy? You are always complaining that you don't have anything. A million dollars will go a long way."

She said, "No, I think I will hold out for two million."

I said, "Two million? Hedy really, a million dollars is quite impressive."

I think that deep down inside she just really didn't want to do it at all, and that was just her way of talking herself out of it. She didn't want her "present-day" face to be shown on television. She made it absolutely impossible for the producers to come to an agreement. She was never seen in public after a certain time in her career.

Naturally, one of the biggest scandals that occurred in her career came in 1991 when she was charged with shoplifting at one of the department stores in Florida. On one occasion I asked her, "Hedy, what was the truth about that?"

She said, "I don't know what got into me. But I got tired of waiting for someone to ring up my items at a cash register. Then I thought to myself, 'Throughout my entire life people have taken things from me.' They took blouses from me at the studio, and autograph seekers have taken things from me. Everyone seems to wants a souvenir from me. Why can't I take something for a change?" With that logic, she stuck a couple of lipsticks and some other insignificant items into her purse.

I thought to myself, "She's got the mind of a child sometimes." She was very simple in the way she deduced certain things. In her mind that made perfect sense. She didn't think of the consequences, she just acted on her own whim.

Well, that cost her dearly. She was accused and found guilty of shoplifting. That turned out to be a really careless move on her part. She was surprised that everyone made such a fuss over this event. Just because someone else has taken things of yours, doesn't mean that you get to turn around and steal someone else's belongings. And, in this case it was the department store's merchandise that she had stuck in her pocketbook. Life does not work that way. The items which she stole were just inexpensive items. Just like they later did with Winona Ryder, back then the press crucified Hedy as well.

Hedy had money problems all the time I knew her. The money she made from the studios was not invested well. She went through life like a child who had never grown up. Reality was really something that she could not cope with. She was absolutely always in some dilemma or another. She was living in The Blackstone Hotel in New York City at that time.

At one point she said to Willi, "Come and get all of my jewelry, and take it away from here. I don't feel that it is safe here."

He came and got the jewelry that was left at that point. Then he rented a safe deposit box, and put all of her jewelry in it. But, he had to pay for it. Hedy certainly wasn't going to pay for it.

He told me at one point, "I feel very uncomfortable about this. I am the only one with access to her jewelry. If anything happens to her, everyone will come to me and claim that I stole it. I don't want to find myself in that position."

I said to him, "You shouldn't have to take care of her jewelry for her. That is crazy, and it should be her responsibility, not yours. Take it back to her and make arrangements so that it can be safe under her control. It is not for you to deal with."

Well, he did that, and then while it was back in her possession most of the jewelry somehow disappeared. I have no idea what had happened to it. Then Willi really felt terrible about it.

Hedy was supposed to marry my friend Willi. In fact there was mention in the press which reported that Willi was set to become her "Husband Number Seven." He would jokingly say to me, "Look at what they have promoted me to."

I said to him, "Why don't you marry her?"

And he said, "No, that would never do. If I were to marry Hedy, I would be her slave. She would make me her slave for sure, and I would have to cook for her, and do everything. And, that I don't want. I would rather she come and visit me every once in a while and have a great time. I would even dye her hair for her. But, I can't have her on a permanent basis, she would drive me nuts. She stays up watching movies until four o'clock in the morning, and then she sleeps until four in the afternoon. I have to go to work, she does not. She has no concept of an organized routine."

Hedy was not an efficient and orderly housekeeper, or for organizing her life for that matter. She couldn't seem to manage her own life at all. It is a shame to think that in 1950 she had four million dollars, and she was mismanaged by her managers. Somehow her fortune dissipated, like trying to hold water in her hands. Hedy, trusting soul that she was, was left penniless at the end. It is really amazing when you see her films and you see how truly beautiful and lovely she was back then. However, she eventually lost control of her own life. It was a sad story about Hedy.

Whenever the three of us were together—Hedy, Willi and I—we had a great time. We were just like brothers and sisters. Unfortunately, Willi died much too early.

Willi's nephew was the famous soccer player, Rudy Völler, who was known all over the world. I remember taking Rudy to the museum, and he just loved it. We went together to the Trustee's dining room at the Metropolitan Museum of Art and had a wonderful lunch there.

However, I was very disappointed in Rudy. He was in training in Miami, and Willi was in New York where he was deathly sick at the time, dying of cancer. He would have loved to have had a visit from his nephew Rudy. However, Rudy never came to visit his uncle.

I even telephoned Rudy personally and begged him to come and visit.

He said to me, "I will see what I can do." But he didn't come. I was so disappointed in him for that. Willi had gone out of his way to show Rudy a good time when he was visiting New York. And this stinker couldn't take the time to fly up from Miami to see his uncle who was on his deathbed and loved him so dearly. It was awful. It still hurts me to tell this story.

I will never forget telling Willi, "He is not coming. He can't seem to get away."

It is so painful to see that kind of disappointment in someone's eyes.

After Hedy's death, her son Tony produced a 2004 documentary film about his famous mother, entitled *Calling Hedy Lamarr*. However, in my opinion it is not as good as it could have been. It admittedly has some great footage of Hedy, looking absolutely glamorous. She was the most beautiful person in the world, but the film does talk about that a bit.

Anthony, who was born in 1947, is her son from her third husband, John Loder. Unfortunately, Tony used this film project to promote himself more than he produced it as a tribute to his famous mother. He makes believe that the project is about Hedy, but it is really all about promoting him. It is an ode to him, and he may as well have entitled it, *I Want to Be a Producer*. He even goes so far as to sing a song called, "I Want to Be a Producer," several times in the film.

The documentary, *Calling Hedy Lamarr* was featured at the 2004

Hampton's Film Festival. I found it repetitious and dull. It was really a shame. If he had included more about Hedy, and had he made it more biographical, it could have been great. I wanted to learn more about her husbands, and her personal life. But the costs would probably be very high to license all of the old film clips and to reproduce them. I am sure it would be a great movie if he had done so, as the theater was completely full that evening. It was gratifying to see that the name of Hedy Lamarr could still draw a crowd.

The documentary showed footage from the film *Ecstasy*, and featured the segment that she had them edit out of the film: the famous naked swim scene. You can imagine that she was told by the director, "Don't worry, because of the lighting you won't be seen as being naked on the screen."

However, there was the uncut footage where she emerged from the water, which showed everything. All I can think of while viewing that sequence was: "What a beautiful girl!" She is stunningly beautiful in it. The documentary shows this long lost sequence in its entirety.

Tony also used a very wonderful idea, having people who knew her talk about her with a telephone in their hands, as though they were speaking on the phone to Hedy. That cinematic ploy was actually brilliant. In fact, several of the people who knew her submitted to being interviewed for this film. This aspect was very carefully done. However, I am afraid that it was not as successful a film as it could have been.

There should have been much more biographical information about Hedy in this film. It left the audience wondering: "How many men did she marry?" "What was her love life like?" "What about her affair with Howard Hughes?" Oh well. The film ran way too long, and too much of the screen time is a self-promoting commercial for Tony.

Apparently Tony had a very strained relationship with his mother. Hedy told me that he once complained to her, "Mother, you gave us everything: you gave us money, we had gifts, we had toys, we had all of these things. But we didn't have you! You didn't give us your love. You were occupied, and we suffered. You shouldn't have had any children, because we were really orphans to your career." One must understand that this was during the era in which the studios literally owned the actors, and the actors had to do whatever the studio demanded. I was rather upset to see that Tony really let her have it, *Mommy Dearest* style.

Hedy once told me with a sense of indignation, "I gave him the best education. I gave him everything."

One day a friend of mine, Barbara DeGroot, invited me to go to The River House, where Mrs. Kelly was having an Easter brunch. It was a very nice day, and I sat next to her. Also there was George McManus, the garden architect who had brought a friend with him who sat on my right side. And we had a very lively conversation.

We started talking about planning a party, and I said to them, "Will you come to this party that I am giving?"

And they all said, "Oh yes, we would love to."

Mrs. Kelly was the one of the oil and gasoline Kelly's. She once sat under a hair dryer in a beauty parlor, which exploded in her face. Her face was left scarred because of this horrible accident. After that she started wearing big dark glasses to cover much of her face. She had a lot of plastic surgery and reconstructive operations, but her face was still badly disfigured. Today, modern plastic surgery would have dealt much more successfully with the damage she encountered.

I don't know how she knew all of these people whom she invited to her house. I had my party, and these two gentlemen were there, and I found in my guest book a very nice note which read, "Thank you for the party..." and it was signed by "King of Afghanistan in Exile. 1982."

About two weeks after the party I received a phone call from somebody, who informed me, "Hey, your nice 'King in Exile,' did you read about him in *The New York Post*?"

"No, why? What was it??"

"Well, he is a real fake! He is not a King, he lives in Brooklyn, and has five children. In my opinion, he is just a golddigger who tries to get the most out of people."

I couldn't believe it. I was so stunned. George McManus was a very honorable man. I said to him, "How did you get hooked up with a scoundrel like him?"

But, that's what he was.

About two weeks after that, Mrs. Kelly was the victim of a hold-up. She was with her car, and she had a lot of jewelry in her trunk and in her baggage. It happened somewhere in Queens. They were stopped and robbed of their suitcases. And, I am sure that this "King in Exile" guy must have had something to do with it, because he was probably so deep in debt that he probably tried to use everything possible to make ends meet. Anyhow, I never found out if he was involved, and I had no desire to get involved any further.

But that was just another funny thing that happened on the way to the forum!

Since I had promised myself that I would one day take all of the trips that I didn't have time to take while Francois was alive, in the 1980s I made the decision to start traveling extensively with Raymond. One of the first vacations that he and I took together, was my return to The Mauna Kea Beach Hotel resort. I had so loved it when I visited it in the 1950s, that we made plans to go there.

We rented a car, and we visited the famous active volcano that is on the main island of Hawaii. It wasn't like you had to look for the volcano, as there was solidified lava right along side the road. It was very interesting to see that, and the contrast, when we arrived at the hotel, it was quite impressive.

Here we were driving along, and next to us was a mass of recently molten lava, which had flowed right up to the street. Then, the next thing we knew we found ourselves amongst the lush tropical greenery of the hotel grounds. What a beautiful setting! Raymond adored this resort, and we went out on several day cruises, and sight seeing excursions. In the evenings we would frequent one of the hotel's beautifully decorated dining rooms. We even had a butler who was stationed outside of our suite and was at our beck and call throughout our stay. If we needed anything, he was right there for us.

One evening we went to have dinner in one of the very beautiful restaurants, with its lovely decor. We had an exquisite meal, and then we went to the bar to have several of the traditional Hawaiian cocktails. That night I especially loved the Mai Tai's. However, my body was not used to drinking alcohol in such quantities.

At one point, Raymond excused himself and went to the bathroom. When he came back to the bar, he looked for me, but he couldn't find me. He walked outside, and heard the pool attendant yelling, "Please, madam, get out of the pool. Get out of the pool."

It was too late to be swimming, and the pool attendant was busy adding chlorine to the water. To do so, he wanted me out of the swimming pool. However, when I got out of the water, Raymond was shocked to see that I had simply dropped off all of my clothes poolside and I had jumped into the pool naked. It was the Mai Tai's that made me do it!

Raymond threw a towel around me, and took me back to the room. I spent the rest of the evening in our bathroom hugging the toilet, as I was sick to my stomach from too many cocktails. That was the end of my drinking Mai Tai's.

In the early 1980's I bought a small house at Bayberry Close in East Hampton, where The Seaspray Hotel burned down and was not permitted to be rebuilt. The ten cottages make up the Bayberry Close complex. One was formerly the laundry for the hotel. Another one was the owner's living quarters for the hotel, and some of the cottages were rented out for the summer.

It was my friend Gerdy DuBoisky who took me to the Bayberry Close. She told me, "This is where you belong. Because everything is taken care of by the manager and gardener, and you are free of all worries about the house and yard."

First the hotel had burned down, leaving the cottages without a hotel to service. So, in the early 1960s Dr. Blume-Sachs purchased all ten of the cottages for the sum of $170,000, and she made a co-op out of it. Some of the people who had previously rented the cottages, purchased them. The unsold ones had to be carried by Dr. Blume-Sachs for several years. But finally, all of them sold as residential cottages, and they function very well as such. Proprietary leases were issued, common grounds were designated, and the backyards of each cottage then became the responsibility of the individual owners. The garage building was divided into storage, offices, and utility space.

I saw Cottage Number One, and I decided to buy it in 1981. It was fun to have and it is wonderful to stay there. I later bought the largest cottage—Cottage Number Ten—in the complex, which belonged to the owner of The Seaspray Hotel. Raymond designed several improvements on the cottage which enlarged it, and lightened it up via the addition of several dramatic windows and sliding glass doors. I am very comfortable there. I visit it practically every weekend to enjoy the fresh ocean air.

No wonder painters find the light in the Hamptons to be so different, and so much of an inspiration to paint. It is just fabulous. It is really a great retreat, and it is very refreshing to be there.

As one friend of mine said, "You extend your life just by going there and breathing the wonderful air. And, you also leave with this air in your lungs. So it is rejuvenating."

One of the people who lived next to me in cottage Number Nine, was Grace Fippinger. Grace was the person whose image you saw on every AT&T share of stock. She started working for AT&T when still they had the plugs and wires in the telephone switchboards. Some people may not know what I am talking about, but you can see them in 1930s movies and in the museums now.

Grace had originally taken a job with them, and worked herself up to become the treasurer of AT&T. She sat on the boards of ten different corporations during her career. Her friend Miriam Siebert was the first woman to have a stock exchange seat. The three of us once had a very nice dinner, at Alison by the Sea. I enjoyed their company very much.

Grace, who died in the meantime, was part owner of the Poxabogue Golf Course on Highway 27th in Wainscott. And she and two other gentlemen were the owners. Sometimes she liked to be at the cash register.

According to her, "I love to handle money. It's in my blood."

I went to see her one day and I said, "I want to talk to you."

She said, "Well, let's talk right here."

So, I took an egg crate as a seat. I sat there and talked to her from my egg crate, while she stood at the cash register, taking money from the people who came there to golf.

She was a very, very bright woman. The C.E.O. at Gulf & Western invited her for lunch every week to pick her brain, because she was so wonderful and clever. She was really an impressive woman, and the director of ten important boards. It was too bad that she had to die so early, in her early 60's.

Grace was looking forward to retirement, and I said to her, "Oh that's great. You are going to enjoy being retired."

She lamented, "I have only the people from my business as company."

I assured her, "Don't worry, you will find others, and they will be retiring too. Go and meet them."

She later admitted, "I should have retired sooner."

To which I said, "I told you so!"

She was such a lovely person. Too bad she couldn't get more out of her retirement, the way that I certainly have.

Chapter Ten:
At the Center of Everything

I have always had a great love for, and ultimately a vast knowledge and appreciation of art. Francois was also an enthusiastic art lover, and in his lifetime he collected many incredible paintings. In the 1960s I also started amassing a fantastic collection of beautiful art.

One day I saw in a magazine that there was a forthcoming auction of art in Zurich, Switzerland, from Gute Kunst Und Klipstein. One of the pieces was the cover artwork design for a playbill for a theatrical production called *Le Chariot de Terre Cuite* in which Félix Fénéon played the part of "Buddah." The original artwork was drawn on cardboard by Henri de Toulouse-Lautrec. The auction specified that the art for sale included not only the blue crayon sketch with gauche by Lautrec, but also a copy of the finished lithographed 1895 playbill that it yielded. Also, on the back of the sketch Lautrec had personally dedicated it to Fénéon.

I sent by mail my bid on this Toulouse-Lautrec art, and I was the winning bidder. And so began my collection. Since that time I have added several more pieces to it.

Another piece I have is a bronze statue of a dachshund by Pompon. I bought that at the Parc Benett auction house at 980 Madison Avenue.

I also bought *The Alpen Veilchen* by Ludwig Kirchner. On the back of that painting of a small potted flower is still another painting by Kirchner, entitled *Amselfluh*, which is of a mountain. If you study Kirchner's life, you will learn that he was always broke and could never afford to buy canvas. This being the case, he had a habit of painting on both the front and back of his canvases.

Francois' had a very impressive collection of art which he dearly loved. Towards the end of his life, I had the idea of publishing a limited edition book of color plates with all of his fantastic art work. Amongst them were works by Picasso, Renoir, Dufy, Signac, Chagall, Sisley, Seurat, and Degas.

A friend of mine, by the name of Reto Conzett, printed several books on art and art history. He was a great printer in Switzerland, and had a company called Conzett & Huber. They did such fabulous work, that they would print very prestigious and expensive books for art lovers, for the Metropolitan Museum and the Frick Museum.

Francois had always wanted to have a book of his art collection printed, so I met with Carla Gottleib who taught art at The New School in New York. I became acquainted with her in 1962 while taking one of her courses, specializing in Art Appreciation. At the time I was trying to learn as much as possible about art for practical purposes. Francois had always been an interested and knowledgeable collector, primarily of French Impressionists. As his "Gal Friday," he expected me to know as much—if not more than he did—and to help him locate good and affordable pieces for him to buy. We had been studying a catalogue of important galleries, attending their auctions, and adding an occasional work to his growing collection.

Ultimately, the book which Conzett published of Francois' art was called *Privately Owned*. However, this was not an easy process. Although Carla was a brilliant woman in her field, she also had a knack for driving people crazy. Francois met with her several times. He wanted her to do extensive research and to write the text to accompany the book of his collected artwork. It wasn't long before she drove him nuts, and he asked if I would deal with her instead, and so I did.

We went so far as to send Carla to Europe on a fact-finding tour so that she could research these specific paintings. Following her extensive research, she ended up presenting us with a huge and exhaustively researched manuscript. It was so overly-detailed that it even discussed what the artists ate for breakfast and lunch. But her demands on the rights to the manuscript made her impossible to deal with. We finally pulled the plug on her work.

I found myself having to replace her for this task. I approached Edgar Munhall, who was the curator at the Frick Museum. He persuaded Joseph Focarino, editor of the Frick Collection Catalog, to get Francois Daulte to write an introduction for the book. Daulte was the author of several of his own books on art, and he was acknowledged as an expert on Impressionist artists and painters.

Since it was about his personal collection of art, Francois Schwarz wrote the "Foreword" to the book. In it he stated:

Is there a difference between a *collection* and an *accumulation*? I believe there is, although many dictionaries list the words as synonymous. To me, an accumulation is something that merely happens as a result of reluctance to part with a variety of acquired items. A collection, on the other hand, is brought together with affection and care because of an appreciation of the beauty and merit of its components.

Finally, in 1974, the year that Francois died, the book *Private Collection* was released. I still have several copies of it. It became a fitting tribute to Francois and the art that he so dearly loved.

I was invited to a dinner party given by Reto, where I met a woman named Lisa Koch. She was responsible for deciding which items are sold in the gift shop at the Metropolitan Museum of Art—which is fondly referred to by New Yorkers as "the MET." It was also Lisa who also made certain that all of the MET's items were sold around the world. When I spoke to her, she suggested that I could express my love for the MET by volunteering at the museum, which I gladly did. Since that time I volunteer as a worker at the Information Desk, specializing in assisting visitors who speak German and French. I started doing this in 1992, and I continue to do so every Thursday that I am in New York City.

Through the MET I became acquainted with Christa Kleffel who approached me very shyly, and asked if I could help with a question that had nothing to do with the MET, but was more personal in nature.

Christa had just moved from Germany and was starting to furnish an apartment in Manhattan. Her husband was being transferred by the New York office of the Commerz Bank, overseeing the regions of Canada, Mexico, and the U.S. I was very happy to tell her where the various items that she wanted could be purchased. We met for lunch, and I continued to give her the addresses of the stores and shops where she could find the things that she desired.

She became a docent at the MET, and was delighted to introduce German tourists to the museum and its incredible collection. We developed a real nice friendship.

After five years, I was sad to see her return to Europe when her husband was transferred back to Germany. Reluctantly, she moved back Dusseldorf. However, she often comes back for her regular "fix" of Manhattan. I always look forward to her annual visits to New York City.

Many years had passed since I last saw Bobby Hirschkron. Throughout all those years Bobby and I had exchanged Christmas cards, but that was about all. He had gotten married, and had a family. Eventually his mother, who was a friend of my mother, had died. By now, all of his children had grown up and he found himself alone. Suddenly, in the year 2000 he called me again. He was a widower, and he wanted to get back in contact with me. It was nice to hear from him.

I figured, "Well, why not look into the situation, and see what we still have in common? Maybe we can get together again."

He came down to New York City from Boston, and he had bought us tickets to see *Les Miserables* on Broadway. We went to see the play, and we went out to dinner afterwards. He took me home, but it just was not right. I realized that I could never move to Boston and the situation that he was in. So, we mutually agreed that we were both marching to different drummers, and that it could never work out.

We said "goodbye," and that was the end of Bobby.

Interestingly enough, one of the people who remained a constant in my life, up past the year 2000, was Meta. One might have thought that because of my role in Francois' life, she might have wanted to part company with me. Quite the contrary.

When Francois died in 1974, Meta was already over 70 years old. Much to my surprise, it wasn't long after she was left alone, that she phoned me to tell me that she wanted to see me. I went over to her apartment, where she confessed to me, "I am completely an ignoramus as far as figures and numbers are concerned. For instance, I don't know what a 'credit' or a 'debit' is. I don't know how to write a check, and I feel very insecure."

I said to her, "Okay, I will sit down and give you a little lesson on how things work."

After I was done, she thanked me profusely, and said to me, "You have the patience of Job."

She seemed unprepared for so many things in life that most adults take for granted. On one occasion she phoned me to say, "The great-grandson of the painter Pissaro wants to come over here and make me an offer to buy one of his great-grandfather's paintings. I don't have a clue what to say to him. Will you come over here and have lunch with us?"

Dumbfounded, I agreed to go over there and have lunch with this man, who was now an art dealer. On another occasion, Meta wanted me to assist her in repairing a damaged painting in her collection. I helped her out by referring her to a restorer who did work for the Frick Museum. I had the painting picked up and repaired, and when it was delivered back to her, I covered it in a bed sheet to ensure that nothing further happened to damage it.

She always asked, "What would I do without you?"

Whenever she wanted to pay me for something, I said to her, "You don't have to. You have credit with me." I never let her pay for anything.

She was also a wonderful hostess. People loved to be invited to her parties.

I had her stay as my guest in my "circle" house in the town of East Hampton with her girlfriend Irmgard, while I stayed at the beach house. I was surprised when the phone rang at midnight and all I heard Meta say was, "Irmgard, I am bleeding to death." That was all it took. I jumped out of bed, threw on my blue jeans, and drove over to the "circle" house.

When I arrived there, I found that Meta had gotten up in the middle of the night, gone to the bathroom, hit her head on the towel rack, and split part of her scalp open. I called "911" and got an ambulance to come immediately. I spent the night at the hospital with her, holding her hand all night long, while the doctor stitched her up.

The doctor said, "When you are older, and your skin is so thin, you have to be stitched up with a fine needle, or you will never heal." It took 53 stitches to sew her up. That's why it took so long.

I was up with her until 7:00 in the morning, until an ambulance took us back to the "circle" house in East Hampton. She said to me, "I am so thankful that you are here and alive to take care of me."

During this era, I was responsible for hiring every employee that Meta had or needed. One day she announced to me that she wanted someone to come and stay with her on weekends. I interviewed a very nice girl by the name of Svetlana. She was a very pretty girl and extremely well dressed, but I had my doubts if she would really work out. I suspected that she was just looking for a good address at which to live and work.

She begged me for the job, and I felt, "Who am I not to give her the chance at this position?" I empathized with her position, and I thought to myself, "How dare I not give her the chance to prove herself?"

So, I hired her with the proviso that in case it does not work out, we would simply sever the relationship.

Well, she worked out fabulously, and my gut feeling was right: she was a very nice girl. Her husband had died of a heart attack in Russia, and he was a film director. Their two sons were aspiring actors. But the immigration laws would not let her sons come to the United States.

Meta's cousin had married a man named Frank. When the cousin died and left Frank a widower, she felt that he should not be left alone in the world. Meta liked Svetlana so much that she suggested to Frank that he marry Svetlana. That way, since their age difference was about 28 years, Frank would have a nursemaid for his old age. And so they were wed.

Svetlana made a lovely home for him and cared for him in a fashion that has been unbelievably terrific. Frank went with her in the ocean swimming every day until October. They live in Brighton Beach, right near the Atlantic Ocean.

Frank reads a lot, and tries to help Svetlana improve her English. They go on trips together, and in Spain they bought a furnished house, at the Costa Brava. It has three bedrooms and a balcony. That way, Svenlana's two sons—with their wives and children in tow—can come and visit and stay away from the harsh winters in St. Petersburg.

Since Frank is now in his 90s, he thought it would be prudent to buy the condominium in the names of her two sons. That would facilitate getting their Spanish visas much easier. It is much easier to obtain a Spanish visa when you own property there.

When Svetlana took Frank to St. Petersburg, everybody fell in love with Frank. He went on trips with Svetlana, where he was so energetic, that he was the first one out and the last one in, from their excursions.

Svetlana told every one in Russia that her husband Frank was actually 72, instead of 92, and everyone believed this small lie. Now, when she applied for her papers to become an American citizen, the interviewer wanted to know how they live together, inquiring if this was just a marriage on paper for the purpose of obtaining her "green card."

She convinced him that she loved him dearly. Now, she and Frank live a happy life in their condominium in Brighton Beach with a balcony overlooking the ocean. Since he has no living relatives, Svetlana really "hit the jackpot." It is a true Cinderella story! Frank inherited 25% of the Estate of Meta Schwarz, and all of the money will eventually come to Svetlana. I admit that she has a golden heart, and is a very sincere and sweet person.

Frank cooks spaghetti for her, and she cooks borscht and other native Russian dishes for him. They fly to Spain together, where their three bedroom apartment waits for them. There they are visited by the children and grandchildren who all adore Frank.

I told her, "Svetlana, you have won the lottery: the Number One Jackpot!" Like Cinderella's story, Svetlana too ended up with a fairy tale ending.

In the last years of Meta's life I found her writing me several very warm and sincere letters, telling me how much she valued my friendship. On one occasion she wrote, "You are better than any daughter could be."

When she passed away in 2002, I was surprised to find that I was not mentioned once in her will. It is not that I expected or needed any sort of gift of cash, but I thought that she would have at least left me one of the paintings from her collection, or one of the books which was leather-bound by her, knowing what an art lover I was. But that was not to be.

My cousin, Francois, currently lives in Brussels. He was the one who was six years old when he and his parents, Aunt Erna and Uncle Jub, left Germany. He has one son, Didier, and two grandchildren—twin girls—Marine and Manon. They are beautiful girls and I wonder what they will turn out to become when they grow up. At present they go to a convent school. Mother Superior accepted them to this prestigious school even though all prerequisites were not met. Instead of being devout Catholics, both parents are religious non-believers, who are not even legally married. I visit with them quite often, and they come to the USA to visit me as well. Marine and Manon are very pretty girls who are charming, and they brighten up any rooms they enter.

My cousin Frank lives in Syosset. He was born an old man. He has two boys and one daughter. The boys are taking after their mother and are entrepreneurs. The daughter, Lisa Marie, is a grade A student and a beautiful girl. It was my hope that she would become what I wanted to be, but did not have the opportunities: a doctor or a surgeon. I put money for her in a trust account, but I am disappointed because she fails to have contact with me. Instead of studying for a full medical degree, she settled for becoming a P.A., or Physician's Assistant. I didn't get to become a doctor, which I thought was a noble profession, so I tried to encourage her to do so. I have the distinct feeling that she resents my trying to live my dream through her. I want her to have the money so she can just relax and study. A lot of people have loans that take forever to pay off, and I wanted her to not have these worries. However, it did not work out quite as I planned.

At present Lisa has two Master's degrees in Science and Education. Her dream was to become a coach for handball or other sports, but her opinion changed. As I see it, she finally realized at this stage of her life, being a coach was going to become a thankless job, and it was not her ideal idea for her future. She is a beautiful blonde, blue eyed, 5'10" and 110 pounds with long wonderful legs. But she is a little bit immature for her age. We have a little more contact now, and maybe she will surprise me. I invited her for dinner because she now studies in New York City, and to my surprise, she arrived with a box of my favorite chocolates attractively presented. The next visit she came with a dozen roses. I had hopes for her that she still will grow up to be a fine doctor one day. She later had a change of heart, and now all is well.

My other cousin, Rudolf Eisemann, Sr. lives in Heidelberg-Spechbach, Germany. He is the son of Hildegard and Alfred Eisemann. Hildegard was my father's only sibling, who married into a Jewish family. My father's mother, Hedwig Mueller, was a very devout Catholic. Her only brother was a Jesuit Monk. Grandma Mueller would go to church every day. She participated in the choir, and was very active in the church. On the other hand, my grandmother Frida Halfen, my mother's mother, was Jewish and very worldly.

Grandma Halfen would say to Grandma Mueller, "Dear Hedwig, you must have prayed very hard to get both of your children married into very nice Jewish families!"

Cousin Rudolf was married late in life, to a very lovely girl who came from the east. Her parents had to leave East Germany in a hurry before the Russians took over, because her father was an outspoken Socialist. In fact, he was an outspoken Socialist journalist—against the Russian regime. They fled East Germany so fast that they barely had the shirts on their backs.

Rudolf Sr. met a pretty girl named Erika who worked in a doctor's office in Heidelberg. He was an umpire for the game of soccer. When the fans at one game didn't like one of his decisions, they jumped onto the playing field, attacked him and broke several of his ribs. How typically German to get caught up in the game to the degree of attacking the umpire! He was taken to a doctor by ambulance, where Erika was a nurse. This is how they met.

Rudolf then married Erika, and I have a lovely photograph of them in their white Mercedes Benz convertible, driving off to their honeymoon. The car's license plate was not registered in Heidelberg, because my Uncle Alfred would not permit such a showy car to be owned by anyone in his family. They called him "Koeniglicher Kaufman," which in German means "kingly or top-notch entrepreneur." In other words, he was low-keyed, and beyond reproach. There were to be no showy displays in his family.

His father was a member of the leading individuals in the local government, without a salary. It was an honor that he valued. But, that did not prevent the Nazis from taking him away—as an old man—to the concentration camp in Auschwitz. That seemed like an impossible concept to him, since in his mind he was an upstanding German citizen, which should have outweighed any other connection. Unfortunately, he was mistaken in the way he was perceived by the devious Nazis.

Towards the end of the Second World War, Rudolf rode his bicycle towards Mannheim, and found out that the Americans were crossing the Rhine River. He came home and said, "Soon the Americans will be here, and the General should immediately leave." The General burned all of his papers in the fireplace, and he left. However, when he walked down the road to go home to his wife and children, one of the Nazi fanatics shouted out, "Deserter!" and shot him in the back, instantly killing him. The fanatic however, still believed that the Nazis would somehow win the war.

While the war was on the villa had been forcibly occupied by the Nazis. Once the Nazis were pushed out of Heidelberg, the villa was again occupied. This time around it was the Americans who were doing the occupying. During the American occupation of Germany, Hollywood producer Kurt Hirsch and actress Hildegard Kneff occupied the master bedroom, replacing the German General. Of course, the situation was in strict contrast to the previous occupant. My aunt and uncle, Hildegard and Alfred, were very happy to have them there, as they were able to obtain all the ingredients for cooking and baking that my aunt could not get during and after the war. My aunt could not get butter, coffee, cocoa, or anything that was rationed at the time. However, Hirsch was an American soldier, who could obtain these things at the local PX. My aunt was happy that they both spoke German as well. My aunt was such an excellent cook that her son often said, "If I would have known that my mother would live as long as I live, I would never get married." Aunt Hildegard always said that, "A man's love is through his stomach." And so, she taught her daughter-in-law everything she knew about cooking and baking.

Curt Hirsch and Hildegard Kneff remained residents of the villa for a long time. He and Hildegard left Germany after the war, and she went with him to Queens, New York to live with his parents. However, the relationship did not work out once they were in America, and she left him. Queens was not the America that Hildegard Kneff was expecting to find. She wanted to be a Hollywood star, and off to California she went.

Rudolf Sr. and Erika had three children: Rudi Jr., Renate—only one year apart—and ten years later, Markus arrived in the family. In three generations of the family, they were hops dealers. Hops are used in the making of beer. Rudi Jr., is still running the family business.

Rudolf Sr. was a very hard worker, and kept abreast of all mechanical advancements and electronic equipment that was established in his lifetime. He insisted that the family move to the suburbs, to a small village called Spechbach. My uncle did not want to move there because he liked his beautiful villa in Heidelberg, and he did not want to make any changes. However, his wife and his son prevailed, and he bought a lot of land in Spechbach, and built a real compound for the family. They still live there to this day.

I understood why he hated to leave his wonderful villa in Heidelberg. While the Germans were occupying their nice villa, my Aunt Hildegard, who was not Jewish, cooked for the German General. The General in turn, was nice enough to close his eyes and allow my Uncle Alfred—who was Jewish—to be hidden in the cellar, which nobody knew. Most likely, my aunt's cooking was so good that it was the talent which saved Uncle Alfred's life. The General was a good man, who was just a soldier, and was simply obeying orders.

My Aunt Hildegard Eisemann ran the family business while Hitler was in power, and was very successful in doing so. Her husband, Alfred, at this point could be visible again and he returned to the business.

After their son Rudi came of age, he began to run the family's hops and malt business, which he greatly expanded. Following the end of the war, Rudi's love of horses caused them to go into the horse breeding business. It became so successful that it got to the point where they received the highest price that anyone had received in Iffezheim at auction for a two-year-old horse—by a private breeder. He was so successful at buying, raising and selling horses that he had the famous "Miss Tobacco," who was a winner in a great way, and a great love of his.

He had a lot of a property, and in the backyard he had a device built for horses to walk and strengthen the muscles in their calves. He read all of the top journals on horse breeding and horse races. He bought from America all of the latest horse vitamins and supplements for his horses. His love of the field was so great that he eventually imported blue grass from America, which horses love.

I was with him in Cologne, where I saw one of his horses win First Place in a top race. I found it very exciting to be included in the Winner's Circle when this horse won the silver trophy. I was there with Rudi and the president of the racing club, as well as the jockey, whose racing colors were white with green hops on it.

Later, in March of 1996, I went with Rudi Sr., his wife Erika, and Raymond to Dubai and saw the famous horse, Cigar, win against all of the Sheik's entries. That was an experience in itself.

On our way to the racetrack, we were surprised to have a beautiful highway, but to the right and left of the highway was sand. The desert was obviously everywhere. Then all of a sudden we saw a gorgeous green golf course. Then we saw very young little boys riding camels to the camel races. We realized how they treated these little boys as jockeys of the camels. The jockeys were supposed to be small of stature, so to achieve this, they didn't feed them much at all. It was very sad to hear the stories of their abuse.

The foreign guests at the race track had huge tents with the finest foods. But when I looked to the spectator's viewing area, I realized that the middle section—which was occupied by citizens of Dubai were men only. Not one single woman was amongst them. The men were dressed in white Arabian robes with head wraps. Also in the hotels, at the reception desk, there were many woman working, but they represented other nations, and no Arabic women could be seen. As we visited the stables there, the handlers were all men or women from other nations.

As Raymond and I went to the marketplace, known as the "Souks," we found an amazing sight. Before we arrived, they had a lot of rain, which flooded the city. At the Souks, we found that they literally had to put down milk crates for us to walk on, or we would have been wading ankle deep in water. Raymond found that at the stores in the marketplace, gold was sold by weight alone, not by workmanship, which made it a real bargain. I received from him a beautiful bracelet and a pair of earrings.

There was so much oil money there that every day they also sold lottery tickets in the marketplace. There was a prize of a million dollars, which was given out on a daily basis. I said to Raymond, "There goes our money!"

I was still amazed at how poorly women were treated in that country. I belong to an organization which is called "Equality Now." It is a group that fights for a woman's rights to decide what is done to her own body, without interference. This group will go into all sorts of dangerous countries and situations, to rescue people who have been unjustly jailed, tortured or abused. In some countries, women who refuse to marry the men they are told to wed, are either jailed or stoned.

I attended the tenth anniversary of the organization, where Meryl Streep dramatically portrayed a woman who was abused and unjustly incarcerated. Her acting was so masterfully done, and so convincing that everyone in the room applauded enthusiastically and gave her a standing ovation.

There was a cocktail reception afterward. At that reception, I spotted Meryl standing alone at the bar. I got up the courage to walk over to her and introduce myself.

I asked, "How can I thank you for the beautiful performance you just gave?

She looked at me, and said, "Just give me a hug."

I was so touched, that was exactly what I did.

Now, they have built in Dubai, the most exclusive hotel in the world. It is a majestic structure that is on an island in the middle of a body of water. The artificial island is designed to look like the top of a palm tree rising out of the water, and on top of the palm tree is a massive structure of metal, glass and steel. The interiors of the hotel are designed by an Asian woman, and the electronic devices installed are beyond belief. They are already calling it the "Eighth Wonder of the World." It is not for the rich and famous, it is for the super-rich and incomparably famous.

Aunt Hildegard died of cancer of the bladder, and some people attributed that to her alcoholism. Her husband Alfred, who was a very fine individual, managed to live into his 90s. When he was 87, one of the horses needed to be ridden, so he volunteered. No one wanted him to get on the horse at his age, but he was insistent. Since he had been a member of the German cavalry in the First World War, he was an excellent rider. But his son convinced him that, since he was 87, and was out of practice with horseback riding, not to do this. Finally, they talked him out of it.

Alfred died at home where he was under the most wonderful care of his daughter-in-law Erika, and her daughter-in-law Hildegard, who previously was a nurse. There was also a male nurse present—so there were three people attending to him at all times. He was well taken care of until the very end.

When Rudi Sr. was diagnosed with cancer, he had all three of his children sign the "Last Will and Testament," to signify that they were all in agreement with the contents of it. By law, anyone challenging this document, would not be eligible for any of the proceeds of the will.

Erika and her daughter Renate were the closest friends and relatives one could imagine. Renate spoke several times to her mother and father each day. She also had a great love of horses, and she continued in the business of the horse breeding. Markus began studying in Berlin. Rudi Jr. graduated from Weihenstephan University in Munich, and took over running the business, while Markus became the eternal student and never did finish his studies. His mother tried to bribe him by offering money if and when he graduated. However these proposed bribes did no good. His liaison with a very lovely and ambitious girl came to an abrupt end when she became a doctor of veterinary medicine, and moved away from Berlin, because she was the one who pushed him to continue his studies. He became quite a computer expert, started his own business in Berlin, and is doing very well with it. Marcus has so much computer knowledge, that when he visits his brother, he regularly brings his brother's computer up to date for him.

As Markus toured around to find a replacement for his girlfriend, in 2004 he won a trip to Vietnam. While he was there he met a girl who already had two children—a boy and girl—and he got them visas to come to Germany. His mother, Erika, and I were up in arms that he could not come up with someone who would fit more suitably into the family than this lovely Vietnamese girl. However, in March 2004, their marriage was performed in Berlin with a Vietnamese interpreter, which was a real novelty for me. But, that's the way he wanted it, and that is the way he has it. He had already moved to larger quarters in Berlin, anticipating this extended family. Now, all I can do is to wish him the best of luck in attaining all of his dreams.

Back to Renate, who once had this wonderful and close relationship with her mother. She broke off communication with her mother, and gave a lot of grief to her. This was the last thing her mother would have expected to happen. I tried to intervene and convince her that the wonderful relationship she had with her mother should not be thrown overboard for—what I am sure—was a minor misunderstanding.

When I intervened, she only replied that I was wrong in my assumption that the disagreement was over financial reasons. From my perspective, the only logical explanation for this rift between she and her mother, could only be money-oriented. What else could it be? Her husband has a very fine business, and she has the horses and races, and now operates her business for herself. The three children—two boys and a girl—are lovely children.

Erika, her mother, is keeping all of the cards and letters and gifts that she has bought for her grandchildren in order to prove that she never discontinued her love for these grandchildren. Her cards and presents which she sends to them, are all returned to her unopened. They will serve as proof that it was not her doing to interrupt the family relationship.

Renata not only discontinued her relationship with her mother, but with her brothers, and myself as well. I find it very disturbing that a family that was once so closely knitted together should be so broken up and destroyed by a minor disagreement. While my cousin was alive, it was a model family—more like a close knit dynasty than a family. Now it has all fallen apart and is a dysfunctional family.

To this day I continue to remain in close touch with as many of my family members as I can. It seems that even when they aren't talking to each other, they are all talking to Ruth! I am the catalyst for many of the people in my family to be in touch with each other, and I thoroughly enjoy being at the center of so much wonderful activity.

Chapter Eleven:
Exploring the World

When I was at the golf club in October of 2004, one of the girls said to me, "I have a letter for you."

I asked, "What kind of letter?"

"My husband worked for General Foods, and I understand that you once represented them."

And I said, "That's true."

"Here's the letter," she announced as she proudly handed it to me.

When I opened it up, I found that it was an interoffice memo from 1950 which stated, "We are in dealings with Francois Schwarz, and the object at this point is to get the 'Cafe Haag' representation to Schwarz."

In French it was called "Sans Caf" which became "Sanka"— without caffeine. "Sans" means without, and "caffeine" was abbreviated to "ka."

The letter stated, "Well, as soon as I get the findings from Hamburg—who distributed 'Cafe Haag'—then we can continue to work and see if we can give the representation to Schwarz."

That was very early in our dealings with General Foods. And this woman's husband worked for the company. After he retired, he cleaned out his files and he came across this letter, and he thought I would find it of interest. Indeed I did. It was fun to read, and in doing so it instantly brought back so many of my fond memories of Francois, and the company he had created. It was hard to believe that over 50 years had passed.

I still am in contact with many of my friends from Germany. For instance, Lory and her twin sister Ann, and I all live in New York City.

We see each other a lot, and we all have opera subscription tickets together. We also all have a subscription to the ballet as well. I consider Lory and Ann to be two of my best and closest lifelong friends.

In the 1950s I went with on a trip to Mexico with Lory and her husband. While there, we had an excellent German guide, Mr. Fuchs, who lived in Mexico. He took us around, to the wonderful ruins, as well as to several other places of interest. He took us to a marketplace that was filled with all sorts of foods. We saw many kinds of exotic looking things to eat. Suddenly, I spotted a small cubicle filled with a terrific display of cheese that looked absolutely delicious.

I said to Mr. Fuchs, "I would really love to buy some of that cheese to eat. It looks so good."

He replied to me, "You are not going to do that unless you make me the 'soul heir' in your 'Last Will and Testament' first. You Americans and your pristine digestive systems, would surely die from some of the bacteria which are plentiful here in Mexico. Although the locals are immune to this, it would probably kill you."

I was disappointed because the cheese looked so good, but he sure had a valid point.

He took us to La Jose Perulla, which was a spa and a nightclub. The nightclub had water running under the dance floor like a little brook, and it was lit from underneath. The spa was not at all to my liking, but I remember that the massage was really good.

Then he took us to a place which was very much off the beaten track. We saw a schoolhouse which could hardly be described as such. It was more like a little shack. There was no seating inside, and there were holes in the ceiling. I was further stunned when I saw a little girl about the age of six or seven, holding her baby brother in her arms.

I was so disturbed by the sight of such abject poverty. So, Lory and her husband, Jules, and I donated some money in hopes that it would improve the condition. It turned out that Mr. Fuchs took us there, because he was having an affair with one of the teachers.

He opened up a suitcase while we were there, and it was filled with several newspapers. I asked him what they were for. He replied to me, "So I don't get grass stains on my pants." I didn't dare ask for a more detailed explanation.

The next day we went on a boat, and we mingled with the more affluent Mexicans, who were rather friendly. We were rather relieved to see them, as opposed to the sights we had seen in that shack of a schoolhouse. I am so happy that Lory and Ann and I have remained friends all these years.

Another trip that I went on with Lory, was to Indonesia in early 1996. I was very much impressed by the cleanliness of Singapore. But I also called it "The city of 'NO.'" There were signs all over the hotel which stressed: "The nation should come before the community. Society should come before self. The family is the basis of society. Community support and respect for the individual. Consensus not conflict. Religious harmony."

I am not quite sure that I would like to live in such a strict society. Maybe I prefer our way of life. Every second word in Singapore is "No." No smoking cigarettes. No chewing gum in public or you will be caned. No noise. No urinating in public. No crossing the street against the traffic light—or you are issued a ticket immediately. That wasn't even a feasible option, as the cars raced through the streets at such a fast speed that I am certain they could not possibly stop for the right-of-way for a mere human. The street cleaner has only permission to pick up leaves in the street. There is not to be a single cigarette butt or piece of scrap paper. And, to top it off, upon entering the country, your passport is stamped in red ink with the words: "Drug Trafficking Has a DEATH PENALTY."

However, the subway system is fabulous. It is fast, and there is not a scrap of paper anywhere. But, I would rather have a little bit of dirt, and a more relaxed atmosphere. After all the "no's" that we heard, we did say "yes" to Singapore Sling cocktails at Raffles, which tasted fantastic.

I must say that in Singapore they sure love hot and exotic spices in their food. Of course, Lory and I were dying to sample some of the native cuisine. We went for dinner at the Oasis for the traditional Indonesian Rijsttafel. Fourteen lovely young girls brought various dishes to our table, balancing them on their heads. They put various local food on our individual plates, so that when they were done serving it, we each had 14 different food items on our plates to sample and eat. After the first bite I had to run like a thief through the whole restaurant, towards the kitchen. People must have thought that I had run amuck. When I got there my mouth was on fire. I demanded, "MILK PLEASE!" Needless to say, that was the end of my Indonesian dinner that evening.

I found that the people are so friendly and happy there, even though they are mostly very poor. If I were much younger I think I would try to make a difference in their lives, and in mine, but time is too short for me to join the Peace Corps.

Since the end of FLS, one of the constant delights in my life has been my close and wonderful relationship with Raymond Griffis. While I was working, I did not have the opportunity to take a lot of the trips and vacations that I had always wanted to do. Once I sold the company, I not only had the money to do so, but I also had the time.

All of my life I had wanted to have my Bachelors of Art degree, and I accomplished that. It was time for some really extensive travel. Raymond invited me to go to Alaska to visit his good friend Dale Barker who lives in Anchorage, and I agreed. We flew up there one summer and met Dale, who took us sightseeing in his small Stetson plane.

We flew up to Homer where we had to stop and wait for clearance, because the weather was bad. We had all kinds of goodies in the backseat next to me, while Raymond was sitting in the front next to Dale. This was the first time I was in such a tiny aircraft, and I felt very uneasy to be in such a small plane.

I said to Dale, "Can't we just turn around?

Dale said to me, "No, we can't turn around, or we would be in the water."

We were bound for Pearl Island, where one of his friends had homesteaded some property. However, we couldn't land because there were cattle on the landing strip.

At one point Raymond turned around, and commented that I was white as a sheet.

Then they shooed the cattle off the landing strip, and we landed. It was very primitive there and fascinating to see. What I liked very much was our trip to the ocean early the next morning. We stopped and picked and ate salmon berries off of the bush. They were delicious.

Dale's friend had a pet pig named Petunia, and she followed us to the beach like a dog. I couldn't believe it. She was so nice, mannered and tame, that she even put her snout in my lap and expected to be petted.

I felt a wonderful sereneness being in Alaska, and it was so rejuvenating for me to be there. I was just on Cloud Nine.

Then I was brought back down to earth that evening when it started to rain, and I had to go to the bathroom. It was so rural there, that the bathroom was not in the house. In that torrential rain, it seemed that the outhouse was a mile away. It was literally a board with a hole sawed in it. This is what it must have been like back in the 16th Century! I realized how spoiled we are, living in luxury in the big city—with flush toilets and modern plumbing.

In Anchorage, we took a car and went to the glacier. That was really an awe-inspiring sight to behold. It was a bright and sunny day, and we were walking on ice and breathing all of that clean air. While we were at the glacier, Raymond suddenly realized that he had locked the key in our rental car. Fortunately, there was a handsome ranger who helped us out.

I was also amazed to see how big the flowers were in Alaska. I had been used to living in such temperate climates, I was amazed to find that up there, the flowers and vegetables grow to be enormous. This is due to the nights of constant sunlight in the summer and the short but intense growing season. Also, it never seemed to get cold up there during our visit.

A very good friend of mine through the years is Aenne Burda. She was born in Offenburg, Germany as Magdelena Lemminger. However, she never liked her birth name. She was educated in a convent school. In 1930 she met the man she was to marry a year later, Franz Burda, who was a printer and publisher. After she married him, she not only changed her last name to Burda, but she changed her first name to Aenne.

An expert at trends and design, in 1949 she took the helm of a small fashion magazine. She proceeded to advance it to where it became a really great and influential magazine, under the title *Burda Moden*. In the magazine there would not only be photographs of the latest dresses and clothes for women, there would also be patterns for reproducing them. *Burda International* became a respected global publication, and she branched out into cooking with her magazine *Burda-Kochstudio*. She is the Martha Stewart of Germany, and her subsequent publications encompass several other fields of focus from cooking to knitting to sewing. Today, *Burda Modemagazin* is available in 16 languages and 89 countries. Aenne did it all on her own.

On one occasion, I was invited to Aenna's birthday party at The Brenner's Park Hotel in Baden-Baden. Preparation was underway as the tent was assembled and behind it was a backdrop for a delightful evening of music, models and merriment. And as I sat on the terrace facing the old trees with their branches hanging down to the ground and swaying in the wind, I thought of previous visits to this hotel. Melancholy overcame me and I was stopped by the arrival of my unbelievable, beautifully served and presented halibut lunch. The dessert was "Rote Grütze" served with vanilla sauce. The 20 models who were there for the show that evening, sat on the lower terrace having their lunch. The lonely professor had a white dog resting at his feet, as he sat opposite me. His dog was very well trained, I heard not a "peep" out of him, and he could hardly be seen.

The tent for the evening's show was almost completed. The music was tested, as well as the lights. It was a real theatrical production. The models walking around tried to coordinate to the music and light for the evening. Most of them were six feet tall, with tiny waistlines, around 17 years old, each possessing white skin with a fresh tint like peaches. It suddenly became a painful for me to see. Where had all of the time gone? It seemed like it was only yesterday when I was a young girl that age.

After my lunch I walked through the clean village, and looked at the neat stores, and the walking mall with pink flowers profusely displayed. As I walked along the promenade there, I saw in a store window, a beautiful pair of Mobé pearl earrings. However it was ten minutes until 6:00, which was closing time. I walked into the store, they took the earrings out of the window, and in ten minutes they were mine. They were so efficient, that in that amount of time, not only were the earrings on my ears, but all of the paperwork was done. This included the paperwork for me to obtain my Value Added Tax refund, when I left the country with the merchandise.

I went to the coiffeur in the hotel, got my up-sweep hairdo for the evening, and found my dress pressed and ready to wear in my room. Everything was perfect, except that I felt terribly lost at that point.

As the evening unfolded, it was of course beautifully orchestrated in all areas. When one of Aenne's great-grandchildren took the microphone and wished Aenne "Happy Birthday," it was wonderful to see the young 12-year-old child with such presence and poise. Aenne said to me, "This child is my reincarnation." She saw in her great-granddaughter all of her own qualities. This impressed me more than all of the other high dignitaries who were guests that evening.

One of the most impressive things that Aenne has accomplished in her career, was to bring women's and men's fashion to post-Communist Russia. How she did this was to appeal to Raissa Gorbatschowa. Aenne made her motto, "Fashion knows no borders." The Minister of the Exterior of Germany, Hans-Dietrich Genscher even proclaimed, "She accomplished more than any three ambassadors together."

How Aenne did this was to print issues of *Burda Moden* in Germany, which were translated in the Russian language. Two huge trucks delivered them to Moscow, where they proved to be a huge hit with the culture-starved Russian public. She took very pretty models with her to Russia and staged a fashion show. Aenne's warm heart and fashion sense, teamed perfectly with the Tchaikovsky music that was played, and the sight of the fashions on professional models conquered Russia with warmth in a way that not even Napoleon—with guns—was able to accomplish.

During one of my trips to Russia, I had a guide for myself, and I told her that I would like to see a fashion show. I had to get permission from the authorities, and the next day the permission was granted. At 3:00 we went to Gump Department Store. There was a room full of young Russian women who were very eager to see the fashions that were to be shown on the runway. A very heavy-set Russian woman with her hair in a bun, a cane, and a very large red Lenin medal on her lapel, sat in the first row. She was probably one of the original members of the Communist party.

But as I looked around the room, I saw that 90% of the women there were dressed in very plain white blouses, and either blue, or black, or brown skirts. The material looked to me like it was made of material left over from old parachutes.

Two beautiful models with high cheekbones presented an array of dresses and suits, and finished the show wearing a great shearling coat and hat. Then two male models came out on the runway with colorful shirts in red and green, and jackets which were covered in sequins, which looked as if they were fit for Liberace on the stage.

We all applauded at the end of the show, and then went downstairs to purchase the outfits which we had just seen. I especially wanted one of the shearling coats. I got in line. In front of me was a man sitting behind a window, at a booth that looked like a banker's cage from the 1940s. I told the man the numbers of the outfits I had decided on, and much to my surprise, he handed me patterns.

I said, "No, I want to purchase these outfits, not the patterns to make them."

My guide said to me, "No, he is correct. You buy the pattern and get a dressmaker to sew it for you. Of course you have to secure the material, which is not always easy to find. In other words, what you saw were all ideas for you—and everybody else—to make whatever you want out of it."

My disappointment was beyond belief. I could not talk to my guide because the person who introduced the fashions, very quickly announced the corresponding numbers of the clothes so that you purchased the correct pattern to produce them. Great applause was given for the accomplishment. Of course, when these shows were seen in other European countries, they were very envious of the great economic advancement that the Russian people made. But in reality, it was something of a hollow victory. It was a far cry from going to the house of Dior in Paris, where you could witness a fashion show, and leave with a fantastic outfit.

Aenne received a great number of decorations and honors throughout her career. And one can honestly say that she really made a significant difference in the fashion world.

Raymond and I had been invited to Aenne's home in Salzburg, Austria, on Burda Strasse, which was named after she and her husband. She gave great parties and among her very illustrious friends was Mrs. von Karajan, wife of the famed Berlin conductor, Herbert von Karajan.

When Raymond and I went to the Barbados, and stayed at the Sandy Lane, by sheer accident we ran into my friends Christine Esswein and her very close friend, Aenne Burda. What a delightful surprise. In the afternoon while we were at the beach, Raymond told Aenne that he would love to dance with her sometime. Aenne mentioned that she would only dance with him if he greeted her with a red rose. This was not something easily found in the Barbados. A hibiscus blossom maybe, but a red rose is a rarity in the island. In Raymond's usual fashion, he found what he was looking for.

That evening at the dinner in the garden, where lovely music was playing, Ray reached up into the inner cuff of his pants and pulled from the inside leg, a real long-stemmed red rose which he had taped into the inside of his jeans.

In perfect German, he said to Aenne, *"Darf ich Sie um den nächsten Tanz bitten Gnä dige Frau?"* Which means, "May I have the next dance with you gracious lady?"

In the 1980s I went with Raymond to Brazil on a tour that the Wildlife organization had put together. We flew into Rio de Janeiro, and from there we took busses and small planes to various destinations.

In the capitol of Brasilia, I found that it was a city very much like any city in Russia. In Russia there is a lot of utilitarian Russian housing and buildings with absolutely no character or design elements. Brasilia was much like this: very plain. One building looked just like the next. They stood there like soldiers, every one identical.

The owner of the travel agency was our guide on this trip. He had invited us to his home for dinner, where he also invited several ministers from the government. We sat at several round tables, which the owner's mother from Germany had arranged with nice flowers and attractive china and glasses.

At dinner, I sat next to a woman who was the Minster of Education of Brazil. I was heartbroken when I saw the poor people outside of our "five star" hotel. I questioned the Minister about why there were so many poor and uneducated people.

She said to me, "I have no educators. I first have to educate the educators. I am starting from the bottom, and it is a long time process. And people have no time. They want immediate advancement and better living conditions."

The farmers there also present a big problem, because they burn the forest to have grazing fields for their cattle. But that lasts only for five years, then the earth is no longer fertile. We touched on many subjects, and had a most informative evening about Brazil.

Then we went by bus to the World Wildlife Organization research station down the Pan American freeway that extends from Brazil, across the continent. It had rained very hard that day, and it was still drizzling. Our bus, like so many of the cars on the freeway, slid off of the road. We had to take our shoes off and walk in the wet and messy mud for about 500 feet, where we met a pickup truck that was waiting to take us up a mountain to the research station. It was a pickup truck which had wooden planks for us to sit upon. I had a plastic shopping bag on myself as a raincoat, which read in big letters, "I Love New York."

This research station was one which people could only visit once a year, because the rainforest and the nature there was not to be disturbed.

While there we encountered an encampment where four men lived. They had hammocks for everyone to sleep on. Down the hill was a lake—which was the bathroom. Up on the hill were the hammocks, and a brick oven where they could cook. Upon this stove, they grilled for us a lunch of fish and some unidentifiable local starch dish—like couscous.

The four guys stationed there found us to be a very interesting distraction from their everyday work.

We left the people in the rainforest and continued on our way to the next stop. We boarded a bus, and on the first step within the bus was a short Brazilian man with a machete, which was almost as big as he was. He was to accompany us on this trip for protection. Together we proceeded to our next stop which was on a mountain top.

Our accommodations there were the poorest I ever could have imagined. There was no running water. The shower was a barrel of water, and we had permission to use only seven pitchers of water apiece. The toilet had such a small eliminating tube that the used paper had to be deposited in a small barrel next to the toilet.

The hired cook and helpers had to make a fire to cook for us. The lights were carbon lamps. The females had one room and the males were in another one. It was so hot that we hardly covered ourselves with a sheet at night. The men had to walk through our room to get to the "bathroom"—if you want it call it that.

The bugs were a lot of bother, and the smell of anti-insect spray was everywhere in the air. They warned us before embarking on this excursion: "Bring one outfit for this three day side trip, and at the end, and as you come down the mountain again, we will burn it."

I wanted to go to town and see what was there, but our guide would not let me go, because that morning in town some people had been killed. It seemed that there had been a big dispute over the rights to a local gold mine, and it ended up with someone's death.

At the airport I met a nice man who very badly wanted me to come on his plane to fly to see his own goldmine. I was sorry—I think—that I could not go, as our tour guide insisted that I stay close to him at all times, and not go astray!

In 1992 I went on an African safari with my dear friend Lory. One of the places where we stayed was the Amboseli National Park. We arrived at the lodge we were to stay in, and we hurriedly dropped off our belongings in our rooms. We wanted to go out on an afternoon game run right away. We left our rooms very quickly.

When we returned and were on our way back to our rooms, we spotted what looked like several aluminum foil candy wrappers strewn on the walkway in front of our door.

"They sure don't keep this place very neat," I said to Lory.

While we were discussing this, one of the workers there came over to us and scolded us for not reading the big sign in our room.

"What big sign?" I asked.

He explained to us that one of the first things that you have to do when you check into the lodge, is read all of the signs.

"There is a sign in the room which says, 'Do Not Leave Windows Open, As Animals Will Enter Your Room,'" he told us.

Then as we opened the door to our room, it looked like it had been ransacked and we had been robbed.

Our belongings were strewn everywhere. Our lipsticks were on the floor and open. Our unused rolls of film were unspooled and lying on the floor. I had brought a large box of chocolate flavored Exlax laxative on the trip with me.

What had happened was that we had indeed left the windows open, and about 20 monkeys came into the room, and had a field day with our things. Since monkeys absolutely love chocolate, they ate the whole box of Exlax. Those were obviously the empty aluminum foil wrappers we saw on the walkway.

Lory and I had a big laugh over our theory as to the reaction those poor monkeys must have had when they got back to their habitat and the chocolate-flavored laxative took effect!

Another trip that I took with Raymond was to China, Mongolia, and Russia in October of 1993. We went with a group from the Metropolitan Museum of Art. Our guides were Olivier Bernier, and Professor Ralph Clem. It was Professor Clem who helped Jelsen draft the revised Russian constitution.

We started out by flying to Tokyo, Japan. Then we flew to Beijing, China, and went to The Grand Hotel where they had arranged a nice reception there for us. Then we went to Tiananmen Square, which reminded us of course of the tragic events that happened there not so long before. I am of the opinion that the handling of the Chinese government was the only way of avoiding civil war, which might have very easily been started. With the millions of people over there who would be effected, it could have been really horrible.

The grip of the old Communist regime has been little-by-little loosened. However the doses of freedom that the people receive are given in small quantities. We as outsiders might not understand why things are the way they are. Compared to what it was, it is already showing improvements. One of the most positive changes is that the Chinese people no longer die of starvation. Francois was right, China *IS* the coming power of the world.

We went to the Great Wall of China, which dates back 2,000 years and stretches from Beijing, across the north of China to the Gobi Desert. Of course we went to "The Forbidden City." In the afternoon we went to the Lama Temple, which is one of the most elaborately restored sacred buildings in Beijing.

We toured several museums, including the former Old Observatory which was established by Kubla Khan. There we saw several Ming and Qing astronomical instruments.

From Beijing we took the Chinese Orient Express, also known Trans Asian Express train, from the Kuangzhang Station to Erlian. The colorful paper decorations and Chinese rice paper lanterns in that train told us right away that we were in China. The service was also very much in the Communist style. By that I mean, you were told, "Go over there and get it yourself," as opposed to, "Yes, I am happy to get that for you."

In Erlian, we changed trains from the Trans Asian Express to the REAL Orient Express, which is run by the Swiss. When we stepped onto the platform to switch trains, suddenly everything changed.

We were met by uniformed waiters, each with a white napkin over their forearm, and a silver tray in their hand. On the trays were beautiful glasses of champagne which were graciously offered to us. That set the tone for the rest of our trip on this train. Our accommodations were very First Class. Our beds were only lower berths. Every guest had their own compartment, and compartments had adjoining doors, which you could open if you desired. During the day the bed served as a couch to sit upon.

One train car had only showers, to which we had to go to take our morning showers. We had to stand in the aisle waiting for use of the showers. We were standing there looking at each other, as we were all dressed in identical navy blue robes, naked legs, slippers, and towels over our arms. We laughed at each other as it was such a funny sight to behold.

After we took our showers, we went back to our individual rooms, to get dressed. Then we went to the well-appointed dining car, where we were served delightful French food. There were beautiful fresh flowers on the tables. We never saw any materials loaded onto the train, or any garbage removed from the train. That was all done in the middle of the night, so we never witnessed any of that.

The Pullman Parlor cars had wide center aisles, with room for lounging and dining. The decor had marquetry—or inlaid wood—by Rene Prou and etched glass relief's by Rene Lalique. The bar car was appointed with tufted red leather upholstery, and there was a bartender, and a pianist to entertain us.

Along the way, we went through the center of the Gobi Desert. We stopped there and boarded an old dilapidated automobile, with five of us passengers per car. We went to visit the homes of some of the local people who were part of a nomadic tribe. They lived in round tent-like residences with peaked roofs made of felt. Each of these tents are known as a "yurt." The walls were of a woven material. I gave a couple of the children hard candies which were wrapped with paper. They put them in their mouths paper and all, as they didn't realized that they weren't supposed to eat the paper as well.

Then we got back on the train and continued through Mongolia. In one of the hotels where we stopped, there was one room where you could purchase cashmere sweaters and other items. I was surprised to find that there, in the middle of the desert there was a machine with which you could charge your purchases on your American Express card. It was such a bizarre contrast to see.

However, the sizes of the clothing there reflected the sizes of the Asian people. Being small of stature, I was able to buy a sweater for myself, but no one else seemed able to purchase anything in their size—aside from scarves or other items in which size was not an issue.

From Ulaan Baatar we went towards Irkutsk, Mongolia. At a small village between those two cities, the train stopped and we were permitted to go out into the natural scenery. We walked down a hill to Lake Baykal, which is one of the largest fresh water lakes in the world. And, at 5,319 feet in depth, it is also the world's deepest lake. It also has 1,000 species of flora and fauna that exist nowhere else on Earth. It was such a strange feeling that this luxury train seemed to stop in the middle of nowhere. However, the scenery was breathtaking to behold. It was such an unexpectedly beautiful sight.

From Mongolia, we proceeded into Siberia. From the 17th Century when Ivan the Terrible was in power up to the 1917 Bolshevik Revolution, it was the men who were formally condemned to live out their lives in desolate Siberia. However, their wives went along with them too, and they took many of their personal effects with them. The reason for this was that Empress Elizabeth in 1753 abolished the death penalty in Russia in favor of a life in exile, where prisoners were forced into labor. That way there would be a captive work force. In 1917, the Provisional Government restored the death sentence for many criminal offenses. After that, it was a still a site where political dissidents were sent to live out their lives behind bars. We toured one home which was restored to reflect the era. The furnishings were turn-of-the-century Russian circa 1899, along with the costumes on display there, and the music that they played.

In Novosibirsk, Russia we were surprised to find a huge bust of Lenin still on display there. People spoke and behaved as though the old Communist system was still in place. I was thrilled to see a show that was put on for us. Amidst the show were two young ladies who were fascinating contortionists. I had never seen such agile performers. They had the balalaika music, and the men were in traditional Russian tunics. It was there that I learned to drink straight vodka. At first I tried to take tiny sips, but I was corrected. The proper way to drink it is to throw it down your throat so that it doesn't remain on your tongue very long at all.

On our way to Moscow, I was startled when all of a sudden a rock hit one of the windows of the train, and shattered the glass. The rock had been thrown by a disgruntled citizen who protested the presence of our train full of affluent Westerners. Apparently this was a common occurrence on this route through some of the poorer areas of Russia. Without missing a beat, the train workers fetched a brand new window from a storage room, popped the old window out—sill and all—and replaced it. The window replacement was completed and done in less than 15 minutes. It was explained to me that because this happened all of the time, they carried several replacement windows aboard the train for just these purposes.

We then proceeded on to Moscow. About 50 miles outside of Moscow our train was stopped. We were told that we needed special permission to travel to Moscow, because at that very moment their version of The White House was on fire. Finally permission was granted, and the extra delay did not throw our tour off in any significant way. After several days in Moscow, we proceeded to our last stop on the tour, St. Petersburg. From start to finish, it was a truly memorable trip, and both Raymond and I had a wonderful time.

In 1996, Raymond and I went to the Caribbean island of St. Marten. While we had a wonderful time at the resort of La Samannia, we had dinner at the open air dining room overlooking the ocean, and the birds came up to the edge of our table and picked up the crumbs. We found that the very colorful birds were not afraid of us at all.

An Italian jeweler, by the name of Scavia, had a great exhibition at the poolside and we admired the wonderful artistic pieces that were on display. I was especially impressed by an aquamarine and diamond ring in white gold. Ray wanted me to buy it, but I did not want to do it. After dinner Ray announced that he wanted to get some fresh air, but when he came back to the room, I spotted an odd, square, bulge in his pants where his pocket was. Against Ray's wish, I explored, and found that the bulge was indeed the box containing the aquamarine ring, which I had admired. He had wanted to give it to me for Christmas, but I spoiled his surprise.

Another unforgettable trip that I took with Raymond was a voyage to South Africa in 1997. This was another great adventure for us. However, when we got there we found that things in South Africa were changing—and not for the better.

We had a tour guide in Johannesburg who told us that she had two sons, both of whom left the country to study medicine. They were not allowed to take any money out of the country. She told us that she really felt imprisoned. She cannot go out alone in the streets, she always had to have someone else with her. She also told us that crime was absolutely rampant. She claimed that before the Apartheid was abolished, everything was so organized and everyone had work. But the minute that Apartheid disappeared, the unemployment rose to 50%. There are acres of little wooded shacks—a virtual shanty town—and even the police are afraid to go there. In my mind, the changes that this new regime has implemented are nothing short of shameful.

Johannesburg, South Africa is known as being the greatest mining town in the world. We visited the nearby diamond mines where we learned about mining diamonds, and its history. Since I have always had a love of diamonds, this was quite fascinating to see. From the Premier Mine that we toured came the world-renown Cullinan Diamond. It is the largest gem-quality diamond yet to be discovered, originally weighing 3,106 carats—almost one and one third pounds. It was so large that it was cut into nine separate diamonds. While there we were shown a lot of the equipment that is needed for cutting diamonds, which is a fascinating process unto itself.

The manager at the diamond mine, who was showing us around, felt very badly about the situation there. She was from Belgium and had two sons in school. She said to me, "I feel that we are going to have to leave here to go back to Belgium, because I no longer feel safe here." This seemed to be a recurring theme in South Africa.

But, as soon as we got outside of Johannesburg we saw the beauty of the countryside and the wildlife there. Gazing at some of the incredibly breath-taking scenery in other parts of South Africa, our memories of frightful Johannesburg soon vanished.

One of the first places we went to by bus, was the city of Pretoria. In

Pretoria we saw the history of how the Dutch first came there, and at the Voortrekker Monument we learned some of the hardships they encountered when they came to South Africa to settle there. We went by train from Pretoria to Cape Town. The train we took was known as The Blue Train. Although it seemed like such an elegant name, the train itself was really quite ordinary. It didn't live up to my expectations, but it was nice to see the beautiful countryside from the comfortable vantage point of the train. The distinctive Dutch architecture could be seen everywhere, and the imposing Table Mountain in the background was quite a sight to behold as well.

In Cape Town, I saw an interesting sight that illustrates what the changing face of Africa is all about. I spied a black family who had white servants. This would have never have happened in the old Africa.

From Cape Town we went to Stellenbosch and Paarl. Stellenbosch was named after the great 17th Century wine booster, Governor Van der Stel. Stellenbosch has more beautiful buildings than any other city in South Africa. Grapes are grown all around there, and small restaurants offer a variety of local wines.

That morning, we walked down the main street, and on the other side of the street I saw a group of teenagers. They were all boys, who wore wine-colored blazers, which were the uniforms of their school. However, the white boys all carried umbrellas to shield their black fellow students from the sun. Here again were the white citizens serving the black ones.

We saw a lot of oak trees that were planted by the first settlers of South Africa who came there in 1679. We next motored to George where we saw the "Little Karoo." It was there that we visited the Cango Caves where we saw the incredible stalactite and stalagmite formations.

From there we continued to an ostrich farm and saw a race of ostriches. We also saw mother ostriches sitting on her egg to keep it warm. I was amazed to see that the size of the egg was at least ten inches in length. Tourists are allowed to ride the ostriches there. Of course I had to sit on an ostrich, which is not very easy, as they can bite. As a souvenir, I purchased a nice purse made of ostrich leather.

Next we went to Durban, where we saw the Zulu's present habitats in the Valley of a Thousand Hills, created by nature millions of years ago. They put on fascinating shows for us, demonstrating their native dances and customs.

In Sun City we went to a national park to view some of the natural wildlife roaming around the hills. Sun City is a beautiful, fairy tale-like place. There were elaborate fountains, and the hotel room was fantastically appointed. All of the fountains and artwork glorified the wildlife of Africa. There was one fountain with a huge head of an antelope in the middle of it.

In our hotel there was a massive swimming pool with a waterfall. Raymond and I celebrated my birthday there. Of course, Raymond had found a surprise for my birthday again. While we had been walking around the shopping area I had seen a black and white pearl necklace that was strung and twisted with gold beads of the same size. It also had a matching bracelet, which could either be worn on your wrist, or attached to the necklace to increase its length. At dinner that night, Raymond presented me with a chocolate birthday cake, and the necklace and bracelet that I had so admired.

From Sun City we returned to Johannesburg, and took a short flight to Mala Mala. Once there we went to Kruger National Park, where all kinds of wildlife could be seen roaming around in their natural habitat. We also went on safaris after dark to view nocturnal creatures on the hunt for their dinner.

In Mala Mala we were chaperoned with rifle toting rangers wherever we went—whether it was to lunch, or if it involved escorting us to our own individual huts. Just recently, a local lion had gotten up the courage to come up to the swimming pool to taste the water, and they weren't going to take any chances with our safety.

The jeeps always had one driver, and one attendant who had a gun. They took us to see the big game that roamed nearby. The food was all wonderful, and this small inn in the jungle was professionally run. Everything was immaculate, from the linens on the tables to the linens on the beds. The rangers were very helpful and polite, and we had a great time. We just loved it.

The three days at this inn in Mala Mala was included in the well-organized tour that we were amidst. I later found that if we had booked a three day stay there on our own, it would have been frightfully expensive, so the tour package worked out well for us.

Of course, one of the most harrowing things to have happened in recent history was the destruction of the World Trade Center, on September 11, 2001. That very week, Raymond and I were invited by Mrs. Maren Otto to come to a great party in Berlin. It was to be an elaborate event, and Mrs. Otto had worked on the preparations for over a year.

It was very rainy and Ray's plane from Richmond, Virginia was delayed. He spoke to me on his cell phone, and he told me that I should try to go ahead on the evening flight as planned, and he would follow the next morning. I agreed.

I had my luggage in the car and the car service drove me to JFK airport. When we arrived at the terminal, the driver got out of the car and she wanted to help me get my luggage out of the car so that it could be checked. At that point I suddenly started yelling like a madwoman. "Don't touch the luggage," I snapped at her. When I yelled, I even startled myself. It was like I was not speaking in my own voice at all. The poor porter who was standing there was so shocked he started walking backwards away from me.

My driver, who is a nice woman who always drives me around, looked at me like I had lost my mind. I said to her, "Take me home." I sensed that something was very wrong, and I didn't know what it was.

I did not speak one word with her on the whole trip back to Manhattan. I was already in bed when Ray finally arrived from Richmond. He was so surprised to find that I was at home, and not on a plane bound for Europe.

I could only tell him that I had some strange feeling that made me stay home. The next morning at 9:00 my cousin from Heidelberg called and said, "Isn't it terrible?"

And I said, "What?"

She said, "Turn on your TV immediately, and I will call you later."

I did as she suggested, and I was in shock to see the twin towers of the World Trade Center aflame.

One of the most upsetting stories from "9/11" was one that I heard from the mayor of East Hampton. At the time the tragedy hit, his daughter was working in one of the towers on the 78th Floor. He was so afraid for her safety, especially when he found that he could not reach her. I was relieved when she finally called him around 1:00 in the afternoon to let him know that she had escaped from the burning building and was alive. She walked across one of the bridges to Brooklyn, and arrived back at her apartment in one piece.

She told me that she could not forget the brave firemen and police officers whom she met on her descent down the emergency staircase. She told me that she found them to be very good at calming everyone down, and assuring people that it all would be okay. However, all of those brave firemen were killed when the building collapsed. Although she had escaped with her life, she was so traumatized by this experience that it took her over a year until she was able to function normally.

After a few days, Raymond and I went to East Hampton, and I stayed out there for about a week. Ray returned to Richmond, only after he knew that I was fine. It was a shocking time for everyone to witness in New York City. It is a part of recent history that none of us will ever forget.

About a year later, Ray and I were in Europe. While we were in Berlin, I phoned Maren, she invited us to dinner at her new house, which she had built for her husband—who was born in Berlin. We had missed the originally-planned inauguration of this impressive villa, which was nixed by the advent of 9/11. For that particular evening she invited us to come up to the house to have dinner with her, just the three of us. I knew that she had so many obligations, so I was very impressed that she took the time out of her schedule to extend an invitation and to show us her very beautiful new house. She surprised us with the most wonderful dinner we could have imagined. It was great to be able to drink a toast to her, in her luxurious new residence.

Including the Arctic region and Antarctica, my travels have taken me to all points of the world and every continent. Along the way I have learned the differences and similarities of national groups and the influence of climate, terrain and proximity to neighboring countries; the predictable energy and unrest in latitudes that require activity to survive, and the lassitude and contentment that prevails where natural provisions are plentiful. There is nothing like seeing the world, and meeting the people who live there, to understand how all of us inhabitants of the Earth coexist and survive.

I can honestly say that I am a creature of habit, and that I have to be programmed. I am someone who likes to get up in the morning and have a concise plan for the day. For that reason, I have a specific schedule. On Tuesdays, I play bridge with a group of my friends. Weather permitting, on Wednesdays I go to Ladies' Day at Knollwood Country Club in Elmsford, New York to play golf. I continue my work at the Metropolitan Museum of Art on Fifth Avenue in Manhattan, where I volunteer every Thursday. And, every Friday—also weather permitting—I drive myself to East Hampton.

I am a great reader of history and of biographies. One of the main reasons that I so much wanted to write this book, was to put on paper the stories of so many of the wonderful people I have known in my lifetime, many of whom never got a chance to tell their own stories. The memories that I have put on these pages finally put in order so many happy occasions, as well as several unpleasant ones.

Recently, on a rainy day, I was at the fourth floor café at the flagship store of Saks Fifth Avenue. At the next table was a woman who handed me a handwritten note as she was getting up to leave. I took the note from her and began to read it. On the small piece of paper she wrote, "Many blessings to you! You seem to have a wonderful spirit. I would love to have your style and class when I am your age." After I read the note I looked up to thank her, only to find that she had already disappeared. I thought it was such a pity that I could not have said something nice to her in return. I found it amusing that she had no idea what my actual age was. However, I was touched and flattered by her kind sentiment. Her kind note gave me a big smile.

People nowadays always ask me how I stay so active in my 90s. I am a firm believer that you have to take care of your mind and your body. One of the ways that I do that is by doing my yoga exercises every morning, and I highly recommend it to everyone. I used to be able to stand on my head, but I don't do that very much any more. However, I now prefer yoga instead!

Life is often a mysterious journey. We do not know why things happen the way they do. After I had arrived in America, my mother revealed to me that before I was born, she had an abortion. Had she not, I would have had an older brother. How would that situation have altered the course of my life? How, if my father had not died in 1937, would that fact have changed things? We might have not left Germany when we did, and we might have been blown up when the bombs were dropped. What if I had not met Francois again in America? There are so many "ifs" and "buts" of what would have been and could have been. Since there is no answer, I will have to follow the philosophy of Spinoza, and believe that all things happen for a purpose, or that everything is planned and happens accordingly.

Although this book comes to an end, my story and my life still grows and changes every day. Throughout it all, my life continues to be a great adventure, and I look forward to every new episode.

CPSIA information can be obtained at www.ICGtesting.com
Printed in the USA
LVOW09s1610020914

402044LV00003B/655/P